D0873880

THE FORTUNATE FEW

THIS VOLUME *has been published with the aid of a grant from the Program of African Studies, Northwestern University.*

NORTHWESTERN UNIVERSITY African Studies

NUMBER EIGHTEEN

THE FORTUNATE FEW: A STUDY OF SECONDARY SCHOOLS AND STUDENTS IN THE IVORY COAST

BY REMI CLIGNET & PHILIP FOSTER

NORTHWESTERN UNIVERSITY PRESS 1966

Library of Congress Catalog Card Number: 66–25368
Manufactured in the United States of America
Designed by Maria Josephy

Remi Clignet is Assistant Professor of Sociology at Northwestern University. Philip Foster is Associate Professor of Education at the University of Chicago and author of *Education and Social Change in Ghana*.

To A. M. C. and P. H. F.

PREFACE

THE NEW NATIONS OF AFRICA are confronted with the enormous task of modernizing their social and economic structures as rapidly as possible, and undoubtedly formal education will play a key role in this process of transformation. Yet the rapid growth of schooling in most African states has not been accompanied by a commensurate amount of research that might demonstrate what kind of role the schools play in development. The almost complete absence of data on the social and economic functions of formal education makes it extremely difficult to make sound assessments of the consequences of current educational policies or to plan meaningfully for the future. It is hoped that this present volume will make some contribution to an understanding of the role of a most crucial segment of the educational enterprise, the secondary schools.

The Ivory Coast commended itself initially as a particularly appropriate area for a case study in view of its strikingly high rate of educational growth during the last decade. In this sense it could be regarded as a model for predicting further developments in other less advanced African states. Moreover, this nation afforded a good opportunity to test certain hypotheses that had been developed in an earlier study by one of the present authors in the adjoining nation of Ghana.

It would be difficult to acknowledge all those individuals and institutions that rendered assistance to the authors during the investigation. However, we must express our thanks to the Carnegie Corporation, without whose help the study could never have been undertaken. In the Ivory Coast itself we were most grateful for the encouragement and aid afforded to us by Son Excellence, M. Alcide Kacou, Ministre des Travaux Publics; Son Excellence, M. Lambert Amon-Tanoh, Ministre de l'Education Nationale; M. André Clerici, Directeur des Méthodes au Ministère de l'Education Nationale; and M. Henri Benoit, Directeur des Cours de la Chambre de Commerce. Of course the success of the investigation depended greatly on the cooperation of the schools themselves and we express our heartfelt thanks for the kindness of faculty and students who manifested a genuine interest in the outcome of the enterprise.

In France itself we were greatly indebted to Michel Debeauvais for his encouragement and to the Institut de Service Social de Montrouge, which extended its facilities to us. In the United States we received valuable advice and comment from C. Arnold Anderson and Robert J. Havighurst of the Comparative Education Center of the University of Chicago and extend our sympathies to Arlene Rubin and Rena Appel, who wrestled manfully with innumerable drafts of the study. Last but not least, our field work could not have progressed without the hard work and devotion of our assistant, Frédéric Kouassi. The merits of this study are in part due to the cooperation of all these persons and institutions; its faults are entirely our own.

REMI CLIGNET
PHILIP FOSTER

CONTENTS

FIGURES AND TABLES

FIGURES

TABLES

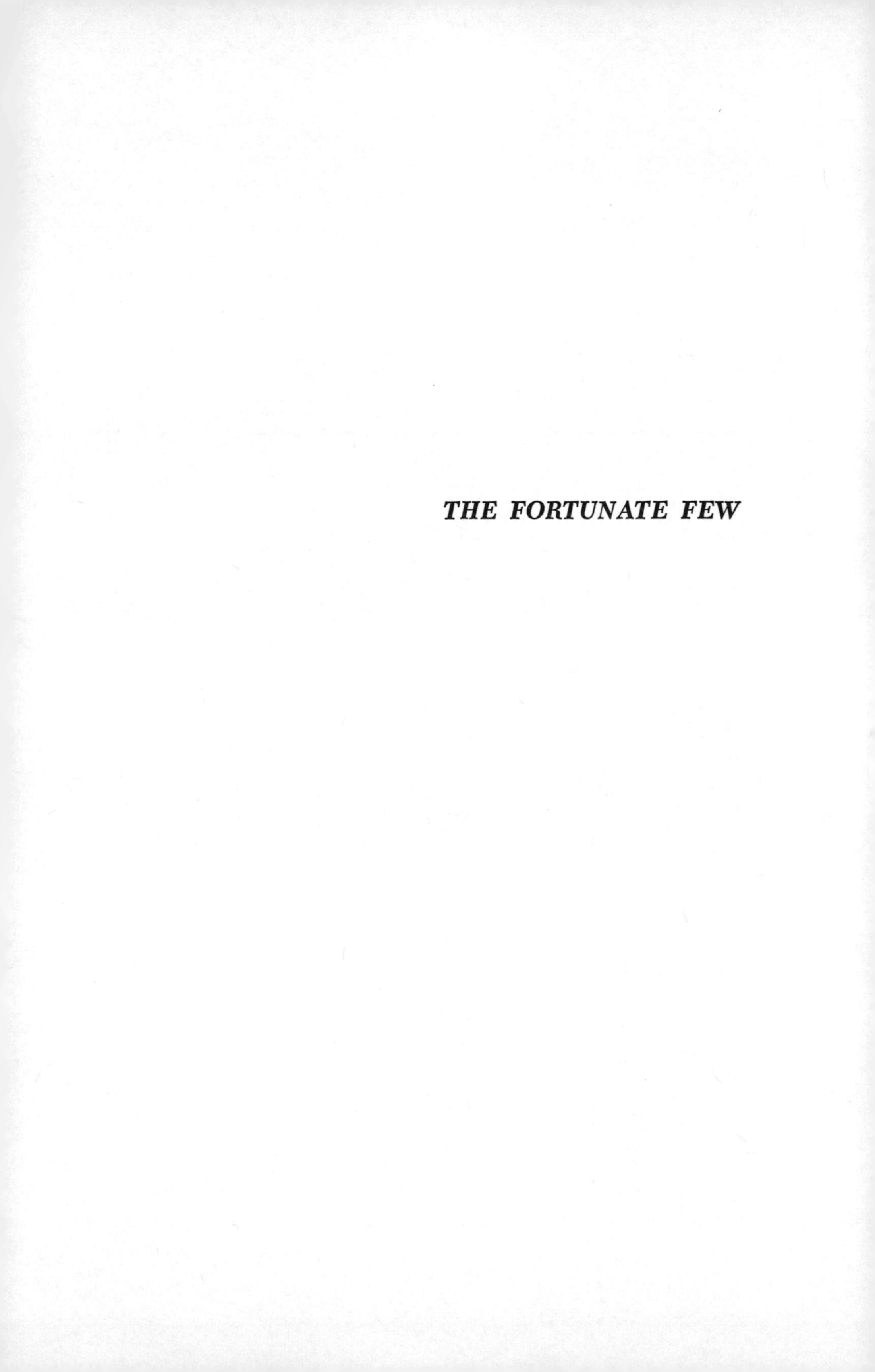

THE FORTUNATE FEW

CHAPTER I

Introduction

ALMOST UNIFORMLY the newly independent states of Africa are characterized by a formal commitment to educational expansion as one of the primary tools of modernization and development. In no small measure the thrust for independence during the colonial period was linked with the demand for an increased diffusion of schooling. Indeed some of the most bitter current criticism of colonial overrule by contemporary African leadership stems from the belief that little was done to increase the quantity and improve the quality of colonial schools.

The new political elites are under immense pressure to fulfill at least a part of the educational promises made to the masses upon assuming office. Their political future depends in some degree on their ability to make substantial progress in the eradication of illiteracy and the provision of at least a basic education for the child population. In some areas primary school provision is conceived as the major problem; in other educationally more developed states, such as Ghana, considerable demand already exists for postprimary schooling, and funds must be increasingly diverted to this sector. What is indeed striking in present-day Africa is the rapid intensification of pressures on educational systems as a result of accelerating public demand.

Mass demand for schooling usually came very late in African territories. The typical historical pattern was one of an initially high level of resistance to Western education, which lasted for a considerable period. This stage was followed by a trickle of demand, which then tended to expand at an ever increasing pace. There are only a very few areas in Africa where Western education was initially demanded on a mass basis without a previous long period of "gestation." Indeed these aberrant models are instructive because they usually occur in a rather atypical kind of traditional social organization. We have argued elsewhere that certain types of systems which traditionally emphasized individual mobility through personal achievement would be more likely to incorporate Western educational institutions, sometimes with a minimal disruption of traditional authority patterns.[1] More typically, however, where status and power were allocated on the basis of primarily ascriptive criteria, there was a tendency for Western education to disrupt traditional organization. As a result, the initial demand for schooling remained limited to a few specific deviant minorities in the population.

In short, other things being equal, traditional structures differed in their capacity to assimilate Western education. Nevertheless, other things are rarely equal, and, in fact, crucial variations occurred in the intensity of European influence in different areas. Thus in West Africa in particular the coastal zones had often been long exposed to European contact, with the concomitant development of urban centers and an exchange economy based on trade and commerce. Obviously missionary endeavors were also heavily concentrated along the littoral or in the immediate interior. Such activities frequently preceded by many years the establishment of political hegemony. In some cases Western education was reasonably well entrenched long before the middle of the nineteenth century. By contrast, the vast hinterland remained far less affected by the European impact and was incorporated into the colonial framework at a far later date; its economic and educational development, compared with that of the coastal zones, remained minimal.

Virtually every new African state presents a similar picture of highly differentiated internal development. In turn, a certain level of economic development often constitutes a necessary precondition for

1. See Philip J. Foster, *Education and Social Change in Ghana* (Chicago: University of Chicago Press, 1965), particularly pp. 26–27 and 124–33.

educational demand. Popular pressures for schooling tend to expand more rapidly in precisely those areas where economic change is already under way and where elaboration of the occupational structure is most marked. This is particularly true in urban centers where the development of an exchange economy and the emergence of new-type occupations create a demand for schooling, thus reflecting African desires to gain access to new occupational opportunities. Further, it can be shown that, in some rural areas, this demand tends to follow the development of lucrative cash crops. Conversely, it has often proved difficult to enlarge the educational system in areas where traditional social structures remain relatively intact and where subsistence economic activities are overwhelmingly important; here educational demand may remain at a low level.

The corollary of this has been that nearly every African country exhibits marked differentials in levels of schooling between regions. Mean levels of education may be low for a nation as a whole, but these may be secondary to gross inequalities on an area basis. Levels of child enrollment in primary school may be at 60 or 70 per cent in urban centers, but may decline to 3 or 4 per cent in outlying rural districts. Further, these inequalities are often associated with ethnic differentials in access, where leading or laggard areas are inhabited primarily by distinct tribal groupings. Finally, it would seem that regional and ethnic differentials are extremely difficult to eradicate. Certain minorities that achieved initial advantages in educational provision still tend to maintain their early lead, even where educational demand is beginning to expand rapidly among laggard groups. Therefore the first salient point concerning the development of African education is the whole question of inequalities of access along regional, ethnic, or socio-economic lines. It must be stressed again, however, that these differentials have rarely been due to conscious planning. They have arisen largely as the result of the historical pattern of European penetration into various areas and concomitant variations in the rate of internal socio-economic change.

The Character of Colonial Educational Policies

Another factor which has tended to influence African attitudes toward formal schooling was the difference in educational policies among the major colonial powers.[2] In British territories in particular, the administration initially adopted a fairly laissez-faire attitude toward the growth of education. In most areas development was largely in the hands of the missions, which were free to multiply the number of schools—sometimes with, and often without, government support. It is probable that this policy did result in the more rapid proliferation of schools in British territories than in those administered by France. In the French territories mission activities were sometimes more vigorously controlled or even looked upon with disfavor, and there was a more serious attempt to regulate school outputs in the light of what were perceived to be the demands of the economy. The consequences of these different approaches have been twofold: First, although educational provision was generally larger in British territories, there was probably a greater variability of standards between schools than in French territories, where general academic requirements were more strictly enforced. Second, the French did make a greater conscious effort to develop more specific forms of vocational training, with the consequence that many formerly French areas possessed a more highly differentiated (if smaller) postprimary system than did most ex-British areas.

However, even if British policies were less consciously planned than the French, both powers were aware of the economic implications of schooling. It is hardly accurate to suggest that the colonial regimes were oblivious of the role formal education might play in the economic development of the colonies. Nor are we justified in portraying the development of colonial education solely as a process of thoughtless transfer of metropolitan educational structures and curricula into African territories.

To be sure, the very earliest missionaries and government officials involved with education in most African areas attempted to structure their endeavors along metropolitan lines. It is difficult to see what else they could have done. They had no other models available, and it was natural that they should wish to extend a system which seemed to work tolerably well in the metropole itself. They could hardly be expected to possess the retrospective insights of those contemporary

2. We have restricted this brief discussion to French and British policies while acknowledging that developments in the Belgian Congo would merit considerable examination. For a more protracted treatment of the situation in British and French territories, see Remi P. Clignet and Philip J. Foster, "French and British Colonial Education in Africa," *Comparative Education Review*, Vol. 8, No. 2 (October 1964), pp. 191–98.

observers who have been so vocal in their criticism of colonial educational practice.

It was not long, however, before educators in both French and British territories began to suggest how metropolitan practices might be modified in the light of African social and economic conditions. In parts of British West Africa especially, sporadic attempts were made from the mid-nineteenth century onward to restructure the curricula of the schools. These attempts were largely in the direction of providing a more practical bias to the curriculum, with a greater emphasis on agricultural and trade training as opposed to mere bookish education. Very often it is assumed that the Phelps-Stokes commissions of the 1920's were instrumental in launching a new phase in British educational policies in colonial territories. Yet virtually every recommendation of these bodies is to be found in varying forms in earlier writings on African schools. The wider publicity given to the work of the commissions merely reflected the existence of an environment far more favorable to their ideas than that experienced by earlier reformers. It was no accident that the period of their work coincided with a heightened interest in theories of indirect rule and increasing anthropological criticism of the supposedly disintegrative impact of Western schooling upon traditional societies. Educational adaptation was largely the analogue of political speculation about indirect rule.

Also apparent is the fact that French policy-makers were very early concerned with the character of colonial educational systems as these seemed to affect economic and social development. It has been fashionable to regard French aims in Africa as essentially assimilationist in orientation, with the implication that colonial educational practice was simply a reflection of the metropolitan precedent. Yet actual educational developments in French Africa by no means adhered closely to metropolitan models. The Education Ordinances of 1903, for example, attempted to create a system of village schools with a markedly agricultural emphasis. Superimposed upon these institutions were a number of regional schools designed to recruit the best pupils from the lower system; once again the curricula of these higher institutions included substantial vocational and agricultural elements. Only within a special cluster of urban schools designed for the offspring of French residents and a minority of assimilated Africans was it considered desirable to maintain metropolitan standards and curricula. The reforms of French West African education enacted in 1924 further attempted to develop a form of schooling which would be specifically adapted to West African conditions, with a heavy emphasis on vocational and agricultural subjects.

However, it is not our purpose to describe in detail the vacillations and shortcomings of British and French educational policies, but rather to stress that the adaptation of colonial schools to African and social and economic conditions was a lively issue throughout the colonial period.[3] In a very crude way colonial regimes did recognize the potential contribution of education to economic development and made some effort consciously to harness the schools to the requirements of both rural life and the demands of the occupational structure created by European economic penetration and exploitation of overseas territories.

It cannot be said, however, that these efforts at adaptation met with great success. In some cases lack of sufficient resources, bureaucratic apathy, and outright hostility to educational change on the part of administrators partially explained the inability of African schools to reorganize themselves on nonmetropolitan lines. A more fundamental reason lay in the resistance of educated Africans themselves to educational innovations. Where formal education was the primary instrument of upward social mobility within the nascent socio-economic structure created by European overrule, it was almost inevitable that Africans would press for educational parity with the metropole. Conversely, variations in educational structure or curriculum which were specifically oriented to the realities of African life were inevitably regarded as attempts to relegate the African to a permanently inferior status.

In this respect African opinions reflected a hardheaded and realistic assessment of educational opportunities and an acute perception that parity with the colonial elite could only be achieved by parity in educational experience. Paradoxically, therefore, African views in the colonial era were often more assimilationist than those of French or British administrators. For example, it is customary to regard the assimilationist attitudes of some French policy-makers as a mere re-

3. One of the major distinctions to be drawn between French and British practice lay in the use of language as a medium of instruction. Particularly in the later colonial period, British administrations emphasized the use of the vernacular at lower levels of instruction. By contrast, in French areas the language of the metropole was used from the lowest stages of schooling. However, the decision to use French was dictated as much by a recognition of the practical difficulties attending the use of the vernacular in polylingual areas as it was by an assimilationist ideology.

flection of their ethnocentrism. Indeed it was the most progressive officials who advocated the creation of metropolitan forms of education in Africa, with the expectation that the barriers between African and European would thus be eradicated. Their fundamentally liberal orientation is too often forgotten, since their aim was that both groups should enjoy parity of opportunity and that merit, not cultural or racial origin, should be the primary determinant of social and economic status within the French community. Intent and practice are very different things, but it was this essentially liberal strand in French thought which commended itself to African opinion. At the same time the proponents of schools with an African bias and with a heavy emphasis on vocational and agricultural content often received support from groups whose motives were more suspect—the *planteurs* and *colons* of French Africa.[4]

In short, developments in colonial education were influenced by two sets of contradictory forces which tended to push systems in one direction or the other. On the one hand, there were pressures to develop specific forms of education suited to the economic needs of the territories, a view often associated with the worthy, if contradictory, aim of effecting economic change with a minimal disruption of traditional African social organization. On the other hand, a basically liberal ideology suggested the expansion of metropolitan-type opportunities to Africans to ensure ultimate parity of status between European and African elites, a policy whose temporarily painful consequences could be justified by its basically egalitarian aims.

Historically it seems clear enough that educational systems in both British and French territories tended to become more like those of the metropole as the colonial period continued. Whatever plans were mooted for broad-scale educational change either remained largely unimplemented or met with relatively little success. Thus in British territories an expanding base of primary education was usually capped by an extremely limited provision of academic secondary schooling modeled mainly along metropolitan lines. In French areas the provision of both primary and postprimary education was usually more limited in extent; yet postprimary schooling in particular became

4. It was no accident that the Brazzaville Conference of 1944 recommended the abolition of any form of distinction between African and metropolitan curricula, largely as a result of direct pressure from African representatives. See Jerry B. Bolibaugh and Paul R. Hanna, *French Educational Strategies for Sub-Saharan Africa: Their Intent, Derivation, and Development* (Stanford: Comparative Education Center, 1964), pp. 43–46.

rapidly organized on the complex multitrack basis so typical of the metropolitan system itself. The academic *Lycée,* though it came very late to French West Africa, almost immediately acquired more prestige than any other type of institution within the postprimary sector.

In summary, despite the manifold and often justifiable criticisms leveled against colonial educational practice, the development of African schools along metropolitan lines was unavoidable. The schools could never have been effectively adapted to local economic conditions, and most educational planners were unaware of the very real constraints placed upon educational innovation.

The Postcolonial Period

Granted all this, it can still be argued that independence constitutes a watershed in educational development. Freed from the constraints of the colonial situation, the new African nations are certainly in a better position to develop their schools along nonmetropolitan lines and to structure them so that they may make a maximal contribution to economic and social development. Yet this is only partly true. To be sure, African states have, for the most part, expanded the overall provision of education with great vigor. The dramatic rise of school enrollments in most territories testifies to a genuine commitment of the new elites to provide schooling for the masses. At the same time, however, they have been reluctant to make radical changes in curricula or alter the basic structure of the educational enterprise. Indeed the similarities between the system of schooling in the ex-colonies and the metropole have often increased since independence.

The reasons for this are not hard to discover. Metropolitan education still commands considerable prestige, and although it is easy enough to speak of a need for the "Africanization" of the curriculum or the adaptation of the schools to local realities, it is extraordinarily difficult to translate these general rubrics into concrete reality. The plain fact is that effective innovation is extraordinarily difficult in an entrenched educational structure—particularly when local planners themselves have been schooled in metropolitan higher institutions and are ambivalent about change.

A more important reason is that no clear guidelines for policy exist, and few research findings are available that might provide data essential to rational decision-making. As a result, educational development becomes the toy of the enthusiast, and changes with changing fashion. Do the needs of development argue for the heavy vocationalization of the educational system at the primary and secondary levels and a deemphasis of the bias toward general and academic education? Is a short-term emphasis on the expansion of secondary education justified at the expense of primary schooling, whose ultimate returns may be real enough, yet indirect and difficult to assess? Does curriculum revision, even properly planned and effected, have any crucial impact in creating dispositions and attitudes among individuals that might be considered more conducive to modernization? There is no shortage of opinion on these matters, but evidence is singularly hard to come by. *Faute de mieux,* educational policy-makers in the African states must base their major decisions upon little more than dogma and educational folklore. Even some of the hard lessons of the colonial past appear to have little effect on current planning.

Above all, education competes for limited resources with other forms of investment, and increasingly African leadership has stressed that educational expenditures must be justified by some form of economic payoff. Earlier optimism concerning the inevitable returns to investment in schooling is now being replaced by a more guarded attitude concerning the possible role of education in development. The rapid expansion in primary school provision has created a new and formidable problem, that of unemployment among individuals with a few years of basic schooling. Paradoxically, at the same time that the new states argue for a major effort in the provision of schooling, they are unable to utilize its products effectively in the context of development. In consequence some African states are already diverting an increasing proportion of their resources to postprimary, as opposed to primary, schooling, and these policies would appear to find justification in some current writing on the relationship between education and economic growth.[5]

As yet, there are no satisfactory rubrics which might provide adequate guidelines for educational policy in the new states. Much contemporary research on the enonomics of education has reached somewhat contradictory conclusions, which are in part attributable to the distinctive approaches adopted by different investigators and to con-

5. For example, emphasis on secondary school expansion in the early stages of economic growth is strongly argued by Frederick Harbison and Charles A. Myers in *Education, Manpower and Economic Growth* (New York: McGraw-Hill Book Company, 1964), pp. 49–72.

siderable variations in the quality of the data upon which they are forced to rely.[6] Further, it must be stressed that tentative findings concerning the possible role of education in development in the West cannot be automatically generalized to the new states. For example, the growth in the national income of some Western nations is not explainable by increases in physical and labor inputs alone, and the improved quality of human capital can be regarded as a residual factor explaining discrepancies between these inputs and growth in national wealth. A priori there seems to be no strong case for extending these conclusions to areas which are only now emerging from the subsistence stage. Few would deny that some diffusion of formal schooling is necessary for modernization, and most would subscribe to the common-sense judgment that increased educational provision is both a cause and an effect of economic development. This kind of judgment, however, does not take us very far. The key issue is the *variable* contribution that education may make at different stages of growth. In terms of policy, this poses formidable difficulties as to the timing and extent of resource allocation to education as a whole and to distinctive levels and types of schooling.[7] At present the kinds of strategies that can be employed are not very clear.

The Crucial Position of the Secondary Schools

In spite of this confusion, there is little doubt that one of the major centers of present controversy concerns the role of postprimary schooling as it relates to economic change and processes of occupational recruitment in the new states. We have already indicated that increased concern with secondary schooling stems partially from some

6. This is very clear if we look at efforts to relate gross national product or income per capita to various indices of educational development through the use of correlation techniques. Harbison and Myers indicate higher correlations between adjusted second-level enrollment ratios and G.N.P. than between first-level enrollment ratios and G.N.P. Harbison and Myers, *op. cit.*, p. 40. Contrast this with the conclusions of Mary Jean Bowman and C. Arnold Anderson, "Concerning the Role of Education in Development" in Clifford Geertz, ed., *Old Societies and New States* (Glencoe, Illinois: The Free Press, 1963), pp. 257–79. In this analysis primary school enrollment appears as a better predictor of income per capita than does level of postprimary enrollment.

7. It should not be forgotten that definitions of educational investment must also take into account on-the-job training and types of instruction within institutions not normally regarded as part of the formal educational system.

disenchantment with the consequences of primary school expansion. Given the sluggish rate of growth in lower level job opportunities in the modern sector of most African territories, it is probable that any nation which succeeds in expanding its primary school enrollments beyond 50 per cent will be faced with growing unemployment among school-leavers. It would seem that where primary education is not very diffused among the general population, a few years' educational experience creates expectations on the part of pupils that cannot be met under present conditions. To be sure, this can be regarded as a short-run phenomenon which occurs at an intermediate stage in the growth of primary schools, but its impact has been sufficient to generate increasing interest in postprimary education as a more rewarding area for investment.[8]

More positively, the concern with postprimary schooling receives impetus from the work of those primarily concerned with manpower resources and their allocation in the developing areas. Almost uniformly, assessments of manpower needs, whether derived from the extrapolation of occupational trends or from employer estimates, have emphasized that the most acute labor shortages are likely to occur at the intermediate level. This category of subprofessional manpower is usually regarded as including technical workers in agriculture and engineering, nurses, teachers, and supervisory personnel. More particularly, it is assumed that this type of worker normally requires a basic secondary education plus a measure of specialized training thereafter.

Our task here is not to comment on the degree of reliance that can be attached to manpower projections, nor indeed to examine the assumption that certain levels of occupational activity need be closely linked to a given level of postprimary education. Rather it is to suggest that such approaches generate a climate of opinion which favors heavier concentration on secondary school development. It is equally clear that in simple quantitative terms the proportion of the adolescent population entering some form of postprimary schooling is uniformly small. Table 1 indicates the proportion of the 15–19 year age group who in 1961 were still undergoing full-time schooling in the 10 most educationally developed states of former French and British Africa. These figures include enrollments at all levels beyond the basic primary

8. More logically, of course, this situation would suggest that every effort should be made to expand primary education as rapidly as possible beyond this level. Once primary schooling is almost universally diffused, it ceases to be linked with distinctive levels of expectation.

TABLE 1. Second-Level Enrollments in Ten African States, 1960–1961

COUNTRY	SECOND-LEVEL ENROLLMENTS * (Percentages)
Ghana	23.5
Kenya	5.5
Uganda	5.3
Nigeria	4.8
Gambia	4.8
Congo (Brazzaville)	4.7
Malagasy Republic	3.9
Gabon	3.8
Zambia	3.8
Cameroun	3.7

* The enrollment ratio is for the age group 15–19, adjusted for differences in the duration of primary and secondary schools in the different countries. The adequacy of these figures varies from country to country depending on the availability of reliable census data. Very probably the enrollment figures are somewhat inflated because of systematic underestimates of the population.

Source: UNESCO, Meeting of Ministers of Education of African Countries Participating in the Implementation of the Addis Ababa Plan (Paris, March 26–30, 1962), p. 13 b.

school course and include individuals in academic secondary schools, teacher training institutions, and other types of vocational training schools, besides those in "senior primary" institutions. Only Ghana is distinctive in that 23 per cent of this age group is still undergoing full-time schooling, though nearly all these students are to be found in "middle schools," which provide a senior primary school education. Only 2 per cent of the age group enter academic secondary schools substantially similar in structure and offerings to English secondary grammar schools.

It is also true that the transition from primary to postprimary schooling is extraordinarily difficult. Opportunities for children to enter primary schooling are increasing rapidly, but the chances of moving from the primary to the secondary level are slight. Indeed, though the chances that a postprimary student will enter some form of higher education, are not high, they are usually better than for his initial opportunity of entering secondary school. In this sense, entry to postprimary education constitutes a major watershed in the careers of students. At present a few years of primary education or even completion of the primary school program does not greatly enhance an individual's occupational opportunities, but completion of some form of secondary education provides access to middle-echelon posts and enables a limited number of individuals to scale the highest rungs of the educational ladder. The crucial importance of secondary schools lies, therefore, in their dual function as both terminal institutions and feeders to higher education, and we are justified in regarding postprimary students as constituting a potential elite in most of the new African states.

Furthermore, two other factors enhance the significance of secondary education. Perhaps in contradistinction to earlier Western experience, few alternative mechanisms for occupational and social mobility exist outside the schools themselves. Throughout the colonial period the possession of some degree of formal education constituted the royal road to recruitment into the occupational structure created by European overrule. The situation has hardly changed in recent years and is indeed accentuated by the extraordinary importance of government as the major employer of educated manpower in most African states. Perhaps more than in the private sector, formal educational qualifications tend to be stressed as the principal criterion for occupational recruitment. If this feature is associated with a relatively slow rate of expansion in job opportunities, then it should be apparent that the educational requirements for access into a given occupation may rise very rapidly. For some sections of the labor force, indeed, a very close fit between level and type of schooling and current occupation is likely to develop, thus making some secondary school experience crucially important.

It is evident, then, that the question of secondary education has a peculiar centrality in the new states, not only as it relates to economic development and occupational recruitment but also as it will increasingly affect the processes of forming a political elite. The immediate postindependence period in any state is often characterized by a rapid Africanization of personnel at middle and upper levels, combined with marked overall expansion of job opportunities within the bureaucracy. At first this may result in rapid occupational mobility for individuals with relatively limited educational backgrounds. Such initial impetus, however, may be followed by a longer period of slower expansion at upper and middle levels, while at the same time the output of educated personnel begins to increase rapidly. Access to occupational opportunities now monopolized by earlier and less educated cohorts * becomes increasingly difficult for younger and more highly trained

* "Cohort" refers to students entering the school system in the same year, so that they could be considered as being in the same class.

individuals. At worst this can lead to consciously articulated political conflict between the educated generations, but short of this, it implies that later cohorts may have to reappraise the occupational currency of their education and adjust themselves to more limited opportunities.

Secondary school systems in Africa are obliged to operate within this kind of context. The schools are not uncontaminated by strong political pressures, and one cannot avoid the conclusion that some planners, particularly those concerned with relating educational outputs to projected manpower needs, are not sufficiently aware of the real difficulties involved in transforming educational systems to meet supposed economic requirements. Even assuming that accurate forecasts can be made, it is still another matter to attempt to adjust educational outputs quantitatively and qualitatively to the putative demands generated by these forecasts.

One of the major sources of difficulty lies in the fact that we have little information on the functioning of existing educational institutions in Africa. We lack, indeed, basic data concerning the secondary schools—data which would provide some solid and meaningful basis for policy decisions. This is quite apart from the more theoretical issues involved in seeing how secondary institutions of a European type tend to operate when transferred into radically different sociopolitical environments. Information on the size of enrollments and their rate of increase or detailed studies of the curriculum content in the schools may be valuable to a degree, but they tell us nothing about the functional interrelationships between the schools and other social, political, and economic institutions in the new states.

Some Research Priorities

If we are to examine some of these interrelationships, our first emphasis must be on clarifying the functions of the secondary schools as recruiting and allocative institutions. Research in the West has already generated a considerable body of information concerning the role of secondary schools in both facilitating and impeding individual or group mobility. Understandably enough, questions of inequality of access have been markedly concerned with recruitment on the basis of "social class," though the frequently substantial regional variations in recruitment rates are sometimes forgotten. However, in Africa recruitment is strongly affected by ethnic differentials. Sentiments and values based on social-class lines may be relatively weak (and we use the term "social class" with considerable reservation), but ethnically focused sentiments are often correspondingly strong. We have seen that under earlier patterns of European penetration certain ethnic minorities usually gained a disproportionate advantage in access to schooling —an advantage which they have frequently been able to maintain. During the colonial period these inequalities often did not lead to open conflict. Paradoxically enough, independence often brings a heightening of ethnic sensibilities and a corresponding demand that all minorities must enjoy equal access to key educational institutions.

This poses painful dilemmas for planners. Demands for equity in secondary school representation may conflict with policies which stress recruitment on the basis of formal achievement criteria. It is clear that the latter emphasis, while justifiable on grounds of efficiency, can facilitate continued overrepresentation in the secondary schools of those minorities who have established early educational traditions. In plain terms, even where secondary school entry is based upon success in impartially administered examinations, certain ethnic groups will still contribute a disproportionate number of students. Moreover, opportunities vary with socio-economic background, which is itself often linked to ethnic origin.

This cluster of factors places marked constraints upon the degree to which secondary school systems can be adapted to national needs and demands. Concern with the content of postprimary education and the size of secondary school outputs often obscures the fact that *who* gets educated is perhaps a more pressing question in the new African states. It is pressing not only because of potential conflict between ethnic groups but also because small African secondary school systems must maintain fairly fluid patterns of access and keep the doors to elite status relatively open. The extent of openness of a system is not purely a function of its size but is related in marked degree to the relative level of educational motivation among ethnic and socio-economic subsegments of the African populations themselves.

A further complication with respect to recruitment is that few postprimary systems are homogeneous. Particularly in areas where educational structures are derived from the French model, the postprimary sector is itself subdivided into a complex of streams and tracks, ranging from terminal vocational schools to the classical division of the *Lycée*. This development is usually based on the assumption that there should be a clear-cut relationship between educational experience and later occupational recruitment. The result is that the prestige of schools is largely determined by the status of those occupations for which they are believed to prepare. In the West different types of secondary school have tended to recruit from distinct segments of the population. With respect to Africa, it is possible to argue that a subgroup may be reasonably well represented in the system as a whole but be distinctly underrepresented in that type of secondary school which provides maximum opportunities for mobility and access to elite status. For example, it could be disadvantageous to an ethnic minority if students from that group were overwhelmingly concentrated in terminal vocational training schools which virtually bar access to higher institutions.

Against this can be set the fact that multitrack systems often contain structural arrangements that may enhance the fluidity of the system. Opportunities may exist for individuals to cross from one track to another on the basis of academic ability (or lack of it). Systems vary greatly in the extent to which individuals are allowed to move into different parts of the school hierarchy, although the incidence of this internal mobility may never be very great. In Africa some ethnic or social minorities may achieve an initial advantage in access to secondary schools of high prestige, but this advantage may become attenuated as a student moves up through the secondary schools. The less able children from these groups may become downwardly mobile. On the other hand, children from some localities or tribes, who may be obliged to commence their secondary school careers in schools designed to provide only a terminal education, may ultimately manage to enter more advantageous types of institutions.

Thus no study of secondary schools will be complete unless the static recruitment picture is supplemented by information concerning the processes of internal readjustment and the reallocation of students that take place *within* the overall postprimary system. This factor is of particular significance to the planner, since it gives some indication of the manner in which initial inequalities may become attenuated and a somewhat more efficient reallocation emerge on the basis of students' academic ability and their tastes or inclinations.

Also of major importance is the whole question of the values and attitudes of African secondary school pupils themselves, particularly as these are manifested in their patterns of occupational preference. All too often educational outputs are adjusted to estimated manpower needs without reference to the role of individual attitudes in the ultimate allocation of manpower. For example, it is common enough for students at agricultural training institutions created in anticipation of a demand for agricultural technicians to regard their training as a forced alternative which may enable them later on to enter some institution of higher education. This is only one of many cases in which the external needs of the system, as defined by planning agencies, differ markedly from the intentions of the clientele of that system.

Typically there have been two ways of dealing with this kind of problem. The first is to accept the fact that a certain proportion of individuals will not enter the kind of occupation for which they have been trained and that standard estimates of "wastage" are thus built into initial planning procedures. Alternatively, an attempt can be made to match outputs with anticipated demand through direct control of labor. This is commonly done by requiring students who have been trained at public expense to serve for a specific number of years in a designated occupation. A more subtle policy which attempts to influence the flow of manpower is the use of explicit differential pricing of occupational positions.

All these approaches implicitly recognize the fact that expectations play a considerable role in ultimate labor allocation. Yet wastage estimates merely assume that nothing can be done about the problem, while compulsory labor drafting has rarely been successful under African conditions. In turn, the provision of special incentives makes unjustifiable assumptions about the factors which really influence job satisfaction and occupational commitment. Unfortunately, little evidence exists concerning the determinants of occupational choice and elements which are crucial in job satisfaction. For example, it would seem doubtful to assume that individuals can be persuaded to enter and remain in the field of primary school teaching through promised salary increases if their preferences for teaching are only loosely associated with its income advantages.

We would argue that data concerning the vocational orientations of individuals and an examination of factors associated with variations in occupational preference should be important elements in any form of meaningful planning. Thus, attempting to match outputs with anticipated demand through stop-gap adjustment techniques might be less profitable than identifying subgroups within the student population who already manifest certain forms of occupational commitment. For example, it is sometimes asserted that much of the economic development in the new states will require a substantial enlargement of the private sector of the economy. If this is the case, it would be worthwhile to identify those ethnic or socio-economic subgroups of students who are significantly more oriented to private employment and who at the same time exhibit greater risk orientations and a propensity to respond to monetary incentives. This approach would seem to make sense also as far as other occupations are concerned, and could result in more realistic approaches to manpower allocation, since, in the last resort, the proclivities of individuals play a significant role in the ultimate allocation of labor.

One caveat must be entered here. We do not assume that the occupational value of an individual is necessarily a function of the kind of formal education to which he has been exposed. This view is often held, either explicitly or implicitly, with the implication that curricular change in the schools constitutes one way of modifying vocational attitudes in a desirable direction. When carefully scrutinized, however, the view finds little to commend it, because such attitudes are likely to be derived from a variety of sources and influences, most of which originate outside the school. Indeed we adopt a very cautious position concerning the effectiveness of the schools as instruments of economic or political socialization. Any attempt to assess their impact would involve longitudinal studies of highly complex design. At this juncture it is sufficient to observe that our examination of occupational attitudes has no curricular implications for the schools. In short, we are merely taking students as we find them, without making inferences as to the factors most crucial in attitude formation.

A closely related problem concerns the dearth of reliable information concerning the actual, as opposed to the theoretical, articulation between secondary school systems and the occupational structure. Little evidence exists concerning the career patterns of secondary school graduates who immediately enter the labor market. Elaborate systems of specialized vocational postprimary schooling, for example, are developed on the assumption that their students will find adequate employment outlets in the vocations for which they have been trained. In actuality, graduates of the academic secondary schools might be dispersed over a broader range of occupations and have more alternatives open to them. Apart from this problem—that is, the degree of looseness or tightness of fit between secondary training and occupational recruitment—it is also important to examine the extent to which secondary school graduates are both horizontally and vertically mobile.

We might expect mobility patterns to be distinctive for different occupational clusters and to be associated with variations in levels of general job satisfaction, current income, and promotion opportunities.

Such an accumulation of evidence can take us a long way toward obtaining a more reliable picture of the major allocative functions of secondary schools in African states. That little has been done in this direction reflects considerable methodological differences in conducting follow-up studies. It is, of course, far easier to examine the educational background of preselected occupational or social groups. However, this latter approach gives us no indication of the general distribution of secondary school graduates throughout the occupational structure, and this picture is most vital for the purposes of educational planning.

In the following chapters, therefore, we shall be essentially concerned with the kinds of research that we have outlined in this introductory statement. To use a simple analogy, we regard a secondary school system as a factory and are concerned with examining the quantitative and qualitative characteristics of the personnel inputs, the allocation of these inputs within it, and the destinations of the finished products.

The Choice of Area

In many respects the Ivory Coast constitutes a particularly suitable area for this kind of investigation. One of the most backward areas in the whole French West African Federation before World War II, it has recently emerged as the most economically prosperous territory in former French Africa. Further, its educational system has been expanding very rapidly over the last decade—in contrast, for example, to Senegal, with its longer traditions of Western schooling and its more established educated elite. The rate of educational expansion that has gone on in the Ivory Coast is, moreover, likely to be typical of developments in many of the other new African states.

On the other hand, the moderate political stance of the country has led to its being regarded by France and some other Western powers as something of a model of harmonious development and sound political judgment in Africa. Whatever the justification for these views, there is no doubt that the Ivory Coast has consequently profited from official aid, international loans, and a growing volume of private investment.

However, the dramatic increase in educational provision has been paralleled by marked conservatism concerning other forms of educational change. More than in any other African state, the structure of its educational system and the curriculum of its schools have continued to reflect metropolitan practice. What France does today the Ivory Coast will do tomorrow. This is an ideal situation for an examination of the shifts in function undergone by a Western metropolitan multitrack system of secondary schooling when it is transferred to the African scene.

Finally, this study gains from the fact that it is not without precedent. Previous investigations of a similar nature have been undertaken by one of the present writers in adjoining Ghana. In many respects these two nations are similar—in the ethnic composition of their populations, their natural resources, their level of economic development, and their internal differences in the diffusion of schooling. They differ, however, in their colonial and, more specifically, their educational traditions. Such a situation provides an opportunity for comparisons of the functions of secondary education in the two states.[9]

9. See Remi P. Clignet and Philip J. Foster, "Potential Elites in Ghana and the Ivory Coast: A Preliminary Comparison," *American Journal of Sociology*, Vol. LXX, No. 3 (November 1964), pp. 349–62.

CHAPTER II

The Social, Economic, and Educational Scene in the Ivory Coast

Geography and Ethnic Groupings

STRETCHING between the fifth and tenth parallels north of the equator, the Ivory Coast is shaped like a square whose sides are approximately 375 miles in length and whose area covers some 140,000 square miles. The size and location of the country have generated a wide variety of climatic conditions; annual rainfall diminishes from almost 80 inches in the coastal zone to about 40 inches in the north. This variability creates marked vegetational contrasts. Tropical rain forests cover the country from east to west up to the eighth parallel, at which point these give way to a transitional deciduous forest zone, which is in turn replaced by open park savannah in the northern areas. These regional differences account in large measure for a highly differentiated pattern of internal economic development.

In 1960 the country was said to have a population of approximately 3.2 million, with a growth rate of about 2 per cent per annum.[1] This

1. There has never been a complete and systematic census of population in the Ivory Coast, and present figures are only estimates. The geographical and numerical distribution of the major Ivory Coast ethnic groups is given in Ministère du

FIGURE 1. Principal Ethnic Groups and Towns

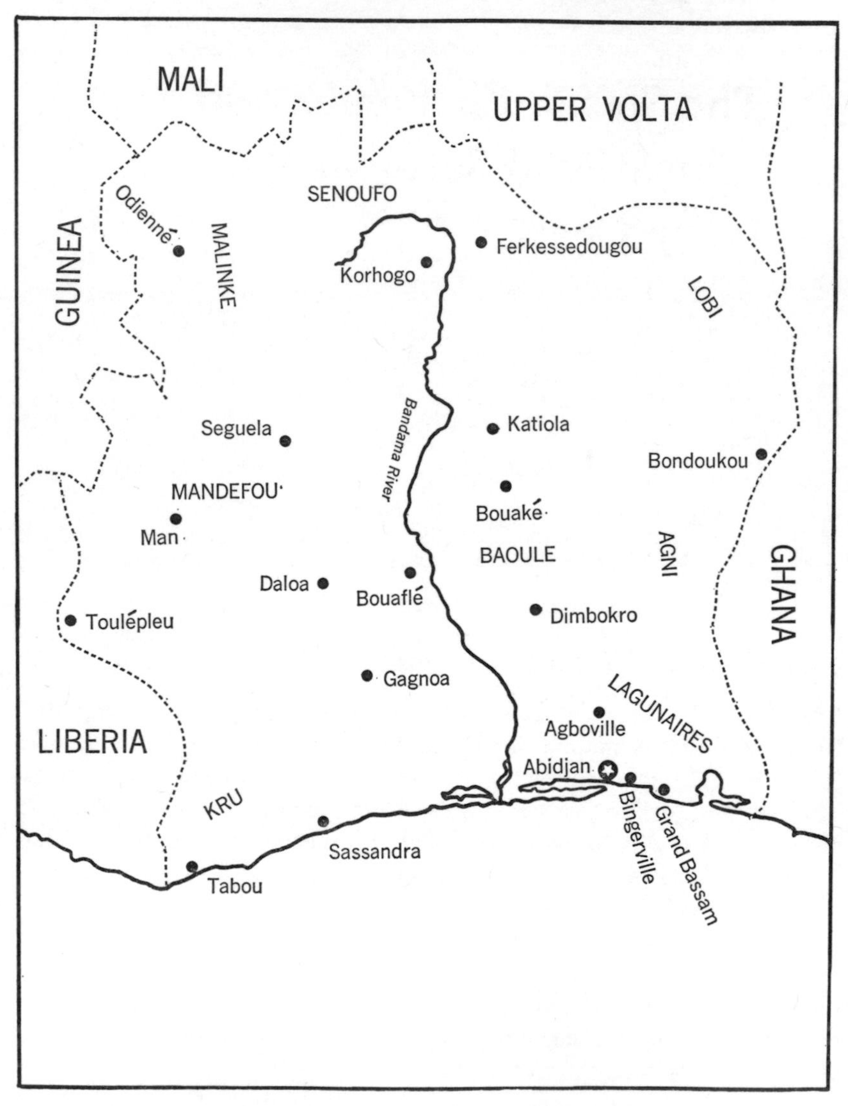

population represents eight major ethnic groupings (Figure 1). The Agni and Baoulé, comprising about one-fourth of the population, are closely related to the Akan peoples of Ghana, and occupy the south-eastern region and part of the central portion of the Ivory Coast. The eastern half of the littoral is inhabited by the Lagoon cluster of peoples (Lagunaires), which is composed of no less than eight distinct tribal groupings. To the west are the Kru peoples, comprising about 18 per cent of the population. Part of the central portion and all the northern portions of the Ivory Coast are occupied by four additional major groupings: the peripheral Mande (Mandefou), the Mande (Malinke), the Senoufo, and the Lobi.

These various peoples differ greatly in size and social organization. The Bandama River, which runs southward, roughly constitutes the borderline between matrilineal and patrilineal societies. To the east, the matrilineal Agni developed a complex political and social organization, with lineages of chiefs whose authority was subject to the elaborate checks and balances of the typical Akan system so well described elsewhere. However, the Agni differed from other Akan models in that well-defined age groups had a variety of military, economic, and social functions. As with most Akan peoples, the ancestral cult occupied a central position in the religious life of the society.[2]

The Baoulé are culturally rather similar to the Agni, although their traditional political structure was less hierarchic and their social organization less clearly matrilineal. The Lagoon Cluster of peoples are extraordinarily heterogeneous.[3] Though it has been customary to regard them as matrilineal in organization, there is actually a wide variation among them. For example, the Ebrié and Adioukrou seem to

---

Plan, Services de la Statistique, *Inventaire économique de la Côte d'Ivoire, 1947–1955* (Abidjan: Imprimerie du Gouvernement, 1958), p. 26.

2. For a general description of Agni society, see Gabriel Rougerie, "Les pays Agni du Sud-Est de la Côte d'Ivoire forestière," *Etudes éburnéennes,* VI (Abidjan: Centre IFAN, 1957). An interesting study by A. J. F. Kobben compares this group with the Bété: "Le planteur noir," *Etudes éburnéennes,* V (Abidjan: Centre IFAN, 1956). Some information concerning the role and organization of age groups in this type of society is given by G. Niangoran Bouah in "Le Village Abouré," *Cahiers d'études africaines,* Vol. I, No. 2 (1960) pp. 113–27.

3. For example, Attié society is described in M. J. Vicenti, *Coutumes Attié* (Paris: Editions Larose, 1914). There are valuable details concerning the organization of Adioukrou society in M. Dupire and J. L. Boutillier, *L'homme Adioukrou et sa palmeraie* ("Collection l'homme d'Outre Mer" [Paris: 1958]). In addition, some comparative material is available in a study of Ivory Coast farmers undertaken by M. Dupire, "Planteurs autochtones et étrangers en Basse Côte d'Ivoire Orientale," *Etudes éburnéennes,* VIII (Abidjan: Centre IFAN, 1960).

follow matrilineal rules of descent, but the Abbey appear to be patrilineally organized, with a structure rather similar to that of the Kru.

On the western side of the Bandama, the Bété represent the most numerous cluster among the Kru peoples.[4] Originally this group of warriors and hunters was organized on a segmentary patrilineal basis, with each clan occupying a definite territory. At present the original social and political functions of the clans have disappeared, and although the Bété are culturally homogeneous, the village remains the maximal unit of social and political organization. The inhabitants of each village can usually trace their descent to a common agnatic ancestor, but unrelated families do reside in some communities, and common daily experience provides a substitute for kinship links. Perhaps the Bété, unlike the Agni, are temporally oriented more to the present than to traditions of the past. Further, the social organization of the village is less differentiated than that of the Agni, and power rests largely with the lineage heads.

In the north the Senoufo, who, like the nearby Lobi, seem to have been previously organized on a matrilineal basis, now follow rules of patrilineal descent and are grouped in large villages.[5] Early Senoufo organization was probably segmentary, but in more recent times there has been a greater integration of the socio-political structure, resulting in the creation of a paramount chieftaincy over all the Senoufo.

The Mande-speaking peoples of the Ivory Coast may be divided into two major clusters: the Malinke, who form a subgroup of the nuclear Mande, and the Mandefou, or peripheral Mande (including the Gouro, Gagou, Webe, Yacouba, and Dan).[6] Both these peoples are patrilineally organized and reside in nucleated villages. Although they share common cultural attributes, social structure is more complex among the Malinke, who have a highly developed caste system. Furthermore, the Malinke are almost uniformly Islamicized, while traditional religious beliefs prevail to a greater extent among the Mandefou. In-

4. The most recent study of the Bété is D. Paulme, *Une Société de Côte d'Ivoire d'hier et d'aujourd'hui: les Bété* (Paris: Mouton, 1962). The social organization of this people is mainly described in the first four chapters of the book.

5. For further details see B. Holas, *Les Senoufo* ("Monographies ethnologiques africaines" [Paris: Presses Universitaires de France, 1957]).

6. See George Murdock, *Africa, Its People and Their Culture History* (New York: McGraw-Hill Book Company, 1959), pp. 61–88, 252, 264. At this stage it should be pointed out that the main classifications of the Ivory Coast tribes established by various authors do not always coincide.

deed Christianity has been diffused more widely among them than has Islam.

In terms of social and cultural organization, then, the Ivory Coast can be roughly divided into four zones. The northern half of the country has been markedly receptive to Islamic influence, whereas the southern zone, originally animistic in belief, has been penetrated by Christianity. The eastern peoples are predominantly matrilineal, while the western groups are overwhelmingly patrilineal. Political organization increases in complexity as one moves northward among the western patrilineal groups, but decreases in complexity among the northern cluster of matrilineal peoples.

The social and cultural heterogeneity of the peoples of the Ivory Coast is not without significance for this study. It is associated with different patterns of recruitment into schools, and in some instances ethnic minorities appear to hold distinctive attitudes and values concerning formal education and other aspects of the process of modernization.

European Penetration

France made its first effective contact with the Ivory Coast during the early eighteenth century.[7] Missionaries, the forerunners of European penetration, were soon followed by military expeditions—whose contacts, however, were sporadic and not systematic in character. New efforts to establish a permanent base for operations were undertaken during the second half of the nineteenth century, when treaties were signed with local chiefs. Under the terms of these treaties the French were obliged to afford protection to the principalities, to refrain from interfering with their sovereignty, and to pay them annual subsidies. In return, chiefs were to accord the French a monopoly over all economic transactions, to afford them free access to the hinterland, and to grant them land for military posts.[8] Interestingly enough, the

7. A Catholic mission was established at Assinie in 1687, but its activities soon ceased. Its development is reported in Paul Roussier, *L'Etablissement d'Issine, 1687–1702* ("Publication du Comité d'Etudes Historiques et Scientifiques de l'Afrique Occidentale Française" [Paris: Librarie Larose, 1935]).

8. P. Atger gives a detailed analysis of the relationships established at that time between local chiefs and French naval officers in *La France en Côte d'Ivoire de 1843 à 1893, cinquante ans d'hésitations politiques et commerciales* (Dakar:

content of these agreements indicates that the French naval officers of the period greatly exaggerated the extent of the local chiefs' authority, considering them monarchs who exerted autocratic power over clearly delineated territories. In this respect the French followed practices similar to their British counterparts in the Gold Coast, recognizing traditional authority while at the same time exaggerating its powers.

The penetration of France into the Ivory Coast followed a definite pattern, as in other African areas. Military control preceded systematic economic exploitation of the region, and the French were at great pains to prevent further British expansion westward from the Gold Coast. To this end a businessman, Arthur Verdier, was appointed as resident in the Ivory Coast in 1878, and Grand Bassam became the base for systematic exploration of the hinterland. Thus the southeast corner of the Ivory Coast was the first part of the country to be subjected to strong and permanent Western influence. Further, while French troops attempted to control the territories located beyond the coastal areas, explorers simultaneously attempted to make their way from the already colonized sections of West Africa toward the Ivory Coast. Binger (in 1882 and 1888) and Monteil (1891–95) penetrated from the Sudan and Upper Volta toward the south. As a result the last part of the Ivory Coast to be subdued by France was not the north, as is often believed, but the central and western portions occupied by the Abbey, the Baoulé, and the Kru. Control of the entire Ivory Coast was not achieved until the end of the First World War.[9] Yet this area had already been included in the larger Federation of French West Africa by a series of decrees signed between 1895 and 1904. There was no concerted attempt to weaken traditional political systems in the earlier period of French expansion. Policies of direct rule, accompanied by more systematic efforts at assimilation, did not emerge until just after the First World War.

In addition, differences in the duration and intensity of contact established between the French and the peoples of the Ivory Coast are reflected in the present production structure of the country and the relative degree of economic development of the various areas. For instance, although the western regions may be potentially as wealthy

Université de Dakar, Publications de la Section d'Histoire, No. 2, 1962). The content of the most famous of these treaties is given on p. 36 ff.

9. Frequent revolts prevented the French colonial administration from establishing definite control over the Abbey and the Bété before 1914. See G. Marty, *Précis historique de la colonisation française en Afrique Occidentale depuis les premiers siècles jusqu'en 1910* (Paris: Editions Larose, 1937), pp. 78–123.

as the east, they have not been exploited on the same scale because of their later incorporation into the colonial system.

Economic Development

Until the end of the First World War the main resources exploited by the French were timber and palm oil. After this period the French administration made strong efforts to develop cocoa plantations, which played an increasingly important role in the economic growth of the

TABLE 2. Decentralization of Coffee and Cocoa Production

GEOGRAPHIC AREA	YEARS					
	1942		1951		1957	
	Tons	%	Tons	%	Tons	%
Southwest	21,920	25	30,610	27	43,825	35
Center	19,600	22	42,500	36	38,709	31
Southeast	46,100	53	43,500	37	41,749	34
		100		100		100

Reproduced from A. R. Zolberg, *One Party Government in the Ivory Coast* (Princeton: Princeton University Press, 1964), p. 25.

Ivory Coast. Until 1952 the territory produced more cocoa than coffee, but since that date coffee production has been more important. However, the development of these crops has taken various forms.

Originally the agricultural exploitation of the south was very uneven, but there is now a tendency for the southwest to catch up with the southeast (Table 2). In the southeast, expansion has been brought about almost entirely through the efforts of local African farmers. By contrast, in the central and western parts of the country the administration first favored the development of large-scale European plantations, although in recent years many Webe, Malinke, and Baoulé farmers have settled there. In short, farmers engaged in growing cash crops are a very heterogeneous group. The general density of population in the area, the nature of traditional organization, and the response to the introduction of new techniques and crops are among the variables which determine the level of economic achievement of these farmers.[10]

10. A. J. F. Kobben, "Le planteur noir," *op. cit.;* M. Dupire, "Planteurs autochtones et étrangers dans la Basse Côte d'Ivoire Orientale," *op. cit.;* and

However, cash cropping is almost entirely confined to the south. The north, which contains about one-third of the population, is an area of subsistence farming, producing principally rice and maize. This implies that certain minorities within the Ivory Coast population have already been drawn into a market economy and have been thereby exposed to many modernizing forces, while other groups have only been peripherally involved in processes of economic change. As we shall see, this distinction has an important bearing on the diffusion of education.

Industrialization is quite recent in the Ivory Coast. Except for one large-scale firm with 1,500 workers, located in Bouaké, the principal town of the central Ivory Coast, and several lumber and sawmill enterprises scattered throughout the forest area, industry is largely concentrated in Abidjan. The most recent additions are a match factory (SOTROPAL), a soluble coffee company (CAPRAL), an auto assembly line (SAFAR), and a flour-milling industry (Grands Moulins d'Abidjan). This concentration is the result of an increased supply of electrical power in this area, from both hydro and thermal sources. It is also associated with the proximity of a well-equipped port, with an adequate supply of skilled manpower, and with a concentration of financial institutions. The rate of economic growth of Abidjan is much higher than that of the hinterland. Consequently the range of income of the various subgroups living within the capital is greater than in any other part of the country.

The only firms controlled by African entrepreneurs are a small plant which manufactures machinery for the decortication of coffee beans (ABI) and two medium-sized construction companies. Apart from this, the Africans are involved in small-scale trading activities and transportation services. The size of European-owned firms varies a great deal, but the most recent activities are large-scale bureaucratic enterprises.

H. Raulin, *Mission d'études des groupements immigrés en Côte d'Ivoire, problèmes fonciers dans les régions de Gagnoa et Daloa* ("Documents du Conseil Supérieur de la Recherche Scientifique Outre Mer," fasc. 3 [Paris: Office de la Recherche Scientifique dans les Territoires d'Outre Mer, 1957]), describe various contrasts between the size and organization of the farms of the different peoples settled in the cocoa and coffee belts of the country. There is also some significant statistical information on this problem in Service de la Statistique, *Etude démographique et agricole du 1er secteur, Côte d'Ivoire* (June 1956–January 1957 [Abidjan: Imprimerie du Gouvernement, 1958]), and Service de la Statistique, *Enquête nutrition, niveau de vie, subdivision de Bongouanou, 1955–1956* (Abidjan: 1958).

Demography and Migration

The uneven rate of economic change within the country has produced two distinct streams of migration. Each year the plantation areas attract a large number of unskilled workers, who are recruited from the younger male elements of overpopulated regions and neighboring countries. This labor force is provided mainly by the Upper Volta (30,000 yearly) and to a minor extent by the Senoufo, Malinke, and Webe from the northern and western sections of the Ivory Coast. Since these migrations have taken place for a considerable period, they have enabled some of the unskilled laborers to settle in richer areas and own their own farms.

The second type of migration results from the concentration of industrial and commercial activities in the larger urban centers. This migration is heterogeneous because the modern sector of the economy attracts both unskilled laborers, generally from Upper Volta, and highly qualified clerical workers from Senegal, Dahomey, Togoland, and Upper Volta. Among the Ivory Coast ethnic groups, the Baoulé, the Bété, and the Malinke are the most heavily represented in Abidjan. Each ethnic group tends to be concentrated in certain kinds of occupations. The Ebrié are most numerous in construction work; the Webe and Guéré are frequently found in domestic service; the Bété are well represented in the ranks of skilled artisans and technical workers.

The population of the Ivory Coast remains overwhelmingly rural, and over 80 per cent of its inhabitants live in villages with less than 5,000 inhabitants. Generally speaking, the density of population is fairly low, except in the most economically developed areas and certain specific backward regions that tend to act as reservoirs of manpower. The first category includes the Abidjan area itself and the agricultural zones around Dabou, Grand Bassam, Alepe, Gagnoa, Lakota, Bongouanou, Tiébissou, and Toulepleu; the second includes the zones which surround Man, Bouaké, and Korhogo.

The urban population is concentrated in eight towns with between 10,000 and 50,000 inhabitants. The largest centers are Bouaké, with slightly over 50,000, and the capital, Abidjan, which has grown more rapidly than all other urban centers and now has a population of approximately 225,000. This difference may be partly explained by the concentration of economic activity in this city and also by the political and administrative centralization of the country, which limits the extent to which the hinterland may enjoy autonomous development.

There are interesting qualitative contrasts between the population of Abidjan and that of the remainder of the country. First of all, men are in the majority,[11] and three-fourths of them are between 15 and 35 years of age. This fact reflects the conditions of the labor market and has certain effects on family structure. Since the composition of the household is related to the age of the household head, the frequency of polygynous families in Abidjan is lower than in many parts of the hinterland.[12] Furthermore, there is a distinct trend toward nuclear family organization, with a corresponding reduction in the extent to which women are directly involved in economic activities. It is also noteworthy that the stability of the nuclear family in Abidjan is dependent upon the regularity of familial income to a greater degree than in rural areas.[13]

In contrast with a large number of other African cities, Abidjan is not divided into ethnic neighborhoods, and its melting-pot characteristics are very evident.[14] However, there is evidence of increasing residential differentiation of Africans along socio-economic lines. Thus urbanization creates distinct patterns of familial organization and association which expose children to experiences quite different from those present within the traditional structure. These facts must be borne in mind when we consider the different characteristics of African secondary school pupils.

Political Development

One of the most salient characteristics of the French bureaucracy is its tendency to centralize political and administrative structures. This

11. See Ministère du Plan de la Côte d'Ivoire, Service de la Statistique, *Recensement d'Abidjan, 1955; résultats définitifs* (Paris, 1960).

12. The following rates of polygyny are given (the number of polygynous women divided by the number of married women): for Abidjan, 14.2 per cent (*Recensement d'Abidjan, op. cit.*, Table 2.24 A, p. 32); for the Agni, 45 per cent (*Enquête nutrition, niveau de vie, op. cit.*, Table 3.8, p. 32); for the Bété, 68 per cent ("Le planteur noir," *op. cit.*, p. 130).

13. In an unpublished survey conducted in 1959 for the Ministère des Travaux Publics, l'Institut Français d'Afrique Noire found that 56 per cent of the families in which all members were living together had a regular income, whereas 71 per cent of those families in which the members had different residences had irregular sources of income.

14. *Ibid.* By contrast, see R. Grivot, "Agboville, Esquisse d'une cité d'Afrique Noire," *Etudes éburnéennes,* IV (Abidjan: Centre IFAN, 1955), pp. 84–107, and H. Raulin, *op. cit.*, p. 121.

characteristic prevails in former colonies as well as in the metropole. As soon as it was incorporated, the Ivory Coast became subject to a centralized and hierarchical administrative arrangement. The governor exerted close control over his district officers, but was in turn obliged to conform to detailed instructions issued by the general governor of the West African Federation and by the Ministry of Colonies (later the Ministry of Overseas Territories). Under these conditions such decentralization as has occurred remains a recent and limited phenomenon. Only a few cities have been incorporated, and these have never acquired substantial autonomy with respect to their finances or development plans.

The newly independent government of the Ivory Coast has accepted this administrative heritage. The constitution is a duplication of the French Constitution of 1958, which accentuates centralization and promotes a tight control by the executive heads of the government upon the economic and social life of the country. Although districts have been reorganized on a broader geographical basis and theoretically have been given legislative institutions (*Conseils Généraux*), their autonomy remains limited.

However, this centralized structure has been obliged in practice to make concessions to minority pressures. To a certain extent the government bureaucracy reflects the organization of the *Rassemblement Démocratique Africain*. During the struggle for independence the party was organized along ethnic lines to promote efficiency and to escape the control of colonial administration.[15] It has never been able to replace its ethnic subcommittees by ward units, defined on a strictly geographic basis. Furthermore, many of the political conflicts in the contemporary Ivory Coast reflect ethnic tensions and dissent.

The Early Development of Education

At the beginning of the colonial period the diffusion of schooling was related to local political necessities. A French primary school teacher, Jean d'Heur, was sent to Assinie in 1887 with the task of

15. The point is fully developed by A. R. Zolberg in "L'Effet de la structure d'un parti politique sur l'intégration nationale," *Cahiers d'études africaines*, Vol. I, No. 3 (January 1961), pp. 140–49. This same author also describes the pattern more fully in *One Party Government in the Ivory Coast* (Princeton: Princeton University Press, 1964), Chapter IX, "Modernization and Control."

opening a primary school in order to attract as many members as possible from the N'zima tribe of the nearby Gold Coast.[16] In order that colonial expansion could continue, it was necessary that France be looked upon as a more desirable master than Great Britain. Very rapidly, however, educational development reflected broader economic and political preoccupations, which changed through time.

The first systematic educational policy in French West African territories was developed by Faidherbe, whose plan was to train a restricted elite locally and send its more gifted students to metropolitan institutions of higher education. Initially this elite was to be recruited from the sons of the chiefs. Talented children were also supposed to be given opportunities for advanced education.

> We are ready to help any child who displays extraordinary gifts during his studies to become a professional. . . . Already, the children from *Christian* families in *St. Louis* who have received good grades during their primary schooling go to France in order to attend Lycées and come back ready to occupy the most important positions in the colony.[17] (Italics added.)

Although it was thus agreed that educational development should ensure the growth of a potential elite, there was much discussion about the portion of the population from which this elite should be recruited. As we may see from the above remarks, Faidherbe abandoned his early idea of modernizing traditional authority and was increasingly concerned with the idea of recruiting the elite from among the most acculturated segments of the population.[18] Nevertheless the policy of giving the children of traditional chiefs preferential access to school persisted until the end of the First World War.[19]

The period between 1898 and 1914 was characterized by the preponderant emphasis placed upon the development of a primary school system.[20] Between 1898 and 1903 six schools were opened, with the

16. See *Archives*, Ivory Coast, X, X.2, Enc. 1, Administration générale des Services de l'Ancien Ministère de la France d'Outre Mer.

17. Quoted by H. Brunschwig, *La Colonisation française* (Paris: Calman Levy, 1948), p. 90.

18. It is interesting to note that the criteria used here to determine acculturation were religion and residence. In fact, the Christian "gentry" of St. Louis in Senegal have always occupied a privileged position in the colonial system.

19. See "La Situation d'ensemble de l'enseignement pour la période triennale 1920–1923," *Bulletin du Comité de l'Afrique Française*, No. 2 (February 1924), pp. 112–15. The schools were to train primarily the sons of traditional chiefs.

20. These details have been drawn from *Annuaire du Ministère des Colonies (1898–1914)*. This *annuaire* indicates the number and characteristics of the civil servants employed by the various administrations in each territory.

help of missionaries in Assinie, Mossou, Grand Bassam, and Memmi, in the southeastern part of the Ivory Coast, and two others were founded in Dabou and Jacqueville, further west. Between 1906 and 1910 the teaching force became both more numerous and more differentiated. Twenty-five Senegalese soldiers were utilized as instructors, and a European woman was added to the staff. In consequence new schools were opened in the northern territories at Dabakala and Bondoukou, and in the west at Grand Lahou and Tabou. In fact the distribution of schools tended to follow military expansion. By 1910 the number of schools was so large that an *Inspection Primaire* (superintendency of the school system) was created. At that time the public teaching force included five European men and one woman, one male and one female schoolteacher graduated from the *Ecole Primaire Supérieure* of Senegal, and nine semiqualified instructors. Unfortunately no reliable figures concerning school attendance are available for this period.

Two characteristics underlay the functioning of the school system at that time. The governor general of French Africa was anxious to give a degree of autonomy to his regional deputies in their treatment of local educational problems; the latter had to decide what should be the optimum rate of growth of educational institutions and what curricula should be developed as most appropriate to "local problems and necessities." Simultaneously the central government wished to increase the number of African teachers in primary schools. A school was opened for this purpose in the vicinity of Dakar, and the number of its graduates increased regularly. Between 1906 and 1912 no less than 160 were appointed as schoolteachers.

In 1923 a *circulaire* of the governor general unified the educational structure of the entire West African Federation and attempted a clearer definition of the nature and function of various types of educational institutions than had been provided by an earlier ordinance in 1903. At the primary level there were to be two types of schools, rural and urban. The first had a two-year program (*Cours Préparatoire* and *Cours Elémentaire*), which was supposed to be directed by an African teacher or instructor. Beyond the rural schools were regional institutions established in the larger villages to recruit the most able pupils of the rural schools for a four-year program. The early expansion of this primary system is indicated in Table 3.

At the postprimary level, one-third of those students who had gained the *Certificat de Fin d'Etudes Primaires* (C.E.P.) were sent to

TABLE 3. Expansion of the Rural and Regional Schools in French West Africa, 1920–1939

YEAR	RURAL SCHOOLS		REGIONAL SCHOOLS	
	Number of Institutions	Number of Students	Number of Institutions	Number of Students
1920–1921	227	16,363	63	4,791
1921–1922	246	19,552	69	4,828
1922–1923	275	22,110	69	4,831
1938–1939	310	26,195	96	21,196

Computed from *Bulletin du Comité de l'Afrique française*, April 1924, pp. 112–15, and September 1939, p. 188.

a single vocational school. Two-thirds entered an *Ecole Primaire Supérieure,* which constituted a preliminary stage for entrance to a teachers' college (*Ecole Normale*), a clerical school, or a nurses' training program. In 1923 there were six such *Ecoles Primaires Supérieures* in West Africa, with 540 students. The profile of the entire system at that time is indicated in Figure 2.[21]

Dadier has observed that during this period there was a permanent conflict between two schools of thought.[22] One group of administrators pressed for the expansion of the primary system in order to supply the increasing manpower needs of the modern sector of the economy, while a second group favored a slower pace of educational development in order to avoid possible social and economic disruption of traditional societies.

The proponents of the first viewpoint did succeed in increasing the

21. The most important administrative texts concerning the development of education in the West African colonies are as follows: (a) The Arrété of November 24, 1903, giving a definition of the distinctive types of education as modified by the *circulaires* of December 30, 1923, January 28, 1931, January 20, 1932, March 30, 1932, and April 8, 1933. All these measures were promulgated by the Gouvernement Général de l'Afrique Occidentale Française. (b) The basic organization of the teachers' colleges (*Cours et Ecoles Normales*) was delineated by the Arrété of November 24, 1903, the Arrété of November 1, 1918, modified by the Arrétés of April 19, 1933, June 6, 1934, and October 9, 1936.

Further, two articles summarize the changes in the educational system which occurred during this period and the motives which underlay them. B. Dadier, "Misère de l'enseignement en A.O.F.," *Présence africaine,* No. 11 (December 1956–January 1957), pp. 57–70, and Ray Autra, "Historique de l'enseignement en A.O.F.," *Présence africaine,* No. 6 (February–March 1956), pp. 68–86.

22. Dadier, *op. cit.,* indicates that the two lines of thought were opposed in the following manner: The alternatives were either to give specialized training to a minority of individuals or to assure every individual a basic humanistic academic experience.

FIGURE 2. Profile of the Educational System in French West Africa before World War II

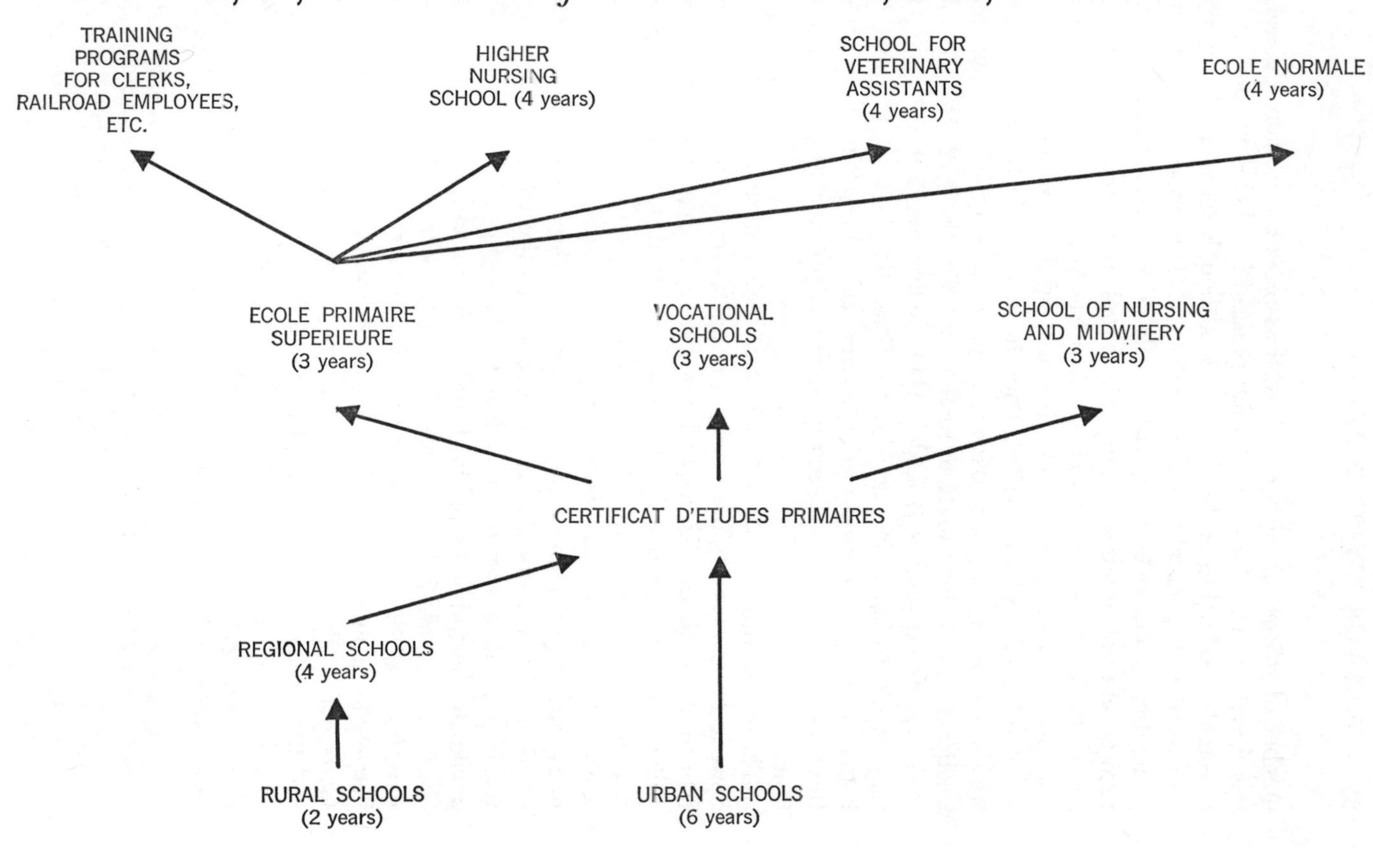

number of schools of all types, as well as providing a more differentiated system. Also, they successfully pressed for the establishment of a secondary school in St. Louis in 1928. Although access to this school was restricted primarily to the children of French colonists in the Federation, some seats were made available to African children. The total number of pupils attending this school rose from 174 in 1930 to 500 in 1936. At the final examination, corresponding to the metropolitan *Baccalaureat,* 7 out of 15 African candidates were admitted in 1930 and 28 out of 53 in 1936. Thus in the middle thirties the first trickle of Africans began to emerge from the schools with educational qualifications commensurate in some cases with those of their French counterparts. At present it is clear that conflict within the contemporary political elite is in part due to disparities in educational level between groups educated in the thirties and others educated during the later period and possessing more advanced educational qualifications.[23]

The conservatives within the French colonial regime succeeded, however, in preventing metropolitan practices from being exported in toto to West Africa and resisted any systematizing of assimilationist policies. For instance, only the two best students of any teachers' college were allowed to continue (for one year) in a specialized course at a metropolitan institution. Furthermore, access to postprimary education was made more selective, on the assumption that too rapid an expansion of the upper segment of the educational system would generate a mass of unemployed educated youth and thus create a climate favorable to political and social unrest. An intermediate course (*Cours de Selection*) was organized between the *Ecoles Régionales* and the *Ecoles Primaires Supérieures,* with the aim of keeping as many students as possible away from the academic schools. Correspondingly, a new impetus was given to vocational institutions, and the *Ecoles Rurales* received a new definition; they were to place as much emphasis as possible on the agricultural component of the curriculum. Between 1934 and 1936 the area of agricultural land attached to rural schools grew from 476 acres to 845 acres, and by 1937

23. Zolberg, *op. cit.,* pp. 279–80, notes that recruitment of officeholders in the Ivory Coast could no longer be limited to "those who fought the battles of the party during its formation years, individuals characterized by an upper primary or Ponty education. . . . The appearance of a new generation on the political stage is also reflected in the doubling of the proportions of members with a *Baccalaureat.*" See also his Table 20, p. 275, which summarizes the characteristics of Ivory Coast officeholders.

each school with a full complement of classes was obliged to plant 2.5 acres of coffee.

In summary, the period preceding the Second World War was characterized by vagueness in the theories underlying the expansion of educational facilities. Some officials stressed the need for the emergence of a Western type of elite. Others emphasized the necessity for adjusting the expansion of education to local conditions, thereby satisfying the demands of the modern sector of the economy by developing clerical and manual workers while at the same time keeping the majority of students on the land.

This period was also characterized by considerable geographical diffentiation in the expansion of education. The proportion of the local budget devoted to education varied from one colony to another, and in this respect the Ivory Coast lagged far behind territories such as Senegal and Dahomey (Table 4). These disparities reflected differences in the local demand for education and contrasting policies followed by the French regime in various areas. European plantation owners, who were the most powerful economic figures in the Ivory Coast until 1958 and whose needs were largely for unskilled labor, were not particularly interested in educational development. During the thirties the Ivory Coast and Upper Volta together produced only 20 graduates annually from the William Ponty School and only 4 university graduates.

The contribution of the African territories to the Second World War obliged the French government to revise the constitutional framework of its colonial possessions. The main lines of a new colonial policy were hammered out at the Brazzaville Conference in 1946, which laid great stress on educational matters. Two goals underlay postwar education policy in colonial areas: An attempt had to be made to eradicate illiteracy, and it was deemed essential that the colonial educational structure should be, in large measure, a duplication of the metropolitan system. "We cannot any longer be concerned with the training of docile servants. . . . We have to build men out of the children that the parents send to our schools." [24] Yet the absence of local resources and the resistance of the French *colons* prevented any marked expansion of the system. To be sure, the organization of the school system was changed; the Federation of West Africa became a *rectorat* modeled on metropolitan lines, and in all the territories of this

24. Speech given by Inspecteur Général de l'Enseignement Delage, quoted by B. Dadier, *op. cit.*

TABLE 4. School Enrollments in Senegal and in the Ivory Coast, 1931–1934

TERRITORY AND YEAR	RURAL SCHOOLS		REGIONAL SCHOOLS		URBAN SCHOOLS		ECOLES PRIMAIRES SUPERIEURES		VOCATIONAL TRAINING SCHOOLS		PRIVATE SCHOOLS	
	Schools	Students *	Schools	Students	Schools	Students	Schools	Students	Schools	Students	Schools	Students
Senegal	61	8,679	13	800	6	657	1	184	1	63	Not available	
1931–1932		470		60		87		...		..		
Ivory Coast	27	4,240	12	363	1	...	1	138	1	90	11	573
1931–1932		253		55		100		...		..		167
Ivory Coast †	43	3,839	19	4,156	1	...	2	245	2	106	19	1,961 ‡
1933–1934		486		513		58		2		...		

* Upper numbers include boys; lower numbers include girls.

† To these institutions should be added one school in the Ivory Coast for children of mixed descent.

‡ No separate figures are available for male and female enrollments.

Computed from *Bulletin du Comité de l'Afrique française* (No. 5, 1932), p. 82, and from Bryant Mumford, *Africans Learn to be French* (London: Evans Brothers, 1935), p. 170.

Federation a general superintendent was appointed as head of the entire school system.[25] In the Ivory Coast the four original *Ecoles Primaires Supérieures* became *Collèges*, and a *Lycée* was opened in Abidjan.

Radical political changes took place in 1950 when a period of agitation in the Ivory Coast was terminated by an agreement concluded between the *Rassemblement Démocratique Africain* and the Minister of Overseas Affairs. This agreement induced the local colonial administration to adopt a new educational policy and enlarge the entire school system. The first efforts in this direction were, of course, focused upon primary enrollments (Table 5). Yet the educational expenditures of the country still lagged behind those of other territories. For example, in proportion to its resources the educational effort of the Ivory Coast was less than that of Dahomey.

A second impetus was given in 1956, when the *loi cadre* was voted and when it became obvious that the personnel of the local adminis-

TABLE 5. Evolution of the Primary, Secondary, and Technical Systems, 1948–1963

ACADEMIC YEAR	SYSTEM		
	Primary	Secondary Academic	Secondary Technical
1948–1949	22,876	1,114	Not available
1949–1950	28,383	Not available	"
1950–1951	32,259	1,121	"
1951–1952	34,537	1,510	327
1952–1953	39,522	1,710	Not available
1953–1954	46,545	2,010	"
1954–1955	57,200	2,480	"
1955–1956	69,181	3,011	1,100
1956–1957	90,907	3,620	Not available
1957–1958	125,727	4,400	"
1958–1959	165,233	6,060	933
1959–1960	200,046	8,180	1,293
1960–1961	238,772	10,824	1,483
1961–1962	265,062	13,709	1,616
1962–1963	298,716	17,528	1,698 (estimated)

Computed from Côte d'Ivoire, Ministère des Finances, *Supplément trimestriel du Bulletin mensuel de statistiques*, No. 2 (1961); Côte d'Ivoire, Ministère de l'Education Nationale, *L'Enseignement du deuxième degré 1962–63* (Abidjan, 1963); *Chroniques d'Outre Mer*, No. 29 (Paris, October 1956); and *L'Enseignement d'Outre Mer*, No. 7 (Paris, December 1955).

25. The *rectorat* of French West Africa was created by a decree of November 27, 1950. The rectorat is the administrative unit which controls all the educational activities within a given area.

tration would be increasingly Africanized.[26] Further, as a result of the growing entente between Houphouet-Boigny and France, the Ivory Coast was chosen as a model upon which the colonial administration was to concentrate its efforts. This probably accounts for the fact that of 469 scholarships enabling African students to attend metropolitan institutions, almost 60 per cent were given to Ivory Coast students.[27]

The increase in primary school provision, however, did not eradicate existing imparities in access to schooling. Female enrollments still lagged behind those of males, and in the academic year 1960–61, 176,000 boys were attending primary school as against only 63,000 girls. Inequalities also persisted between geographical areas. For example, in 1958, 59 per cent of the children living in the Abengourou district were enrolled in primary institutions, as against only 8 per cent of children living in the Korhogo area. Three years later these relative differences had increased.[28]

Within the primary system the rate of attrition was still very high. The first-year enrollment represented 48 per cent of all students in primary schools, while candidates for the *Certificat d'Etudes Primaires* (C.E.P.) represented only 5 per cent of primary school pupils. Attrition was, and is, particularly high during the first three years of schooling. In addition, access to secondary institutions remained limited until 1958, and the percentage of students admitted either to the *sixième* of *Lycées* and *Collèges* or to the *sixième* of the *Cours Normaux* always remained below 50 per cent of eligible candidates.[29]

The Characteristics of the Present Postprimary Educational System

Since the Second World War the organization of postprimary education in the Ivory Coast has increasingly paralleled that of the metropolitan schools and has become more complex (Figure 3). The system is divided into three major streams: the academic, the technical or

26. Law 56–619, promulgated June 23, 1956, constituted the basic orientation underlying the political changes which took place in the French overseas territories between 1956 and 1958.

27. *Encyclopédie mensuelle d'Outre Mer,* No. 70 (June 1956), p. 250.

28. See Côte d'Ivoire, Ministère des Finances, *Supplément trimestriel du Bulletin mensuel de statistiques,* No. 2 (trimestre 1961), pp. 24–26.

29. French educational terminology reverses the usual American or British practice. The first year of secondary study is termed the *sixième,* followed successively by the *cinquième, quatrième,* etc.

FIGURE 3. The Structure of Postprimary Education in the Ivory Coast in 1963

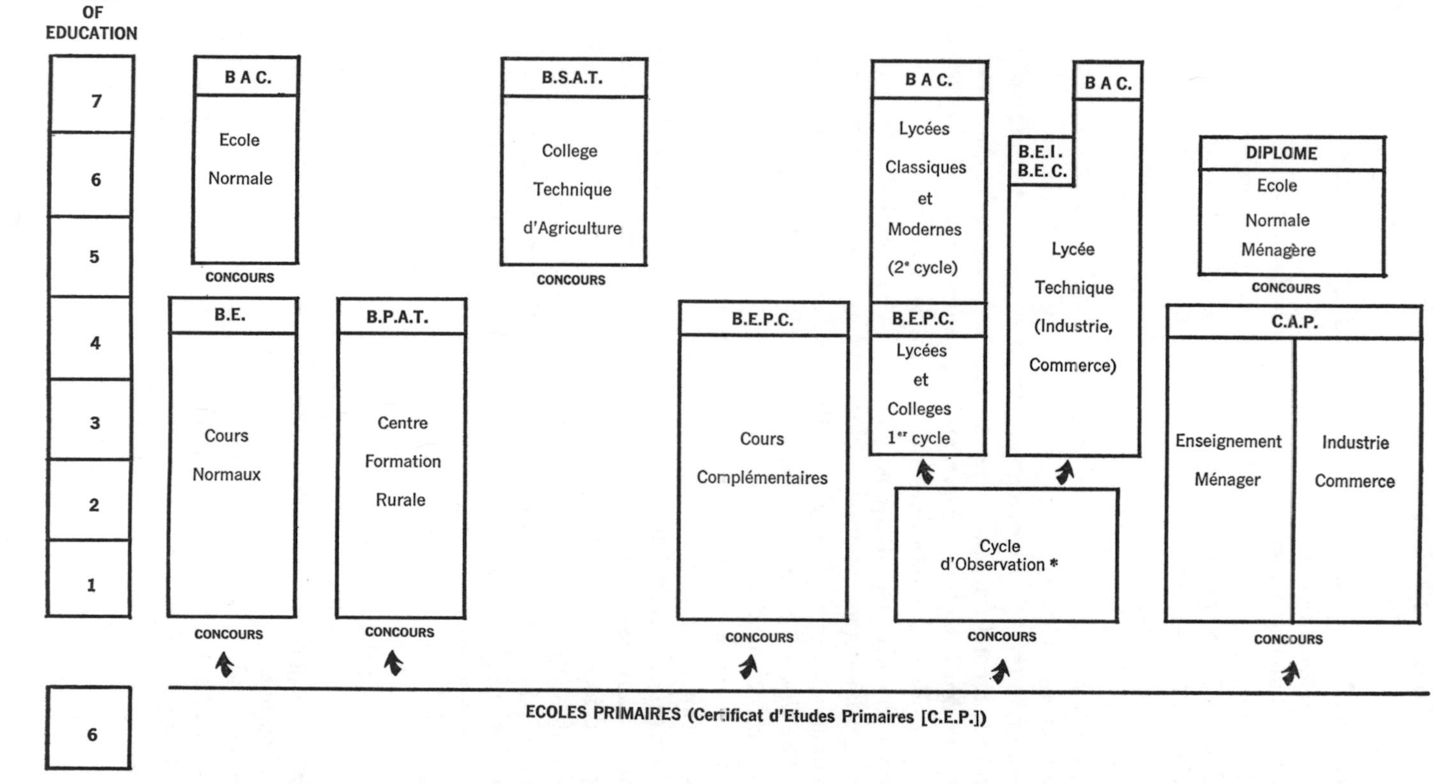

* The *cycle d'observation* is an innovation following recent developments in the metropolitan system. It aims at deferring selection into the *Lycées* and *Collèges* for a period of two years.

vocational, and the agricultural. Let us first examine the academic stream in some detail.

The academic schools are themselves divided into three major types. The academic "long" schools (*Lycées* and *Collèges*), the academic "short" schools (*Cours Complémentaires*), and the teacher training colleges (*Cours Normaux*). The *Lycées* and *Collèges* provide two cycles of study. The first cycle of four years, which ends in the *troisième* class, is terminated by a major examination (the *Brevet de Fin d'Etudes du Premier Cycle,* or B.E.P.C.). Students within the *Lycées* and *Collèges* may proceed to the second cycle of studies leading to the first *Baccalaureat,* which is taken in the *première* class, and the second *baccalaureats,* which are taken in the classes of *Philosophie, Mathématiques Elémentaires,* or *Sciences Expérimentales.* The long academic system does provide curricular alternatives. These include the classical division, with a strong emphasis on Latin and foreign languages, and the modern division, with a bias toward either mathematics and physical or natural sciences, or modern languages.

The *Cours Complémentaires,* which were created in 1957, constitute the "short" academic stream and prepare students only in a single four-year cycle of secondary studies leading to the B.E.P.C. examination. This latter differs in some minor details from the long B.E.P.C. The purposes underlying the development of the *Cours Complémentaires* were ambiguous and have remained so. Clearly they were opened in order to satisfy part of the growing demand for secondary education generated by the increased output of the primary system. Initially none of the *Cours Complémentaires* students, recruited from among the less able children who had succeeded in passing the entrance examination to secondary school, were allowed to continue beyond the first four years of postprimary schooling. Their education was to be terminated with the possession of the B.E.P.C. It was also anticipated that the curricula of these institutions would be regionalized, so that their students would constitute the backbone of a technical bureaucracy specializing in either agricultural or stock-rearing techniques, depending on the region. This decision was never enforced, and there has been no differentiation whatever between the courses taught in *Cours Complémentaires* and those provided in the *Collèges* and *Lycées.*[30]

In practice, until 1963, in spite of provisions to the contrary, some of

30. Personal interview with M. Clerici, Directeur du Ministère de l'Education Nationale (July 1964).

the best students of the *Cours Complémentaires* were allowed to enter the second cycle of the *Lycées* and *Collèges*. In that year an even more drastic step was taken. Recognizing that the *Cours Complémentaires* were merely extension branches of the regular academic system, the government decided to allow all students within them to take an entrance examination into the second cycle, access to which had previously been monopolized by students in the *Lycées* and *Collèges*.

The *Cours Normaux*, which represent the third division of the academic stream, provide a four-year cycle leading to the *Brevet Elémentaire* (B.E.), which is roughly equivalent to the B.E.P.C. and which qualifies students to teach in primary schools. A few students are allowed to proceed further into the *Ecole Normale*, which prepares them for the *Baccalaureat* examinations. In effect, the *Cours Normaux* really offer a short academic training for the overwhelming majority of their students, and in later pages we have found it convenient to group them with the *Cours Complémentaires*.

Let us now examine the structure of the technical and vocational system. In 1959, in order to deal more efficiently with the ever increasing number of graduates of the primary schools, it was decided to differentiate the structure of existing technical institutions and make them similar to their counterparts in France. The existing vocational centers (*Centres d'Apprentissage*) provide their students with a short cycle of three or four years of highly specialized studies in industrial techniques (mechanics, carpentry, building trades, electricity, and ironwork), home economics (sewing, maternal and infant care, cooking, dietetics), and commerce (accounting and secretarial duties). All courses at this level are terminated by the award of a *Certificat d'Aptitude Professionnelle* (C.A.P.) or a *Capacité Commerciale*, beyond which further study is almost impossible.

However, an attempt has been made to raise the status of technical studies by creating a *Lycée Technique*, which provides a variety of courses of between five and seven years' duration. Entry to the *Lycée Technique* is rarely from the *Centres d'Apprentissages*, but either directly from the primary schools or from the academic stream of the secondary system. The full seven-year cycle leads to a *Baccalaureat* in industrial technology or economics, but a shorter five-year cycle prepares students for the *Brevet d'Etudes Industrielles* (B.E.I.) or the *Brevet d'Etudes Commerciales* (B.E.C.). In addition, special qualifications exist in surveying (*Brevet de Géomètre*) and in home economics (*Diplôme des Techniciennes d'Enseignement Ménager*).

The agricultural stream provides the third major component of the postprimary educational structure. Its internal organization is similar to that of the other two principal streams. The *Centre de Formation Rurale* provides a first cycle of studies lasting three years and leading to the *Brevet Professionnel d'Agriculture Tropicale.* On this sequence is superimposed a *Collège d'Agriculture,* which provides another three-year cycle of studies, leading to the *Brevet Supérieur Professionnel Agricole,* with a status equivalent to that of the *Baccalaureat.* The *Collège d'Agriculture* recruits its students either from the *Centre de Formation Rurale* or from those who have completed the B.E.P.C. qualification in the academic stream.

As if this present system of secondary studies were not already complex enough, the government created a variety of new institutions between 1958 and 1963. These were designed to absorb the increasing number of graduates from the postprimary system and to fill new types of openings in the bureaucracy. It can be seen from Table 6 that courses of training in these institutions are highly specialized. Applicants who wish to enter them first require a qualifying certificate, which allows them to sit for a competitive *concours* for entry. This qualifying certificate varies, but the minimum level has risen in recent years.

The extent of the present postprimary system is summarized in Table 7. Two salient features emerge from this picture. The overwhelming majority of educational institutions are public and include 85 per cent of the entire student body. Students in these schools do not have to pay tuition fees. Indeed many are assisted in various ways, and almost half of the students attending public *Lycées* and *Collèges* enjoy free board and/or room. This proportion increases to 70 per cent for the population of the *Cours Normaux* and declines to one-third in *Cours Complémentaires.* Only 20 per cent of the children attending private schools are provided with such assistance. However, the fees of this subsegment of the school population have been recently reduced as a result of grants-in-aid extended by the government to the private school system.

We must also note that most postprimary schools are concentrated in Abidjan and its surroundings. Twelve of the twenty public and private *Lycées* and *Collèges,* six of the thirty-six public and private *Cours Complémentaires,* one of the eleven *Cours Normaux,* and four of the seven technical schools are located in that area. This reflects not only the centralization of the administrative structure of the Ivory

TABLE 6. Training Programs and Schools Available through Concours *to the Students of the Postprimary System*

ACADEMIC PREREQUISITE	COURSE	PLACES AVAILABLE	DURATION
C.E.P.	Assistant nurse	80	2 yrs.
	Assistant social worker	30	3 yrs.
	Post office clerk	65	4 mos.
	Merchant marine	20	8 mos.
	Agricultural demonstrator	80	1 yr.
	Policeman	180	1 yr.
C.A.P.	Building assistant surveyor	20	9 mos.
	Junior prospector	7	9 mos.
	Construction foreman	17	4 yrs.
	Hydraulic technician	8	6 mos.
	Roads technician	20	1 yr.
	Bulldozer crewman	20	2 mos.
	Bulldozer foreman	12	6 mos.
	Public works foreman	...	...
	Naval artificer	7	1 yr.
	Post office foreman	25	4 mos.
	Electrical foreman	10	3 mos.
B.E.P.C.	Nurse	10	3 yrs.
	Midwife	15	3 yrs.
	Social worker	20	3 yrs.
	Construction foreman	17	4 yrs.
	Merchant officer	7	1 yr.
	Post office foreman	25	4 mos.
	Statistical operator	10	9 mos.
	Noncommissioned police officer	50	5 mos.
	Police inspector	8	10 mos.
	Assistant prospector	7	9 mos.
Baccalaureat	R.O.T.C.	100	6 mos.
	School of administration	50	2 yrs.
	Public works officer	5	4 yrs.
	Post office supervisor	15	1 yr.
	Post office technician	15	4 mos.

Coast but the fact that almost the entire secondary teaching force is European and reluctant to live in the hinterland.

The Definition of the Sample

The postprimary system of the Ivory Coast is highly selective. Only 10 per cent of the pupils who enter the first year of primary schooling finally gain access to secondary schools. Further, the rate of increase in the size of the two systems is not the same. The secondary schools tend

TABLE 7. The Postprimary System in the Ivory Coast, 1962–1963

	TYPES OF INSTITUTIONS											
	LYCEES AND COLLEGES		COURS NORMAUX		COURS COMPLE-MENTAIRES		ECOLE NORMALE	CENTRES * D'APPRENTIS-SAGE	LYCEE * TECHNIQUE	CENTRE DE FORMATION RURALE	COLLEGE TECHNIQUE D'AGRICUL-TURE	TOTAL
	Public	Private	Public	Private	Public	Private						
Number of institutions	10	10	8	3	26	10	1	5	1	1	1	76
Male enrollments	5,317	1,475	1,590	314	5,822	276	154	653	623	90	118	16,432
Female enrollments	946	809	320	...	495	6	4	257	165	...	...	3,002
Total enrollments	6,263	2,284	1,910	314	6,317	282	158	910	788	90	118	19,434

* Estimated numbers.
Computed from UNESCO, *op. cit.* (note 31), p. 59, and *L'Enseignement du deuxième degré 1962–63*, *op. cit.*, pp. 4,5, 22 ff.

to grow more slowly. In consequence, although a larger number of children enter these institutions each year, the percentage of students who enter the secondary system after completing the final year of primary school is actually diminishing. In addition, of any given cohort entering the *sixième* of the secondary schools, only 39 per cent reach the *troisième* without being obliged to repeat (or double) a class on the way. Even including those who repeat classes, only 63 per cent reach the *troisième*. Of those who enter the *sixième*, only 2 per cent gain the *Baccalaureat* without doubling, and a further 6 per cent finally achieve this qualification in spite of repeating en route.[31]

Thus entering secondary school means overcoming formidable hurdles, but even then access to higher levels of study is not automatically accorded. In the three streams we have discussed, there are two crucial cutting points: at the end of the first and the second cycles of study. All students at these levels face similar obstacles. Some will proceed to further studies; others will double their present class or migrate to lower status institutions; and a large proportion will go directly into the labor force. It is therefore at these cutting points that a study of recruitment and selection becomes most meaningful, and hence the final sample of students used as the basis of this investigation was drawn from the total student population at the end of the first and the second cycles of postprimary studies. In 1963 this population included all candidates who were preparing for the following examinations: the B.E.P.C. (short and long), the B.E., the first and second *Baccalaureat*, the *Capacité Commerciale*, the *Certificat d'Aptitude Professionnelle*, the *Brevet d'Etudes Industrielles et Commerciales*, the *Brevet de Géomètre*, the *Diplôme de Techniciennes d'Enseignement Ménager*, the *Brevet Professionnel d'Agriculture Tropicale*, and the *Brevet Supérieur Professionnel Agricole*.

In 1963 there were 2,712 African students at these levels in the postprimary system, and it was possible to interview 2,176, or just over 80 per cent, of them.[32] Our universe being now defined and the size of our sample indicated, we can proceed to examine the ethnic and social composition of this rigorously selected group.

31. Computed from UNESCO, *Première mission du groupe de planification de l'éducation en Côte d'Ivoire* (Paris, 1963), p. 61.

32. See Appendix A for a discussion of field-work problems and the representativeness of the sample. Appendix B consists of the questionnaire used in the investigation. Of the original 2,176 questionnaires, 2,074 were completed in such a fashion as to be adequate for purposes of analysis.

CHAPTER III

The Ethnic, Social, and Cultural Origin of Students in the Postprimary School System

A SECONDARY SCHOOL SYSTEM which recruits a distinct minority of any age cohort will never draw equally upon all ethnic or social subgroups of the population; inequality of access to secondary schooling is the inevitable corollary of educational selection. The problem of the relative fluidity of recruitment patterns is particularly crucial in the new African states, and we propose to discuss in turn how ethnicity, socioeconomic background, and cultural orientations influence the selection of students for secondary schools. Irrespective of its absolute size, does the secondary school system of the Ivory Coast recruit from a broad spectrum of the population? Or do these elite reservoirs call upon only a narrow segment of the country's social and ethnic groupings?

Ethnic and Geographical Representation

We have seen that French penetration and colonization moved in a generally northward and westward direction from the southeastern section of the country, producing a staggered pattern of contact with the peoples of the Ivory Coast. We have seen also that the expansion of the educational system clearly paralleled the spread of political control, producing marked inequalities in the access of various ethnic groups to schooling. Such inequalities are marked at the level of primary education and are of considerable political significance, but how far are they manifested at the secondary school level?

The picture of ethnic recruitment provided by Table 8 was to be expected. Considering the profile of male enrollments alone, it is evident that the Agni and Lagoon peoples, who were among the first to be subjected to colonial rule, have maintained a strong position in the secondary school system. This is very clear if we compare groups in terms of their selectivity indices, which are merely the ratios between a group's representation in the sample and its approximate representation in the general population. Thus the index for the Agni stands at 2.9, but indices decline consistently as one moves north and west, dropping to as low as 0.3 among the Senoufo-Lobi cluster. However, Africans hailing from outside the Ivory Coast are very well represented, for reasons to be explained later.

Although ethnic groups are obviously over- or underrepresented in terms of their population proportions, it would be remiss to ignore absolute figures of enrollment. Whereas the Kru, for example, are relatively underrepresented compared with the Agni, they still form the largest single ethnic bloc in the schools. If the secondary school system functions as the supplier of middle- and high-level manpower in the Ivory Coast, a very high proportion of that manpower will be drawn from the relatively underrepresented peoples.

Although the picture of female recruitment generally parallels that of males, the gradients are considerably steeper, and southern ethnic groups form a larger proportion of the female student body. This more constricted pattern is perfectly understandable. The access of girls to secondary schooling lags in all ethnic groups, but this lag is likely to be proportionally greater among peoples whose male representation in the schools is relatively low. Girls are seldom found in secondary schools in any number until the level of male enrollments for a particular group is relatively high.[1] As we shall see, ethnic inequalities in female enrollments are paralleled by similar inequalities with respect to other variables. Actually the proportion of female to total enroll-

1. Irrespective of these factors, we feel that traditional attitudes toward the status of women are likely to have a great deal to do with levels of female enrollment. It would be interesting to speculate, for example, whether societies which traditionally accord women a great deal of economic independence react more favorably to the question of female schooling.

TABLE 8. Distribution of Major Ethnic Groupings in Ivory Coast Secondary Schools Compared with Their Distribution in the Population (Percentages)

ETHNIC GROUP *	PERCENTAGE OF † IVORY COAST POPULATION (1958)	MALE STUDENTS	SELECTIVITY INDEX	FEMALE STUDENTS	SELECTIVITY INDEX	TOTAL	SELECTIVITY INDEX
Agni	5.6	15.9	2.8	21.5	3.8	16.5	2.9
Lagoon cluster	7.3	18.4	2.5	16.0	2.2	18.1	2.5
Baoulé	19.0	16.7	0.9	14.8	0.8	16.5	0.9
Kru	18.3	19.9	1.1	18.1	1.0	19.7	1.1
Mandefou	11.2	8.9	0.8	3.4	0.3	8.3	0.7
Malinke	15.2	9.5	0.6	8.9	0.6	9.5	0.6
Senoufo-Lobi	19.0	6.4	0.3	5.5	0.3	6.3	0.3
Other Africans	3.8	4.3	1.1	11.8	3.1	5.1	1.3
Europeans and others	0.6	0.0	..	0.0	..	..	..
Total	100.0	100.0	..	100.0	..	100.0	..
		(1,837)		(237)		(2,074)	

* Ethnic groups comprise the following subclusters: *Agni*—Agni, Nzima, Ehotilé, Abouré, Abron, Mbatto, Apollo; *Lagoon cluster*—Adioukrou, Alladien, Attié, Abidji, Avikam, Ebrié; *Baoulé*—Baoulé; *Kru*—Abbé, Bété, Dida, Godié, Guéré, Neyo, Niaboua, Kru; *Mandefou*—Dan, Gagou, Gouro, Webe, Yacouba; *Malinke*—Malinke; *Senoufo-Lobi*—Kulango, Lobi, Senoufo, Taguana; *Other Africans*—mostly from Dahomey, Senegal, Mali, and Upper Volta; *Europeans and others*—includes Lebanese, West Indians, etc.

† These figures have been computed from Ivory Coast, Ministère du Plan, *Inventaire économique de la Côte d'Ivoire, 1947–1956* (Abidjan, 1958), p. 26, and from unpublished census materials of the Direction de la Statistique et des Etudes Economiques, Côte d'Ivoire, collected in 1959. Although these figures can be considered as only approximations, there is a high degree of correspondence between the two sources regarding the size of the major ethnic groups.

ments for each group tends to be higher among the most well-represented peoples; girls constitute just over 11 per cent of the total sample but comprise 26 per cent of the sample of African foreigners and 15 per cent of Agni students. Among all other peoples this proportion tends to stabilize at about 10 per cent, except among the Mandefou, whose female representation is markedly lower.

Besides ethnicity itself, the origin and present residence of students tend to be associated with secondary school entry. Columns I and II of Table 9 reveal the rather sharp variations in levels of primary school enrollment between the main geographical zones of the Ivory Coast, but column III shows an extraordinarily tight relationship between the provision of primary schooling and access to secondary education. There is no necessity to infer that this must be the case. To be sure, children usually enter primary schools in the area where they live, but there is no link between secondary schools and their geographical hinterland, for these institutions are largely free to recruit from all parts of the country. Since students are highly mobile in their search for secondary schooling, areas underrepresented at the primary level might be expected to obtain a larger proportion of secondary school places. This is not true, however, and the evidence indicates overwhelmingly that the best guarantee of being able to continue with secondary studies is to be born or resident in an area with high levels of primary enrollment. As column IV also shows, there is a slight drift of students from the majority of areas in the Ivory Coast toward the southeastern zone, centering on Abidjan, where the bulk of secondary school facilities are still situated.

The Socio-economic Dimensions of Selection

Although geographical and ethnic variations are quite apparent, it can likewise be expected that students will be drawn disproportionately from urban families characterized by higher levels of occupational and educational background. Certainly what empirical evidence we have concerning secondary recruitment in a variety of nations indicates a consistent skew in terms of these variables, and the Ivory Coast is no exception. Yet it is the actual *degree* of inequality that concerns us here, since secondary systems may be highly exclusive in the type of clientele they recruit or, alternatively, while favoring some minorities, may still allow access to broad segments of the population. One never expects to find uniformity of socio-economic representation

TABLE 9. Relationship between Population, Primary School Enrollments, and Secondary School Population

ECOLOGICAL* ZONE	I PERCENTAGE† OF TOTAL POPULATION	II PERCENTAGE ‡ OF PRIMARY SCHOOL ENROLLMENTS (1958)	III PLACE OF BIRTH ** OF SAMPLED STUDENTS (PERCENTAGES)	IV PLACE OF PRESENT ** RESIDENCE OF SAMPLED STUDENTS (PERCENTAGES)
Southeast	19.0	38.1	39.0	44.4
Southwest	10.7	13.6	12.8	11.6
Central	44.3	37.9	34.5	32.8
North	26.0	10.3	9.1	8.6
Total	100.0	99.9	95.4	97.4

* These zones do not coincide with administrative districts and are grouped as follows: *Southeast*—Abidjan, Bassam, Aboisso, Agboville, Abengourou; *Southwest*—Grand Lahou, Gagnoa, Sassandra, Tabou; *Central*—Dimbokro, Bouaflé, Daloa, Man, Bouaké, Katiola; *North*—Odienne, Seguela, Korhogo, Bondoukou.

† Computed from Ivory Coast, Ministère des Finances des Affaires Economiques et du Plan, *Supplément trimestriel du Bulletin mensuel de statistique*, 3e Année, No. 2 (Abidjan, 1961), p. 25.

‡ *Ibid.* Primary school enrollments are calculated for the year 1958 (i.e., the median year in which sampled students graduated from primary school).

** Totals exclude students not born and/or not resident in the Ivory Coast and "No answers."

in a secondary school population, but one does find considerable variation in the representation of various subgroups.

Table 10 shows an association between secondary school access and

TABLE 10. Urban or Rural Background of Students in Relation to Size of Birthplace and Present Residence (Percentages)

POPULATION OF LOCALITY	DISTRIBUTION* OF IVORY COAST POPULATION	BIRTHPLACE OF SAMPLED STUDENTS		PRESENT RESIDENCE OF SAMPLED STUDENTS	
		Male	Female	Male	Female
Below 5,000	82.3	70.5	37.6	59.4	30.8
5,000 to 9,999	4.3	9.3	12.7	9.7	12.7
10,000 to 49,999	3.7	8.9	20.7	11.0	16.9
Above 50,000	9.7	7.7	21.9	18.4	35.4
Not born or not resident in the Ivory Coast	...	3.6	7.2	1.5	4.2
Total	100.0	100.0	100.0	100.0	100.0
		(1,837)	(237)	(1,837)	(237)

* These figures can only be regarded as approximations computed from Ivory Coast, Ministère des Finances, *Inventaire économique et social de la Côte d'Ivoire, 1947–1958* (Abidjan, 1960), p. 37.

urban origin or residence. Over 80 per cent of the Ivory Coast population lives in towns or villages with populations under 5,000, but only 70 per cent of our male students were born in such centers. Conversely, just under 4 per cent of the population lives in centers with between 10,000 and 50,000 inhabitants, but these provide over 9 per cent of our male sample. The association between urban birth and secondary school entry is much more striking if we look at female enrollments.

However, the relationship between secondary school entry and size of town of birth (or residence) is not quite linear. True, the proportional representation of students generally increases as one moves from the smaller to the larger towns, but there is an interesting downswing as one reaches urban centers with populations of over 50,000 (i.e., Abidjan and Bouaké).[2] The reasons for this reversal in the trend are not clear.

2. Interestingly enough, this downswing is paralleled by a similar phenomenon in France itself. The proportion of individuals entering *Lycées* and *Collèges* increases consistently as one moves from rural areas to larger towns, then drops sharply in Paris itself. See Alain Girard, "Enquête nationale sur l'entrée en sixième et la démocratisation de l'enseignement," *Population*, Vol. 18, 1963, p. 29.

Some explanation of the concept of urbanization should be entered at this point. In practice, urbanization implies a number of complex, interrelated processes of which size is but one dimension. Our index could be very misleading if it were applied to areas in Africa having large traditional towns, as do the western and northern regions of Nigeria. There one might well argue that levels of education would not be higher than in rural areas. The crucial relationship between educational diffusion and urban growth occurs where urban development is accompanied by the growth of heterogeneous ethnic populations, the extension of a monetary economy, and the emergence of more complex Western-type occupational structures. Under such conditions the persistence of traditional patterns of socio-political organization in their entirety is manifestly impossible. It is within these towns, therefore, that formal education is first perceived as a desirable acquisition, leading to access to present-day occupations and roles. It is within these towns that schooling is first looked upon as providing high returns in terms of status, income, and power. The growth of a demand for education is itself an intrinsic part of the whole process of urbanization and modernization. In the Ivory Coast, where urbanization is a direct result of French influence and economic change, the size of a town is closely associated with other aspects of the increasing scale of the society. Thus the relationship between education and social change is not a fortuitous consequence of the fact that towns are merely convenient places for building schools in the midst of concentrated populations.

Let us now ask how far the fathers of our students are representative of occupational categories for the Ivory Coast adult male population. Table 11 indicates that our sample is drawn disproportionately from the higher occupational levels. The male offspring of managerial and clerical workers are markedly overrepresented, and the sons of farmers are proportionally underrepresented. The son of a managerial or clerical worker has approximately nine times the chance of entering some form of secondary school as the child of an Ivory Coast farmer.[3] But this tells only part of the story. For the sons of farmers constitute over 70 per cent of enrollments, and the selectivity index for the group stands at 0.8, not far below the full quota. In fact, an

3. Besides occupational level another significant feature is the type of employer worked for. Almost one-fifth of the fathers of students are employed by the administration, as against only 3 per cent of the adult male labor force in the Ivory Coast as a whole.

TABLE 11. Relation between Occupations of Fathers of Students and Occupations of the Adult Male Population of the Ivory Coast

OCCUPATIONAL GROUP	PERCENTAGE OF IVORY COAST* ADULT MALE POPULATION (1961)	MALE STUDENTS		FEMALE STUDENTS		TOTAL	
		Percentage	Selectivity Index	Percentage	Selectivity Index	Percentage	Selectivity Index
Managerial † and clerical workers	2.0	14.3	7.2	48.1	24.1	18.1	9.1
Uniformed services	0.5	2.5	5.0	3.0	6.0	2.6	5.2
African traders and businessmen	3.3	5.0	1.5	9.7	3.0	5.6	1.7
Manual workers (skilled, semi-skilled, unskilled)	7.9	6.6	0.8	9.7	1.2	6.9	0.9
Farmers and fishermen	86.3	71.6	0.8	29.5	0.3	66.8	0.8
Total	100.0	100.0	..	100.0	..	100.0	..
		(1,837)		(237)		(2,074)	

* Computed from UNESCO, *Première Mission du groupe de planification de l'éducation en Côte d'Ivoire* (Paris: UNESCO, 1963), p. 19, and from UNESCO, *Situation et perspectives de l'emploi dans le cadre du plan décennal de développement* (Mimeo, 1963), Table II H.

† Includes higher technical and professional personnel.

overwhelming proportion of the potential elite of the Ivory Coast is still being drawn from rural farming families. This, we would argue, is in marked contrast to early patterns of secondary school enrollment in Western nations, when secondary institutions were in short supply and the occupational profiles of the countries were similar to the contemporary Ivory Coast profile.

However, this fluidity in recruitment patterns is far less characteristic of female enrollments. Girls are much more likely to be drawn from restricted occupational groups and highly atypical segments of

TABLE 12. Educational Level of Fathers of Students (Percentages)

LEVEL OF EDUCATION*	MALES	FEMALES	TOTAL
No education	74.0	31.2	69.1
Some primary school	12.3	16.5	12.7
Completed primary school	5.6	21.9	7.5
Above primary school	8.1	30.4	10.7
Total	100.0	100.0	100.0
	(1,837)	(237)	(2,074)

* No comparable figures are available for the educational level of the adult male population of the Ivory Coast. However, in a 1955 study of the Abidjan population, only 23 per cent of adult males could read and write French. These figures for Abidjan are certainly far higher than for the Ivory Coast as a whole. Ivory Coast, *Recensement d'Abidjan, 1955* (Abidjan: Ministère des Finances des Affaires Economiques et du Plan, 1960), p. 37.

the population. Further, we can again see that the less proportionally represented a group is as a whole, the lower is the proportional representation of girls within that group. For example, girls constitute 30 per cent of all enrollments from managerial and clerical families but only 5 per cent of enrollments from farming families.

Data concerning fathers' level of education are less satisfactory. Although no figures exist showing general levels of schooling among the adult male population, we can infer from the results of a recent survey of Abidjan that the level of paternal education of secondary school students is much higher than that of the general adult male population of the Ivory Coast.[4] Table 12 indicates, in addition, striking and consistent differences between male and female patterns of recruitment. Almost three-quarters of the fathers of boys have had no

4. Côte d'Ivoire, Ministère des Finances des Affaires Economiques et du Plan, *Recensement d'Abidjan, 1955* (Paris, 1960), p. 37.

formal schooling whatever, but this figure drops to just over 30 per cent of the fathers of girls. At the other extreme, it is quite remarkable by Ivory Coast standards that nearly one-third of fathers of girl students have even gone beyond full primary school.

Needless to say, there are vast disparities between paternal and maternal levels of education in the families of students. About one-third of the fathers have had some formal education, as against less than 8 per cent of the mothers. Maternal education varies markedly along ethnic lines. For example, almost 13 per cent of Agni mothers have had some schooling, as against 2 per cent of Mandefou mothers. There is also an expected high correlation between paternal and maternal levels of education; and over 95 per cent of the mothers who have attended school are married to educated men. However, three-quarters of the fathers who have attended school have illiterate spouses. The limited diffusion of schooling among adult women implies that all educated mothers are married to men highly educated by Ivory Coast standards. The association of these two factors vastly enhances the chances of their offspring's attending postprimary school.

Religion, Family Structure, and Parental Demands

Although little reliable evidence is available concerning the overall religious composition of the Ivory Coast population, it seems probable that about one-third of its people are Moslem. On this basis it is clear that Moslems are underrepresented in the system, while Christians are probably overrepresented (Table 13). We could anticipate this kind of pattern, of course. Nevertheless, before arriving at hasty conclusions we should consider these points: There has always been a tendency to

TABLE 13. Religious Background of Students (Percentages)

RELIGIOUS AFFILIATION	MALE STUDENTS	FEMALE STUDENTS	TOTAL
Roman Catholic	65.7	73.4	66.5
Moslem	14.9	19.4	15.4
Protestant	10.8	6.4	10.3
No affiliation	6.9	0.4	6.2
No answer	1.7	0.4	1.6
Total	100.0	100.0	100.0
	(1,837)	(237)	(2,074)

attribute the lower levels of Moslem enrollment in Western-type schools to a traditional ideological antagonism between Islam and Western secular schooling—an antagonism which is particularly strong with reference to female education. To be sure, in many parts of Africa south of the Sahara, Moslem enrollments are relatively low, but in some portions of these areas, the Islamic populations were incorporated relatively late into the colonial framework. For example, low levels of school enrollment in northern Nigeria tend to be attributed to the hostile influence of Islam, while it is conveniently forgotten that northern Nigeria was not occupied until the early twentieth century. This is partly true in the Ivory Coast, because the different zones of European penetration and economic development tended to coalesce with zones of religious difference. As a result, the pattern of educational development might have been different if the Islamic groups had been coastal dwellers.[5]

The negative stance of Islam vis-à-vis educational development has perhaps been exaggerated. At least one thing is made clear by Table 13: Moslems may be underrepresented as a whole, but Moslem girls seem to do just as well as their Christian counterparts in obtaining secondary education. Females constitute over 14 per cent of the total Moslem enrollment but only just over 12 per cent of the Christian student population. This fact alone should make us wary of attributing variable recruitment patterns to religious differences.

Another factor of considerable importance is the type of family environment from which students come. We have already seen that pupils are disproportionately drawn from urban centers and educated families. It would not be unreasonable, therefore, to infer that their families are likely to be monogamous, with value orientations of a European type. But this is not the case. Even among these educated families there is a remarkable persistence of traditional patterns of familial organization. Over 50 per cent of students of either sex come from polygynous households.

This incidence of polygyny among the families of our students is probably higher than that prevailing in the Ivory Coast as a whole, leading us to question the occasional assertion that children from

5. In general we deprecate this tendency to speak of Islam as producing a homogeneous set of attitudes toward Western schooling. West Africans tend to be very pragmatic in matters of religious belief, and we seriously doubt whether ideological barriers would prevent them from sending their offspring to school, providing the monetary and status rewards were sufficient.

monogamous households are likely to obtain more consistent support for their education. The prevalence of polygyny in these families is probably due to two factors: [6] First, the fathers come from older age groups, and there is certainly a correlation between polygyny and paternal age. Second, it is probable, though by no means demonstrable from our data, that these fathers (including those who are farmers) enjoy considerably higher financial status than the majority of Ivory Coast males.

Most striking, however, is the fact that socio-economic status as measured by paternal occupation is not clearly related to family type. Over 47 per cent of the fathers in managerial and clerical occupations have more than one wife, as against only 52 per cent of the farmers. The relationship between patterns of urban residence and family structure is a trifle clearer. A little over half of the students living in rural areas come from polygynous households, as against 40 per cent of those living in the largest towns. Paternal level of education, as might be expected, also accounts for some differences. Fifty-two per cent of the fathers without schooling are polygynous, as against 43 per cent of those who have completed at least primary school. Since all these differences are statistically significant, the urban child from an educated family is more likely to come from a monogamous household. However, the correlation is by no means striking. The evidence points to the tenacity of polygynous family organization, and we can demonstrate this even more clearly: Two extreme groups were drawn from the sample. The first was composed of male students from towns with a population of over 10,000 whose fathers had completed at least a full primary school education and were employed in administrative and clerical occupations. This group, comprising 116 students, was designated as the "maximally acculturated" segment of the student population. The second group included all male students living in towns or villages with a population of below 5,000 whose fathers had not attended school and were occupied as subsistence farmers.[7] This

6. Of course, there are variations in the extent of polygyny among different ethnic groups. See A. J. F. Kobben, "Le planteur noir," *Etudes éburnéennes*, V (Abidjan: Centre IFAN, 1956), p. 130. Kobben's sample shows only 32 per cent of married Bété women belonging to monogamous households, as against 54 per cent in the Agni area. See Côte d'Ivoire, *Enquête nutrition, niveau de vie, subdivision de Bongouanou, 1955–1956* (Paris, 1958), p. 32.

7. In previous tables we have grouped all farmers together. However, most students gave details about the crops grown by their fathers, which provided a reasonable basis for differentiating between cash-crop and subsistence agriculturalists.

group, numbering 198, was described as being "minimally acculturated" for the purposes of this study.[8]

One-half of the "lows" came from polygynous households, as against one-third of the "highs." This difference is sizable, but far less so than might be expected in view of the extreme polarization of the two groups. The plain fact is that among the parents of our students, whatever measures of "acculturation" or "Westernization" are used, economic and social attributes are not dramatically associated with the institution of polygyny, the frequency of which remains high at all levels.

Nevertheless there is a close relationship between maternal education and the structure of the family; educated women are far less frequently found in polygynous households.[9] In any event, the high rate of polygyny among the families of our students suggests that plural marriage is less detrimental to school attendance than is sometimes supposed.

So far we have drawn attention to certain characteristics of the family background of the students. Although it is easy enough to demonstrate that urban children with educated parents are better represented in the schools than are rural children from illiterate homes, we must now see whether such differentials are correlated with contrasts in perceived parental expectations. Do urban parents attach more importance to academic achievement than rural parents? Further, are there marked differentials in this respect between ethnic groups and distinct socio-economic clusters?

What parents consider to be appropriate behavior for their offspring varies between social groups. One way of measuring such variations is to ask children to rank the parental demands imposed upon them. We asked our students to do so with five types of obligation most likely to be of considerable significance to African parents: to display respect to senior members of the kin group, to help parents carry out their daily chores, to assist in the care of siblings, to achieve well in school, and to look after family belongings.[10]

8. In succeeding pages we shall refer frequently to these two polar groups, calling them simply "highs" and "lows."

9. Thus 55 per cent of the uneducated mothers belonged to polygynous households, as against less than one-quarter of those who had some education. Only 4 per cent of women belonging to polygynous households had attended school, as against 12 per cent of the mothers in monogamous households.

10. Students were asked to rank-order these items for each parent. A mean score was then computed for each separate item.

Overwhelmingly, irrespective of ethnic or socio-economic background, respect for senior kin remains the most important demand made of children by their parents. Students perceive both parents as attaching considerable importance to academic achievement, which is ranked second, although fathers score more highly than mothers. Fathers also appear to stress assistance in domestic chores more than care of siblings, whereas the position is reversed with mothers. Finally, both parents seem to attach least importance to the handling of family belongings.

Ethnic affiliation, urban or rural residence, and socio-economic characteristics do not affect the rank order of parental demands. However, this is not to say that these factors make an equal contribution to the character of the response. We are most concerned here with parents' emphasis on educational achievement, which, as we have seen, is uniformly ranked second. We can see that the intensity of this concern varies with the sex of the child and that of his parents. Mothers of male students attach much more importance to educational achievement than do mothers of girls. On the other hand, fathers of girls are relatively more concerned about their daughters' academic success than are fathers of boys. This paradox is easily explained if one recalls the marked differences in the level of education of the fathers of male and female students. Furthermore, where the level of maternal education is high, both parents attach great importance to educational achievement.[11]

In summary, the parents of these students appear to be far from apathetic about the academic progress of their offspring. To be sure, some subgroups score more highly on educational demands than others, but the differences are not great, and the rank order is invariant. Thus the presence of children in secondary school is usually associated with a high level of perceived parental concern over education.

However, it is not only parents who are intimately involved with the academic progress of students. Other members of the kin group play a considerable role, and no less than 27 per cent of students indicated that the person primarily interested in their academic career was a close relative rather than their own parents. In most of these cases, elder siblings ranked first, followed by maternal and paternal uncles.

11. For some interesting comments on the attitudes of educated and uneducated women toward the education of girls, see Claude Tardits, "Réflexions sur le problème de la scolarisation des filles au Dahomey," *Cahiers d'études africaines*, Vol. III, 2me Cahier, No. 10, pp. 266–81.

Nonetheless the role of these other members of the immediate and extended family diminishes significantly as the level of paternal occupation and education increases. Nine-tenths of the students whose fathers were engaged in professional or clerical work indicated that one of their parents was their main educational sponsor; this figure dropped to two-thirds among the offspring of farmers. Correspondingly, only two-thirds of those students whose fathers had never attended school viewed one parent or the other as their principal sponsor, as against almost nine-tenths of those whose fathers had been to school. It would appear that the traditional extended family does contribute to the education of its junior members, though its participation is more limited when fathers are directly involved in the modern occupational structure.

Ethnicity and Socio-economic Background

We have seen that the various ethnic groups of the Ivory Coast are very differentially represented in the postprimary schools. Ethnicity has two distinctive connotations. In the first place, ethnic groups differ from one another in terms of traditional organization, language, and culture. We are not concerned here with this aspect of ethnicity, but rather with its second implication in the contemporary context: the differing socio-economic characteristics of various groups. Some peoples who have had more experience with modernization than others may be more urbanized and more educated, and may have had greater access to the higher levels of the occupational structure. For example, the northern Lobi is likely to be a rural, illiterate subsistence farmer, while his southern Agni counterpart often possesses a degree of formal education, operating as a cash-crop farmer or as an employee within the modern sector of the economy. What implications does this variability have for secondary school recruitment?

It is tempting to argue that variations in ethnic representation in the schools will be closely associated with similar variations in the socio-economic background of the students. In other words, students recruited from ethnic minorities that are well represented in the schools will rank higher than others in urban background and paternal levels of occupation and education. This general hypothesis, however, is only partially borne out.

To begin with, there is no relationship between ethnic representation and urban origin or residence. In fact, students from ethnic groups whose selectivity index is high (above 1.5) are just as likely to come from small rural communities as are those from ethnic minorities with low selectivity indices (below 1.0). Conversely, there is no correlation between residence in the largest urban centers and the level of the selectivity index.

The same observation is generally true with respect to paternal occupation. Variations in ethnic selectivity indices are not usually associated with differences in paternal occupational background. For example, the proportion of fathers occupying managerial and clerical positions is almost identical for minorities whose selectivity index is above 1.5 and those whose index is below 1.0. There is only one important exception to this general statement. Although the proportion of farmers remains constant at about 65 per cent for all groups, the proportion of cash-crop to subsistence farmers increases substantially as the selectivity index rises. Thus only 28 per cent of students from minorities with a selectivity index of below 1.0 have fathers who are cash-crop farmers, as against 50 per cent of those students who belong to ethnic groups with an index of over 1.5.

Treating farmers as a homogeneous occupational group might facilitate survey analysis, yet this finding points to the fact that a farmer's degree of involvement in the exchange sector may bear significantly on his children's access to secondary schooling. In fact, the cash-crop farmer is much more caught up in the process of modernization than his subsistence counterpart and is therefore more sensitive to the implications of formal education.

We also find that the level of paternal education is systematically related to the level of the ethnic selectivity index (Table 14). To be

TABLE 14. Relationship between Ethnic Representation and Paternal Education of Students (Percentages)

LEVEL OF PATERNAL EDUCATION	ETHNIC SELECTIVITY INDEX		
	Below 1.0	From 1.0 to 1.5	Above 1.5
No education	76.7	65.4	63.0
Some primary education	9.0	15.0	15.4
Completion of primary school plus further education	14.3	19.6	21.6
Total	100.0	100.0	100.0
	(840)	(515)	(719)

sure, the differences are not great, but of all the factors considered here, level of paternal education explains differentials in ethnic access most satisfactorily.

However, one cannot argue from these data that there is a very strong relationship between ethnic representation in the schools and the socio-economic background of students. In fact, despite their ethnic heterogeneity, the students' social background is fairly similar. This suggests that the extent of socio-economic selectivity varies among ethnic groups. Let us examine this point more fully.

First, we have noted that ethnic minorities are differentially involved in processes of modernization. In particular, levels of education and occupation vary considerably from one group to another. To be sure, we cannot, in the absence of adequate census data, establish a definitive rank order for these characteristics among different peoples. Nonetheless, using current primary school enrollments and limited data on the occupational profiles of ethnic minorities, we can establish three main clusters of peoples on a putative scale of modernization. To the first cluster belong the Agni and Lagoon groups, followed by an intermediate cluster including the Baoulé and Kru. Last come the least modernized elements of the population—the Mandefou, Senoufo-Lobi, and Malinke.

Yet we have noted that students from highly represented groups have social backgrounds very similar to those from poorly represented minorities. This implies that in one case the socio-economic characteristics of Agni and Lagoon students approximate more closely the general profile of the people to which they belong, whereas, in the case of northern groups, students come from atypical socio-economic subsegments of their ethnic group.

We can demonstrate this proposition more clearly in Table 15. Here we present a picture of how students from different ethnic groups compare with one another on three simple scales: one based on level of paternal education; another based on level of paternal occupation; and a composite scale of modernization derived from the addition of paternal educational and occupational scores.

Strikingly enough, African students of foreign origin rank above all Ivory Coast groups in terms of all variables. The variation among Ivory Coasters themselves is minor compared with the differences between them and "foreigners." There is good reason for this, since migration into the Ivory Coast has historically been of two kinds. One group of immigrants has been unskilled laborers, mainly coming from

TABLE 15. Relationship between Ethnicity and Indices of Modernization

INDICES OF MODERNIZATION	ETHNIC GROUP							
	Agni	Lagoon Cluster	Baoulé	Kru	Mandefou	Malinke	Senoufo-Lobi	Others
Putative rank order of modernization	1	2	3.5	3.5	6	6	6	..
Student scores on paternal education *								
Mean score	0.76	0.64	0.49	0.45	0.20	0.59	0.52	1.29
Rank	2	3	6.5	6.5	8	4	5	1
Student scores on paternal occupation †								
Mean score	1.35	1.22	1.03	1.16	0.94	1.58	1.18	1.96
Rank	3	4	7	6	8	2	5	1
Student scores on a combined index of modernization								
Mean score	2.11	1.86	1.52	1.65	1.14	2.17	1.75	3.25
Rank	3	4	7	6	8	2	5	1

* Computed on a scale of 0 to 3, where 0 = no education, 1 = some primary school education, 2 = completion of primary school, and 3 = education beyond primary school.

† Computed on a scale of 0 to 3, where 0 = subsistence farmer, 1 = cash-crop farmer, 2 = manual workers, traders, and uniformed services, and 3 = managerial and clerical workers.

N.B. Some objections can be raised to the weighing of items on these scales, but in the absence of any adequate data, they serve as useful approximations.

Upper Volta. Another group has included highly skilled persons from Dahomey, Togoland, Senegal, and Ghana, who have occupied key positions in the administrative cadres of the Ivory Coast.[12] It is mainly the offspring of this elite alien minority who have gained access to secondary schools.

Turning to the Ivory Coast students themselves, it is apparent that the differences among them are not great, in spite of the probable wide variations among the ethnic groups as a whole. For example, the Agni people rank first in terms of their level of modernization, and the Malinke rank very low on this scale. Yet on the combined index of modernization Malinke students actually have a higher mean score

12. This is still the case. In a separate survey conducted by the present writers in several firms and government agencies in Abidjan in 1963, no less than 16 per cent of higher clerical and skilled manual workers were African foreigners.

than Agni students. This would imply different selectivity ratios within these two ethnic groups and might suggest that among the more backward Malinke the first individuals to enter secondary school are likely to be drawn from very small and atypical segments of the group. Conversely, the background of the average Agni student is likely to be closer to the mean socio-economic profile of the Agni population itself. Similarly, the Senoufo-Lobi students rank higher than the Baoulé and Kru. Since these latter groups are certainly more modernized, we may infer once again that recruitment among the Senoufo tends to be more selective. However, the Mandefou show a somewhat different pattern. This people resembles the Malinke and Senoufo-Lobi in its level of modernization, but the average Mandefou secondary school student is much more likely to come from an illiterate farming family. Thus there seems to be much less selectivity among the Mandefou than among the Malinke.

In the absence of adequate data concerning the general socio-economic characteristics of the major ethnic groups of the Ivory Coast, our conclusions can only be very tentative. We would argue that as the process of educational diffusion begins, the first groups to enter secondary schools will tend to be exclusive in terms of their social characteristics. Then as general levels of primary enrollment rise in particular areas, the secondary schools will tend to dig deeper into the population, and the composition of the secondary school student body will come closer to reflecting the general characteristics of the population. Very loosely we might term this a rising level of democratization in the secondary school system.[13]

There is enough idiosyncratic variation in the ethnic subgroups of our sample to suggest that specific investigations of the process of educational diffusion need to be made among the different peoples of the Ivory Coast. The present study can point only to broad differences in recruitment patterns, but we can do no more than guess, for example, why Malinke students differ so markedly from their Mandefou counterparts despite a substantially similar traditional background and level of modernization among the two peoples. More detailed studies would necessarily involve careful examination of the educational policies pursued in different districts during the colonial period, and particular reference would have to be made to the differential impact of formal education upon variant types of traditional social

13. Of course precisely the same phenomenon applies to the different enrollment patterns of boys and girls.

structure. In short, large-scale survey analysis is not a substitute for intensive anthropological field investigation if inter-ethnic differences are to be thoroughly explored.

Religion, Ethnicity, and Socio-economic Status

We have already seen that the Moslem minority is distinctly under-represented in the secondary schools of the Ivory Coast. But how does religious affiliation link up with the ethnic and socio-economic characteristics of students?

Religion is closely related to ethnicity in the Ivory Coast. Well over 90 per cent of students from all southern groups are formally Christians, although this figure drops to 80 per cent among the more centrally located Baoulé. Further, the Mandefou and Malinke, in spite of their common cultural and linguistic traditions, are now clearly differentiated along religious lines. Almost 92 per cent of the Malinke students are Moslem, as opposed to only 7 per cent of the Mandefou, of whom almost 80 per cent are Christians. Among the Senoufo-Lobi cluster the spread of the two major religions has been more even. About 40 per cent of the students coming from this cluster of peoples are Christian, and another 40 per cent Moslem. These religious differences between students are also associated with variations in their socio-economic background.

First, Moslem students are more likely to come from urban centers. Over 63 per cent of them reside in towns with populations above 5,000, as against only 39 per cent of the Christians. There is also a distinct tendency for them to be drawn from the largest towns—23 per cent, in fact, from Abidjan and Bouaké alone.

Second, Moslem students come from rather distinct occupational groups. A higher proportion of Moslem fathers are employed in administrative and clerical work—almost 27 per cent as against 18 per cent of Christian fathers. The proportion of fathers engaged in trade and commerce shows a like difference. No less than 23 per cent of the fathers of Moslem students are traders, compared with 3 per cent of the Christian fathers. On the other hand, just over 70 per cent of the fathers of Christian students are farmers, as against 38 per cent of the Moslem fathers.

Most important, however, Moslem and Christian groups do *not* differ significantly in paternal educational background; the figures for both groups are virtually identical. This would again support the view that level of paternal education has more influence on children's attendance at secondary school than do the other socio-economic characteristics we have explored.

Although no census data are available concerning the relationship between socio-economic and religious characteristics of the general population, it is likely that self-selectivity is much higher among the Moslem students than among Christian students. There can be little doubt that adult Moslems as a group are far less educated than Christians in the Ivory Coast, and far less likely to be represented in the higher sectors of the occupational structure. Making an informed guess about the overall urban or rural composition of the two groups is somewhat more difficult, but it is safe to say that Moslems are distinctly less numerous in the largest towns of the Ivory Coast, namely Abidjan and Bouaké.

Yet when Moslem and Christian students in the secondary schools are ranked in terms of paternal education or occupation and urban residence, the Moslems rank as high as the Christians or even higher. This can only suggest that the schools draw upon a restricted and atypical subsegment of the Moslem population. Ethnicity and religious affiliation, therefore, tend to operate in a similar manner: As the proportional representation of a minority in the secondary school system declines, its representatives in that system are more likely to be drawn from deviant socio-economic subgroups within that minority.

Summary and Conclusions

Current processes determining the selection of students for secondary education in the Ivory Coast do not result in equal representation of the various ethnic and socio-economic subgroups of the population. The historical pattern of European penetration in the Ivory Coast has led to a differential rate of social change in various parts of the country which is reflected in inequalities of educational provision and access. Undoubtedly children from the southern ethnic groups, particularly those with urban backgrounds and parents of higher socio-economic status, have a better chance of attending these key institutions. Nevertheless our evidence in no way suggests a highly restricted recruitment. Notwithstanding the very small extent of the secondary school system, children from the most humble backgrounds do enter it in substantial numbers. Indeed, this is a system more or less open to talent—at least talent as measured by academic success.

The relation between ethnicity and secondary school recruitment is particularly crucial not only in the Ivory Coast but in most of the new African states. Although certain minorities have been able to maintain a substantial lead in secondary schooling, there is no clear-cut relationship between ethnic representation in the schools and the other socio-economic variables that we have considered. For example, the under-represented ethnic groups are not very different from the others in urban or rural origin, place of residence, or type of paternal occupation. In fact, the variable most systematically related to differential ethnic enrollment would appear to be the father's level of education.

Our evidence also suggests that selection operates in a rather different manner for the various ethnic groups in the population and seems to dig deeper into certain ethnic groups than into others. In similar fashion, although inequalities exist in the representation of various religious groups within the secondary system, we do not imply that the underrepresentation of Moslems reflects an ideological conflict between Islam and Western education. The lag in their representation might well be due to their geographical location.

We have also attempted to examine aspects of family structure which might be expected to have some relevance for recruitment. Our findings in no way suggest that the bulk of students come from monogamous, nuclear-type households. There are almost as many secondary school students from polygynous households as from monogamous families.[14] Indeed the structure of the family does not seem to be so critical a variable as is sometimes supposed. There can be no doubt, furthermore, that polygyny is a tenacious institution, still very common among the most "Westernized" families.

We can see that traditional behavior patterns persist in other areas as well. All students, whatever their ethnic or socio-economic origin, state that respect for senior kin is still the most important demand placed upon them by their parents. Equally striking is their agreement that parental stress on academic achievement is uniformly high. The mere fact of their attendance at secondary school implies that their

14. Whether polygyny tends to lead to a lower need for achievement is beyond the scope of this study. See David McClelland, *The Achieving Society* (Princeton: Van Nostrand, 1961), p. 374. However, even if this is the case, children from polygynous families in the Ivory Coast still seem to be very successful in obtaining secondary school places.

parents will not be greatly differentiated in terms of concern over their children's academic progress.

Finally, although this chapter has laid great stress on inequalities in educational recruitment, we must not forget that talent is the criterion for access to the secondary schools. A great deal has been made of the "elitist" characteristics of the French type of educational system in Africa. If this means that only a tiny fraction of the adolescent population ever enters secondary schools, then the judgment is correct. No change in the situation is likely to occur for some time in most African nations, in view of their sparse resources. Conversely, if the term "elitist" suggests that students tend to be drawn from very limited ethnic and social minorities, then it can in no sense apply to the Ivory Coast. It is striking that a system so numerically small and so academically oriented can recruit along such broad lines. Indeed the fact that the home environment of a substantial proportion of students would seem superficially to be highly unfavorable to academic success suggests that the formal academic curriculum of these schools is not so formidable a hurdle as is sometimes supposed.

CHAPTER IV

The Hierarchy of Postprimary Schools: Its Impact on Ethnic and Social Recruitment of Students

THE SECONDARY SCHOOL SYSTEM of the Ivory Coast is, as we have noted, highly complex. It is made up of a network of schools with differentiated streams and cycles, which vary greatly in prestige. The status of these different types of secondary schools depends in some measure on the distinctive vocational and educational opportunities open to their graduates. In Europe multilateral streaming has been correlated with rather distinctive types of student population.[1] For example, it is hardly an exaggeration to say that in France the *Lycée* has historically been the preserve of the middle classes, while the children of manual workers have been more heavily concentrated in terminal schools of a general or vocational type. Our task here is to see how such a hierarchy of postprimary institutions manifests itself in the Ivory Coast and to analyze the extent to which differential patterns of internal recruitment are beginning to appear.

1. For example, most systems of secondary education in Western Europe have institutions which offer their graduates markedly superior chances for occupational and social mobility. The German *Gymnasium*, the French *Lycée*, and the British secondary grammar school fulfill this function. Multilateral secondary education always implies a hierarchic organization of schools, and to talk of "parity of esteem" among different types of secondary institutions contradicts all the evidence now available.

The Secondary School Hierarchy

First of all, the hierarchy of secondary institutions is based on the actual duration of courses of study. For instance, students currently preparing for the *Brevet Professionnel d'Agriculture Tropicale* complete only three years' work after primary schooling. This figure rises to four years for students working toward the C.A.P., the B.E., and the B.E.P.C. Correspondingly, students in the third year of the *Ecole Normale Menagère,* the *Collège d'Agriculture,* the classes of the *Technique Industrielle,* and the *Technique Commerciale* are completing their sixth year of postprimary education. Candidates for the academic and technical *Baccalaureat* have usually completed anywhere between six and seven years of secondary school. There can be little doubt that the status of particular courses is closely related to the length of secondary education, a factor which is equally apparent in the metropole itself.

Not only this, but the different streams tend to vary in prestige, depending on their curriculum content. As in Europe, the academic system has a considerably higher status than have programs of a technical or narrowly vocational nature for two major reasons: First, students taking academic courses have in the past had a virtual monopoly on access to universities and other higher institutions. Second, a greater number of graduates from academic programs have been enabled to enter the more rewarding occupations. The very generality of academic studies facilitates both vertical and horizontal occupational mobility.

Thus in the Ivory Coast, where postprimary institutions specializing in agricultural, commercial, or industrial subjects have been created, the principals of these institutions have constantly pressed to be allowed to prepare students for examinations equivalent to those of the *Baccalaureat.* Unquestionably the possession of formal academic qualifications improves the occupational prospects of students. In addition, the fact that a school prepares its students for the *Baccalaureat* also enables it to claim a greater share of government resources for the payment of teachers and the improvement of physical facilities.

Another significant distinction in the system concerns public and private schools. While it would be difficult to show that these sectors actually enjoy differential status, the public schools generally obtain greater financial support, and their staffs are usually better trained.

Private schools offer systematic religious instruction and charge tuition fees. Moreover, private schools have smaller classes and give more individual attention to students. As a result, overall rates of academic success for students in public and private schools are not very different, and both types of institution prepare students for the same examinations.

A final crucial difference concerns the relative age of secondary institutions. Students in the older established schools enjoy higher rates of success in national examinations. The longer traditions and larger size of these schools create a more competitive and stimulating scholastic climate. Such higher status schools are concentrated overwhelmingly in Abidjan and its vicinity. They uniformly attract the most highly qualified European teachers, in terms of both background and seniority, and are able to provide superior physical facilities and greater financial help to their students.

Our present task will be to measure the extent to which these various distinctions are associated with differential patterns of student recruitment. We propose to examine these patterns as they are related to the students' sex, age, ethnicity, and socio-economic or cultural background.

There are two ways of looking at this problem: First, since various types of curricula command differential prestige and lead to distinct kinds of occupations, we can make comparisons of students in the academic, technical, and agricultural streams. Further, because of the difference in status between the long and short academic streams, we must also compare students in these two subdivisions. Second, the cycle of studies in which a student is enrolled is of considerable significance, so we must compare students at various stages of their academic careers. Although there are only two formal cycles of post-primary education, we have found it necessary to divide the student population into three groups. The "low" cycle includes all individuals within the *Centre de Formation Rurale,* the *Centres d'Apprentissage,* the *Cours Complémentaires,* and the *Cours Normaux* (included here because access to further education beyond the B.E. level is very rare). The "intermediate" cycle includes students in the *Lycée Technique* who are preparing their *Brevet d'Etudes Industrielles* or *Commerciales* or the *Diplôme d'Enseignement Ménager.* Within this cluster are also to be found students in the *Lycées* and *Collèges* who are preparing the long B.E.P.C. examination. Strictly speaking, this examination is similar to that of the short B.E.P.C. or B.E. However, we have included long academic students in the intermediate group because their chances of proceeding to the *Baccalaureat* level are much better and the prestige of their present course is much greater than that of the *Cours Normaux* or *Cours Complémentaires.*

Finally, the "high" cycle of studies includes all persons preparing for both the technical and the academic *Baccalaureats* and also candidates for the *Brevet Supérieur d'Agriculture Tropicale.* All tables in the ensuing pages which refer to streams and cycles of studies will follow this system of classification.

The Relation of Sex and Age to Recruitment

We have seen that the most striking feature of the female secondary population is its very exclusive background. Girls are far more likely than boys to come from the larger cities and to have relatively well-educated families in which the father is engaged in some professional, managerial, or clerical occupation. In spite of this, girls tend to be rather more concentrated in low-status types of secondary schools. Table 16 shows that girls make up a rather higher proportion of

TABLE 16. Sex Composition of the Secondary School Student Body by Stream and Cycle (Percentages)

SEX	STREAM				CYCLE		
	Agricultural	Technical	Short Academic	Long Academic	Low	Intermediate	High
Male	100.0	73.3	90.8	90.4	85.8	89.1	94.2
Female	0.0	26.7	9.2	9.6	14.2	10.9	5.8
Total	100.0	100.0	100.0	100.0	100.0	100.0	100.0
	(39)	(262)	(708)	(1,065)	(916)	(780)	(378)

students in the technical streams. Nearly all girls in this category are preparing for the C.A.P. examinations in clerical work and domestic science. Girls make up a roughly similar proportion of students in the long and short academic streams, but they tend to be underrepresented in the long academic schools—only 43 per cent, as against 52 per cent of boys.

The table also shows quite clearly that girls are at a disadvantage in the senior cycles of study, constituting over 14 per cent of the student body at lower levels but less than 6 per cent at the senior stage of studies. About one-fifth of all male students reach the highest cycle of secondary schooling, as compared with less than one-tenth of all girls. It could be argued that this pattern tends to reflect some basic attitudes concerning the education of women. Not only have these attitudes led to the late entry of girls into the secondary schools as a whole, but they imply that certain terminal types of postprimary vocational schooling are deemed more appropriate for women. Certainly girls are very poorly represented in the pre-university segment of the system.

Our next step is to determine whether there is a relationship between students' age and the kind of postprimary institution they enter (Table 17). Differences in age largely reflect the operation of

TABLE 17. Mean Age of Male Students by Stream and Cycle *

CYCLE	STREAM	MEAN AGE
Short and intermediate	Agricultural	21.2
	Technical	19.8
	B.E. (*Cours Normaux*)	19.4
	B.E.P.C. (short) (*Cours Complémentaires*)	18.3
	B.E.P.C. (long) (*Lycées* and *Collèges*)	18.2
Long	Agricultural	21.5
	Technical	20.6
	Baccalaureat	20.3

* Girls have been excluded because of their relatively small numbers in each stream. However, their mean age is higher than that of boys.

two factors: Some students begin their primary school career later than others, and some are obliged to double (repeat) classes in the primary school. If for either of these reasons students' entry into the postprimary system is delayed, we suggest that they will be faced with a more limited range of choice in the types of courses they can follow.

There are no differences in age distribution between students in public and in private secondary schools. This suggests that the latter are not obliged to accept the culls of the public school system. Conversely, there are distinct differences in the ages of public school students in the long stream and those in the short stream; the short-stream group is significantly older. This finding is to be expected in the case of students in the *Cours Normaux*, since these programs require the recruitment of older students who will join the teaching force immediately after graduation. However, the same prerequisites are not required for entry into the *Cours Complémentaires;* as we have noted, the examination for entry to this type of school is identical with that for admission to the *Lycées.* In practice, the *Lycées* cream off the most academically talented candidates, and the remainder enter the *Cours Complémentaires.* This implies an inverse relationship between age and academic achievement when level of studies is held constant.[2]

Regardless of the stage of studies, candidates for the final technical examinations are significantly older than their academic counterparts. It might be argued that these age differentials reflect selective recruitment from different ethnic or socio-economic groups, and also that technical students are drawn disproportionately from the less developed sections of the country or the more backward groups in the population, where primary schooling usually begins at a later age. In the following chapter, however, we shall show that this is not the case. Rather, we shall present evidence that technical schools recruit in considerable measure from the dropouts of the academic system—a factor that accounts largely for differential age levels. In summary, it seems clear that the more demanding and rigorous the program of a secondary school, the younger will be its student body.

Ethnic Representation

Because Ivory Coast students have much more difficulty entering one type of secondary school than another, one might assume a positive correlation between ethnic background and recruitment into different types of schools. Thus, since the Agni are proportionally very

2. The difference between the age of students in the short and long streams B.E.P.C. is not great but is significant at the $p = .01$ level. This evidence contradicts current opinion in the Ivory Coast. At present the government erroneously believes that the older students enter the long academic stream and the younger ones enter the short academic stream. This opinion is not based on any empirical evidence but on the assumption that the children who do best in the entrance examination are those older students who have frequently doubled primary classes and who are, therefore, proficient at reproducing rote answers. This erroneous view has been the basis for a reform of the entrance examination to the second cycle. To be sure, we have no direct evidence of doubling at the primary school level in this study, but the younger age of students in the long academic stream would suggest that they double less frequently than does any other group of students.

well represented in the system as a whole, it might be anticipated that students from this group would also be concentrated in the upper levels of the long academic system. Alternatively, it might be plausibly asserted that some of the poorly represented northern groups would also be found more frequently in programs of lesser prestige—the vocational and agricultural streams. Yet Table 18 indicates that the

TABLE 18. Ethnic Origin of Students by Stream and Cycle (Percentages)

	STREAM				CYCLE		
Ethnic	Agricultural	Technical	Short Academic	Long Academic	Low	Inter-mediate	High
Agni (N =343)	10.3	18.3	15.3	17.2	15.1	17.8	17.5
Lagoon Cluster (N = 376)	12.8	13.4	17.5	19.9	16.5	18.5	21.4
Baoulé (N = 342)	20.5	19.1	16.7	15.6	16.7	17.2	14.6
Mande (N = 171)	7.7	7.6	9.0	7.9	8.7	9.0	5.5
Kru (N = 409)	17.9	19.9	19.5	19.9	20.2	20.6	16.7
Malinke (N = 196)	15.4	9.5	9.3	9.3	9.5	8.8	10.6
Senoufo-Lobi (N = 131)	5.1	5.7	7.5	5.7	7.5	4.5	7.1
African foreigners (N = 106)	10.3	6.5	5.2	4.5	5.8	3.6	6.6
Total (N = 2,074)	100.0 (39)	100.0 (262)	100.0 (708)	100.0 (1,065)	100.0 (916)	100.0 (780)	100.0 (378)

proportional representation of each tribe remains remarkably constant, whether examined in terms of stream or of cycle. In fact, each ethnic group tends to get its fair share of places in the different parts of the school system. To be sure, there is a very slight tendency for the southeastern peoples to be less in evidence in the agricultural schools and a little more numerous in the long academic system, but the difference is not substantial. Even if we compare two absolutely polar groups, the well-represented Agni and the poorly represented Senoufo-Lobi, it is evident that 53 per cent of the former are in the long academic system as against 47 per cent of the latter, while about one-fifth of each group is in the higher cycle of studies. These differences are certainly not very large.

Further, since the private system accounts for only about 14 per cent of the places in secondary schools, we should expect the overwhelming bulk of students from each ethnic group to be in the public system. This is generally the case, with one major exception: Whereas the ratio of public to private male enrollments stands at five to one for nearly all ethnic groups, it is only two to one for the Mandefou. The greater concentration of this people in the private schools reflects the considerable missionary effort that has been made in Mandefou country.[3] Conversely, two groups are hardly represented at all in this type of institution. Only just over 1 per cent of the Islamic Malinke students are to be found in private schools, for obvious reasons, and, more surprisingly, these schools enroll less than 10 per cent of pupils from the Lagoon area. This is rather puzzling in view of the fact that historically both Catholic and Protestant missionary activities have been focused there.

In summary, it can hardly be said that ethnic background is clearly associated with enrollment in the various streams and cycles of the secondary school system.[4] The reason is, of course, that ethnicity is itself a rather general term which masks the operation of factors that may be much more important in influencing enrollment patterns. On the one hand, it signifies variations in the pattern of traditional social organization which may have implications for the diffusion of education. On the other hand, the different geographical locations of diverse ethnic groups have led to varying degrees of contact with Europeans. This has created divergences among them both in levels of urbanization and in socio-economic background. These latter factors are far more likely to be linked to differential recruitment into secondary schools.

3. It would seem that the missions have expended a great deal of educational effort among the underprivileged members of the population, notably those in the less developed tribal areas, and among girls.

4. Although in this chapter we examine the school hierarchy in terms of streams and cycles, we have avoided the question of whether schools of a different type situated in the same region have distinct patterns of recruitment. This is indeed the case. For example, the *Lycées* and *Collèges* have a much more national pattern of access than the *Cours Complémentaires* and the *Cours Normaux*, which draw their student bodies to a greater extent from the immediate regional hinterland.

Socio-economic Background and the School Hierarchy

Since urban origin and residence have a great deal to do with the overall profile of secondary school recruitment, it is not unreasonable to expect a similar effect within the various segments of the postprimary system. Urban birth, as opposed to rural birth, seems in no manner to be associated with differential recruitment, but Table 19

TABLE 19. Residential Characteristics of Students by Stream and Cycle (Percentages)

	STREAM				CYCLE		
Size of Place of Residence	Agricultural	Technical	Short Academic	Long Academic	Low	Intermediate	High
Below 5,000	64.1	44.3	59.3	56.7	56.1	58.5	51.6
5,000 to 9,999	15.4	11.5	9.3	9.9	10.1	9.7	10.6
10,000 to 49,999	7.7	11.8	12.2	11.5	12.2	10.5	12.7
Over 50,000	7.7	31.3	17.4	20.1	20.0	20.0	21.9
Foreign towns	5.1	1.1	1.8	1.8	1.6	1.3	3.2
Total	100.0	100.0	100.0	100.0	100.0	100.0	100.0
	(39)	(262)	(708)	(1,065)	(916)	(780)	(378)

reveals some measure of variation if the present residence of students is considered.

The table shows, as we might expect, that rural children provide a greater proportion of students in the agricultural schools, while almost one-third of students in technical institutions come from the largest towns. However, the most striking feature revealed in the table is the weak association between residence and access to the schools of highest prestige in the secondary system. Bearing in mind the nature of the school hierarchy and also the characteristics of the overall pattern of enrollment, one would expect that urban-rural differentials would be very marked within the long academic stream—in other words, that rural students would not hold their own in this most demanding stream within the secondary schools. But they do hold their own and perform almost as well as urban children at the highest levels of the system. Rural students from the smallest communities make up 57 per cent of all students in the long academic system and 52 per cent of those in the higher cycle of studies. To put it another way, almost 52 per cent of the rural children are to be found in the long academic system and 17 per cent in the senior cycle of studies; the comparable figures for urban students from the largest towns are 51 per cent and 20 per cent. Indeed, rural students constitute one-half of all candidates for the academic *Baccalaureat.*

Thus it is quite apparent that although residence pattern is closely associated with access to the secondary school system as a whole, it is

TABLE 20. Paternal Occupation of Sampled Students by Stream and Cycle (Percentages)

	STREAM				CYCLE		
Paternal Occupation	Agricultural	Technical	Short Academic	Long Academic	Low	Intermediate	High
Managerial and clerical workers	12.8	22.5	15.0	19.4	16.9	18.1	21.4
Uniformed services	2.6	1.5	3.5	2.2	3.3	2.0	1.9
Traders and businessmen	2.6	7.7	4.8	5.6	5.3	5.0	7.1
Manual workers	5.1	10.3	7.4	5.9	8.3	6.4	4.8
Cash-crop farmers	46.1	37.0	42.5	37.3	40.5	40.4	33.6
Subsistence farmers	30.8	21.0	26.8	29.6	25.7	28.1	31.2
Total	100.0	100.0	100.0	100.0	100.0	100.0	100.0
	(39)	(262)	(708)	(1,065)	(916)	(780)	(378)

a far weaker predictor of where or how far a student will go within the system once he has entered it. It is interesting that one factor which seems to exert considerable influence in metropolitan France itself should be so unimportant in the Ivory Coast.

The same can be said of the relationship between recruitment and socio-economic background as measured by level of paternal occupation. To be sure, Table 20 shows that the offspring of fathers with high occupational status tend to be proportionally more numerous in the long academic and technical streams and in the higher cycle of studies. Conversely, the short academic and agricultural streams draw a higher proportion of their students from farming families, although the differences here are not great. Indeed almost 55 per cent of the children of managerial and clerical workers are in the long academic stream and 22 per cent in the higher cycle of studies, while the comparable figures for the offspring of farmers are 51 per cent and 17 per cent. One could hardly argue on the basis of these figures that the academic *Lycée* in the Ivory Coast is very exclusive in its clientele, and in no way is the degree of differentiation in recruitment patterns at all comparable with the magnitude of variations in the metropolitan context.

We have attempted to illustrate this point even further in Table 20 by distinguishing between the offspring of subsistence and cash-crop farmers. As noted previously, the children of cash-crop farmers are proportionally more numerous in the system as a whole than are the offspring of subsistence agriculturalists, and it might have been expected that they would also be far better represented in the long academic system and the higher cycles of study. Exactly the opposite is true. The children of subsistence farmers constitute a higher proportion of students in the long academic system and the higher cycle of studies than they do in any other stream or cycle, excluding the agricultural schools. Twenty-one per cent of them are concentrated in the highest cycle, as against only 16 per cent of the children of cash-croppers.

We must, therefore, stress again the relative success of children from subsistence-farming families in entering the most exclusive schools of the secondary system. They not only constitute one of the most numerous groups but are proportionally as well represented in the *Baccalaureat* classes as are students with far superior backgrounds. If we assume that these farm children come from cultural environments that supposedly would not stimulate high levels of academic achievement, then we can only conclude that a substantial number of them have quite outstanding academic abilities.

On the other hand, children from this background tend also to be concentrated in some of the very low-status institutions. In the technical stream alone they constitute 29 per cent of enrollments at the C.A.P. stage, as opposed to only 19 per cent at the intermediate and higher technical levels. By contrast, the proportion of children from cash-crop farming families rises from 35 per cent to over 51 per cent in these two cycles. Thus there is a downswing in the representation of students from subsistence-farming backgrounds as one moves upward in the technical stream and a marked upswing in the representation of those from cash-crop backgrounds. Since this phenomenon is not apparent within the academic stream, it could be suggested that the offspring of subsistence farmers constitute a polarized minority in academic terms; they comprise a substantial proportion of the most able students and also account for a considerable percentage of the least successful.

The technical stream also affords another interesting example of the relation between recruitment and socio-economic origin that is not apparent in the academic schools. The proportion of individuals from managerial and clerical families who are following technical studies is not very different from that of the children of manual workers (15 per cent as contrasted with 19 per cent). Yet there is a substantial difference in the representation of these groups within the high- and low-prestige technical institutions. Over 37 per cent of the first group are concentrated in the *Lycée Technique,* as against only 21 per cent of children from workers' families. This differential representation is rather similar to the picture found in metropolitan France, though the contrasts are less marked in the Ivory Coast.[5]

However, in general, socio-economic background seems to exert only a moderate influence on recruitment into the various types of postprimary study. Does it seem to affect access to private as opposed to public institutions, in view of the substantial fees charged by the private schools? Our evidence suggests that there is generally no difference in patterns of recruitment within the two systems, except in one minor respect: The male offspring of both subsistence and cash-crop farmers constitute roughly an equal proportion of enrollments in the public long academic system taken as a whole. By contrast, half the enrollments in the private long academic schools come from cash-crop families, as against only one-fifth from subsistence backgrounds. This substantial differential reflects the operation of two major factors: First, subsistence farmers are proportionally more numerous in areas of limited missionary influence where Islam is more likely to prevail. Second, cash-crop farmers are obviously in a better position to pay the fees required by private institutions. Notwithstanding this difference, one is justified in concluding that the social *cachement* area of the private schools is not substantially different from that of public institutions. Private schools in the Ivory Coast, unlike those in so many other

5. See, for example, J. Duquesne, *Les 16–24 ans* (Paris: Le Centurion, 1963), pp. 14–20.

areas, do not constitute a more or less socially exclusive subsegment of the educational structure.[6]

Of all single variables, level of paternal education is perhaps more systematically associated with the pattern of internal allocation of students in the secondary school system (Table 21). Students whose

TABLE 21. Paternal Education of Students by Stream and Cycle (Percentages)

	STREAM				CYCLE		
Level of Paternal Education	Agricultural	Technical	Short Academic	Long Academic	Low	Intermediate	High
No education	74.3	63.0	74.3	67.1	71.5	69.9	61.9
Some primary school	10.3	13.4	11.4	13.5	11.7	12.3	16.1
Completed primary school	5.1	9.5	7.2	7.2	7.6	7.4	7.2
Above primary school	10.3	14.1	7.1	12.2	9.2	10.4	14.8
Total	100.0	100.0	100.0	100.0	100.0	100.0	100.0
	(39)	(262)	(708)	(1,065)	(916)	(780)	(378)

fathers have never attended school are relatively more conspicuous in the agricultural and the short academic streams, whereas the offspring of fathers who have had a postprimary education are more numerous in the technical and long academic streams. It is equally apparent that paternal education and level of studies are moderately related. Although this relationship is relatively weak, out of the range of factors already considered the level of a father's education remains the best single predictor of the type and level of postprimary study to be undertaken by his child.[7]

6. This is in basic contrast to the situation in most Western countries, where the pupils of private secondary schools come from families whose social status is usually distinctly higher than that of parents of public school pupils.

7. Variations in maternal background are also associated with differential recruitment into the schools. This is to be expected insofar as there is a substantial correlation between paternal and maternal characteristics. The educated woman in the Ivory Coast is almost certain to be married to a highly educated man, and she in turn is more likely to be occupationally involved in the modern sector of the economy for personal financial gain. If women are engaged in cash-crop farming or trading or are employees in European or government enterprises, their offspring are proportionally more likely to be represented in the long academic stream and

Finally, a word concerning religious affiliation. It can be argued that this factor might play some role in influencing the nature of academic aspirations and thereby affect recruitment to various types of secondary school. We have suggested previously that religious affiliation is

TABLE 22. Distribution of Male Catholic and Moslem Students within Streams and Cycles, by Socio-economic Background

TYPE OF STUDIES	SOCIO-ECONOMIC BACKGROUND			
	Urban Educated Fathers *		Rural Uneducated Fathers †	
Stream	Moslem	Catholic	Moslem	Catholic
Agricultural	5.1	0.5	2.8	2.3
Technical	10.2	15.0	12.5	8.0
Short academic	30.5	27.3	36.1	37.8
Long academic	54.2	57.2	48.6	51.9
Total	100.0	100.0	100.0	100.0
	(59)	(187)	(72)	(613)
Cycle				
Low	42.4	36.9	44.4	44.2
Intermediate	37.3	36.9	43.1	40.9
High	20.3	26.2	12.5	14.9
Total	100.0	100.0	100.0	100.0
	(59)	(187)	(72)	(613)

* Includes students who reside in towns with populations above 5,000 and whose fathers have had at least some primary schooling.

† Includes students who reside in villages with populations below 5,000 and whose fathers have not attended school.

probably less important than is commonly supposed and that frequently, apparent attitudinal differences merely reflect variations in socio-economic background. We have tried to take this into account in Table 22 by comparing the distribution of male Moslem and Catholic students while holding constant residence and paternal level of education. Clearly religious affiliation plays a small apparent role in influencing recruitment into different types of secondary school.

In summary, it is evident that some of the factors which in Western nations seem closely associated with student allocation into the various

in the higher cycles of study than are the children of women not gainfully employed. Almost 60 per cent of students whose mothers are active in the monetary economy are concentrated in the long academic stream, and over one-quarter are in the higher cycle of studies. The corresponding figures for students whose mothers are not so employed are 49 per cent and 17 per cent.

streams and cycles of secondary systems exert a limited influence in the Ivory Coast. Nevertheless they do tend to operate in the same direction, producing a slight concentration of students with superior socio-economic backgrounds in the technical and long academic streams. We can see the combined operation of these socio-economic factors more clearly in Table 23, which shows how the high and low male

TABLE 23. Level of Acculturation of Male Students by Stream and Cycle (Percentages)

LEVEL OF ACCULTURATION	STREAM				CYCLE		
	Agricultural	Technical	Short Academic	Long Academic	Low	Intermediate	High
Highs	2.7	7.9	4.4	7.6	4.8	5.9	11.0
Intermediates	83.8	84.7	81.8	82.8	82.5	83.2	82.0
Lows	13.5	7.4	13.8	9.6	12.8	10.9	7.0
Total	100.0	100.0	100.0	100.0	100.1	100.0	100.0
	(37)	(189)	(636)	(948)	(777)	(689)	(344)

students are distributed among the various streams and cycles of the system. Over 62 per cent of the highs are concentrated in the long academic schools, as contrasted with 46 per cent of the lows, and over one-third of the highs are to be found in the higher cycle of studies, as against 12 per cent of the lows. To put it another way, at the lower cycle of studies only 5 per cent of students are highs, but this figure rises to 11 per cent at the senior cycle. By contrast, the proportion of lows drops from 13 per cent to 7 per cent. True, students from markedly superior backgrounds are rather more likely to enter the long academic and technical streams and have a somewhat greater chance of reaching the higher levels of the system. Although the picture is consistent enough, the magnitude of variations as between subgroups is not very great, and recruitment into different streams and cycles is still extraordinarily fluid.[8]

8. The looseness of the relationship between student social background and allocation in the secondary school system can be demonstrated in a more succinct manner. Using "gamma" as a coefficient of correlation, we find that the relationship between paternal educational background and student stream and cycle of study is only 0.106. Similarly, when we use our strongest measure available, the combined index of acculturation, this relationship is 0.203. See Leo Goodman and William H. Kruskal, "Measures of Association for Cross Classifications," *Journal of the American Statistical Association,* 49 (1954), pp. 732–64.

The Interaction between Ethnicity and Socio-economic Background

Given the fact that the relationship between socio-economic background and student allocation is very loose at the national level, this relationship can still vary markedly between ethnic groups. In a sense, acculturation represents an interaction between pressures toward uniformity exerted by modernization and initially divergent forms of traditional organization and culture. Thus we might well expect to find certain idiosyncratic patterns of variation between ethnic groups.

Some evidence for this is provided in Table 24, where we compare

TABLE 24. Distribution of Male Agni and Kru Students within the Academic Stream, by Socio-economic Background (Percentages)

ETHNIC GROUP	SOCIO-ECONOMIC BACKGROUND	B.E.P.C. (SHORT) AND B.E.	B.E.P.C. (LONG)	*BACCALAUREAT*	TOTAL ENROLLMENT ‡
AGNI	Highly urbanized *	14.7	15.6	26.8	17.8
	Rural †	55.8	48.6	25.0	45.9
	Other	29.5	35.8	48.2	36.3
	Total	100.0	100.0	100.0	100.0
		(95)	(109)	(56)	(292)
KRU	Highly urbanized	11.8	8.5	12.3	10.7
	Rural	61.4	62.4	56.1	59.8
	Other	26.8	29.1	31.6	29.5
	Total	100.0	100.0	100.0	100.0
		(127)	(141)	(57)	(366)

* Includes students who live in urban centers with a population of over 10,000 and whose fathers have attended some primary school.

† Includes students who live in towns with a population of less than 5,000 and whose fathers have never attended school.

‡ Total enrollment figures include additional students in technical and agricultural institutions.

the characteristics of male Agni and Kru students within the academic system—their number being large enough within this sector to justify detailed analysis. Both groups have distinctly different traditional social structures and have been differentially exposed to European influence.[9]

9. It should be noted that in this table the definition of high and low subjects has been modified to make it possible to work with a smaller number of cases. The Baoulé represented the only other group in the sample which was numerous

Clearly the substantial differences in the overall socio-economic composition of the two groups reflect the different levels of acculturation of the ethnic populations from which they come. However, the social composition of the Agni sample changes markedly as one moves up through the academic system, and the proportion of highs rises from less than one-fifth in the short academic stream to well over one-fourth at the *Baccalaureat* level. By contrast, the proportion of lows drops from over one-half to little more than one-quarter between the lower and higher academic cycles. The Kru pattern is distinctly different, since there appears to be no systematic variation in the social composition of the male student body at the various levels of the academic system. In this sense the Agni student population seems to be much more internally stratified than its Kru counterpart.

How does this finding relate to our earlier observation that the higher the general level of acculturation of a people, the more likely it is that its student population will be socially more typical? The schools recruit from a broad segment of the Agni people, but the Agni student body is, comparatively speaking, more stratified than its Kru counterpart. Very tentatively we suggest that this feature is a corollary of educational diffusion: Greater openness in access to secondary education as a whole is correlated with more marked inequalities in recruitment into different parts of the system. In other words, any group that expands its overall representation will become more heterogeneous in terms of the ability and social background of its student body, leading to highly differentiated achievement and variable progress through the system. By contrast, students drawn from relatively poorly represented groups will be much more homogeneous in terms of ability. It may well be that as the problem of access to secondary schooling as a whole becomes less crucial among educationally developed groups, the question of access to *particular* segments of the system becomes progressively more important.[10]

---

enough to justify a similar analysis. In their case, socio-economic gradients were similar to those of the Agni but less marked. In this sense they can be considered intermediate between the Agni and the Kru.

10. This interpretation would certainly seem to fit the European case. In early periods when secondary education was available to only a small proportion of the student population, social background was crucial in determining whether a child would proceed to secondary school or not. At present the enactment of policies to provide some form of postprimary schooling for all children merely enhances the value of particular varieties of such schooling. Thus entry into the stream having highest prestige is invariably associated with higher mean levels of socio-economic background.

Some General Conclusions

In Chapter III, we saw that the overall pattern of recruitment into the secondary schools was relatively open. We can now see that this openness is even more characteristic of access into different kinds of postprimary schooling. Variations in ethnic or socio-economic status are even less pronounced among the streams and cycles of secondary education than they are for the system as a whole. Once a student begins his postprimary education, what stream he enters or what level of studies he achieves seems to be largely dependent on his academic abilities as measured by public examinations. The evidence in this chapter would lead us to conclude that academic achievement is only loosely correlated with ethnic, religious, and socio-economic characteristics. Perhaps one of the most striking conclusions is the extent to which students from the most unpromising environments hold their own against others with superior backgrounds, even in the most demanding part of the postprimary structure—the long academic stream.

However, it must be recognized that the present data are subject to one serious limitation: In comparing the social and ethnic characteristics of students at different levels within the system, we are making comparisons between different cohorts. A more adequate examination of the relationship between recruitment into, and allocation among, the segments of this secondary school structure would necessarily involve longitudinal studies of given groups of students, since the present material provides no evidence concerning the characteristics of individuals who have dropped out of secondary school altogether. Cross-sectional studies like the present one can only indicate that if dropping out does occur, it is not sufficient to produce substantial variations in student characteristics between the *troisième* and *Baccalaureat* levels.

This examination of the internal allocation of students is no idle exercise. The importance of a secondary school hierarchy lies in the fact that various types of schools furnish differential access to higher education and to elite roles within the polity. We have seen that some schools, particularly the *Centres d'Apprentissage,* provide only a terminal vocational education that limits the occupational opportunities of their graduates. Other types, notably the *Lycées,* give their clientele optimum chances for occupational and social mobility. At present in the Ivory Coast the crucial factor is that these differential opportunities are not closely linked to ethnic or social background. So long as the secondary school system can maintain its present openness and fluidity, the question of allocating places in different types of secondary schools is not likely to be raised in a political context. Yet, as the system evolves, if differentials become more marked and inequalities more apparent, there is some likelihood that secondary education may become a focus for conflict between ethnic and social haves and have-nots. Indeed in our final chapter we shall present evidence suggesting that as the secondary school system expands, social and ethnic inequalities could be exacerbated rather than diminished. So far the schools have facilitated open recruitment into the elite from the mass, but one must not forget that they can also contribute to a polarization between the two groups.

CHAPTER V

Student Attitudes and Adjustment to the Postprimary School Hierarchy

We have demonstrated that the postprimary educational system of the Ivory Coast is basically hierarchical in its organization, with the result that the status of particular types of study depends largely on the content of instruction and on whether courses lead to a higher cycle of studies or are terminal in nature. The academic schools stand at the apex of the system, followed by the technical and agricultural institutions. Since there is considerable difference in the status of the long and short academic streams, it may still be preferable, for example, to be in the long technical system rather than a *Cours Complémentaire*. At the same time it has been pointed out that these status differentials are only minimally correlated with variations in students' social and ethnic background. The inference must be, therefore, that student placement overwhelmingly reflects variations in academic ability, as measured by examination success, and is to a lesser degree determined by personal motivations and aspirations.

The students' perception of the relative worth of different types of secondary education is likely to correspond closely to the picture already presented. These student perceptions of the school hierarchy can be learned in two ways: first, by asking students what kind of school they would prefer to attend if they were free to begin their secondary studies again, and, second, by ascertaining their attitudes toward the type of school they are now attending. Their views will then constitute an index of the level of demand for various types of secondary education. Further, if we assume a certain amount of discrepancy between academic aspirations and actual ability we might expect a corresponding degree of internal mobility in the system. Thus students will tend to change their stream or cycle of studies either by choice or, more frequently, because of marked academic success or scholastic inadequacy. In the latter case, for example, a student may not survive the rigors of the long academic system and thus be forced to repeat classes, with ultimate demotion to a secondary course of lower prestige. The following pages will concern themselves, therefore, with this internal circulation of students.

Student Preferences for Alternative Secondary Schools

Let us first consider patterns of choice if students were free to recommence their secondary school career. Column I of Table 25

TABLE 25. Student Preferences for Alternative Secondary School Careers (Percentages)

PREFERENCE	I Aggregate Choice	II Choice Excluding Preference for Present Institution
Short technical	2.7	2.4
Long technical	30.7	41.7
Cours Normaux and *Cours Complémentaires*	5.3	2.2
Academic long *	40.1	24.6
Agricultural schools	15.7	21.0
Other training programs †	4.5	6.7
No answer	1.0	1.4
Total	100.0	100.0
	(2,074)	(1,395)

* Also includes choices for the *Ecole Normale,* which for this purpose can be regarded as part of the academic long system.

† Includes military school, special training programs for social workers and nurses, etc.

shows that the long academic system is most in demand; its prestige is unquestioned, and it still remains the most direct channel to higher education. Yet it is striking that the *Lycée Technique* commands over 30 per cent of the total vote, while the percentage of choices of the new agricultural schools is surprisingly high. Conversely, the relative unpopularity of the *Centres d'Apprentissage, Cours Normaux,* and *Cours Complémentaires* is quite manifest.

Column II of the table shows the distribution of choices when student preferences for the type of institution they are now attending are excluded from the total count. The percentage of preferences for the least popular secondary institutions declines, but so also does the proportion of expressed preferences for the long academic system. By contrast, the level of preference for the long technical and agricultural systems rises quite sharply. The implication is clear: Although the *Lycée* is popular among all groups, the *Lycée Technique* and the agricultural schools have considerable attraction for students in low-status terminal institutions. In effect, the pattern of alternative preferences is related to the type of institution now attended by students, as made clear in Table 26.

This table shows that students place the *Centres d'Apprentissage* at the bottom of the school hierarchy. Only 14 per cent of the students in these institutions would consider reentering them, while over 40 per cent would choose the *Lycée Technique* and one-fifth the long academic system. One must remember that the short technical stream is essentially terminal in nature and does not provide an overwhelming number of recruits for the long technical system. Students are thus perfectly aware that the *Centres d'Apprentissage* offer only minimal opportunities for further study.

The same might be said of the *Cours Complémentaires.* Their relative unpopularity springs from the fact that they constitute a dead end for most students. Originally created to provide regional elites, they have become merely a cheap substitute for the already overcrowded long academic schools. Hence a high proportion of their students would prefer to enter those parts of the academic, technical, or agricultural system that afford some opportunity for further study.

Students in the *Cours Normaux* are in a somewhat better position. Indeed over one-fifth of them would reenter this type of institution or a *Cours Complémentaire* if given another chance (actually, almost all choices in this category are for the *Cours Normaux*). The reasons for this rather greater popularity are twofold. First, unlike the *Cours*

TABLE 26. Student Preferences for Alternative Secondary School Careers, by Present Type of Study (Percentages)

PREFERENCE	PRESENT INSTITUTION					
	Short Technical	Long Technical	*Cours Normaux*	*Cours Complémentaires*	Academic Long	Agricultural Schools
Short technical	13.7	0.0	3.8	1.2	1.6	0.0
Long technical	43.4	69.1	21.8	30.8	29.2	2.6
Cours Normaux and *Cours Complémentaires*	7.7	0.0	21.5	3.8	1.7	0.0
Academic long	19.7	23.5	35.0	34.1	49.6	2.6
Agricultural schools	8.3	3.7	12.8	24.6	12.6	84.6
Other training programs	6.0	3.7	4.1	4.8	4.3	7.7
No answer	1.2	0.0	1.0	0.7	1.0	2.6
Total	100.0	100.0	100.0	100.0	100.0	100.1
	(168)	(81)	(289)	(419)	(1,078)	(39)

Complémentaires, the *Cours Normaux* do train for a specific career in primary teaching, and postsecondary employment is almost guaranteed. Second, it is possible for a graduate of this type of institution to enter the *Ecole Normale* and prepare for the *Baccalaureat.* To be sure, his chances of doing this are not great, and the vast majority of students in the *Cours Normaux* are destined to enter primary school teaching directly after gaining the B.E. Nonetheless the opportunity exists, and raises the status of the institution above that of the *Cours Complémentaires.* Notwithstanding this fact, the high percentage of student choices for alternative institutions reflects the relatively low status of primary school teaching in the Ivory Coast and of the institutions which prepare individuals for this career.

Most striking, however, is the high level of choice for the long technical system and the moderate preference for the agricultural schools. Students already in these institutions show a strong commitment to their present course of study, while a substantial number of students in alternative streams would prefer to join them. Thus, rather surprisingly, almost 30 per cent of the academic long students would like to enter the long technical studies.

The growing popularity of the *Lycée Technique* reveals a rise in status of technical studies following the creation of a new technical *Baccalaureat* which permits entry into higher institutions. At the same time there can be no doubt that the career opportunities of students with higher or intermediate qualifications have improved in recent years. This is true also of the agricultural schools. The status of these new institutions has been enhanced by the creation of a second cycle of studies in the *Ecole d'Agriculture* with an appropriate second-stage qualification.[1] Further, current government stress on agricultural development virtually guarantees occupational placement for these students. As we shall see in a later chapter, the relative popularity of the agricultural schools does not reflect their students' desire to become farmers. Most of them expect to enter the bureaucracy as demonstrators and agricultural technicians in response to the demands of the Ministry of Agriculture.

Students seem able to make a fairly shrewd appraisal of the relative worth of different types of secondary schools, and this demand pattern is linked to differences in current placement. However, it is associated

1. In the same manner that long technical schools have been allowed to offer a technical *Baccalaureat,* there is now strong pressure to create a full agricultural *Baccalaureat* to enhance the status of agricultural studies.

also with other differences in students' background. Although the actual school career of girls is shorter and less differentiated than that of boys, girls' demand for long academic education is more marked. Over half of them would prefer to enter a *Lycée,* as against only one-third of the male students. This variation reflects differences not only in the social background of the sexes but also in the career opportunities open to them. Primary school teaching is one of the first occupations to become open to educated girls, and it is not surprising that 17 per cent of them would prefer to enter teacher training courses, as against 10 per cent of boys. So far, women have comprised a very small segment of the primary school teaching force, but with an accelerated development of education among women, their numbers in this occupational field can be expected to increase rapidly over the next few years.[2]

Choices of different types of postprimary education also tend to vary along ethnic and social lines. The demand for studies in the academic *Lycée* is highest among southern ethnic groups, such as the Agni, the Lagoon cluster, and the Kru, and lower among northern and central peoples. About 36 per cent of southern students would select this type of institution, as against 27 per cent of northerners. The demand for agricultural studies presents a reverse picture, with only 13 per cent of southern groups choosing this type of schooling, as contrasted with 19 per cent of northerners. The relationship is by no means a strong one, but it would seem that the more modernized an ethnic group, the more likely it is to choose the type of secondary education that has hitherto been highest in prestige and most rewarding in the metropole itself.

Fathers' occupational status also tends to exert some influence on educational choices. No less than 43 per cent of the children of managerial and clerical workers would prefer to study at a *Lycée,* as compared with only 29 per cent of the offspring of farmers, while the demand for agricultural studies is more closely correlated with a farming background. Twenty per cent of students from farming families would like to enter agricultural schools, as against only 9 per cent of the children of managerial and clerical workers.

2. Increased female participation in the teaching force has been a well-nigh universal phenomenon where educational systems have been undergoing expansion. This is happening in some African states. In the Ivory Coast, women already constitute some 15 per cent of the total teaching force, but in nearby Ghana this figure has already grown to 25 per cent.

The relationship between choice of school and level of paternal education is even clearer (Table 27). Here it is quite obvious that the demand for agricultural schooling or teacher training is associated with the lack of an educational tradition within the family, while the demand for education in a *Lycée* is more heavily concentrated among students from families in which the father has had some schooling. Though the demand for education in a *Lycée* or *Collège* is high for all groups, it rises from 30 per cent among students whose fathers have had no education to over 50 per cent among students whose fathers went beyond primary school. By contrast, there is an inverse, if not so sharp, relationship between social background and interest in agricultural studies or teacher training. Conversely, a generally high level of interest in technical studies (virtually all concentrated in the *Lycée Technique*) does not vary significantly with students' social background. This lack of variation could be due to the increasing status of technical studies but may be attributable in part to the very newness of this kind of offering. In time, it may well be that preferences for a technical education will be more closely linked to parental background.

If we now introduce our composite measure of acculturation and compare high and low male students, we find that social origin is substantially correlated with educational demand (Table 28). This table supports our general conclusion that family background influ-

TABLE 27. Preferences of Students by Level of Paternal Education (Percentages)

	LEVEL OF PATERNAL EDUCATION			
PREFERENCE	No Education	Some Primary School	Completed Primary School	Above Primary School
Academic long	30.1	34.9	39.4	50.2
Technical schools (long and short)	34.0	34.1	32.2	29.9
Cours Normaux, Cours Complémentaires, and *Ecole Normale*	13.0	10.2	11.0	6.8
Agricultural schools	18.1	14.4	8.4	6.8
Other	4.0	4.9	7.7	5.4
No answer	.8	1.5	1.3	.9
Total	100.0	100.0	100.0	100.0
	(1,434)	(264)	(155)	(221)

ences attitudes toward different types of education. Sometimes it seems to be assumed that the average family in Africa is so remote from the world of the schools that it can have little influence on children's educational choice. Yet it is not unreasonable to infer from these data that students' attitudes reflect the varying importance attached by parents to various kinds of schooling. The findings present a pattern that is familiar enough in some Western countries. Families of lower economic and social status are much more likely to view education in terms of entry into specific occupations; hence, the greater preferences of their children for technical, agricultural, and teacher training schools. By contrast, the more acculturated families with longer educational traditions are likely to be more informed about the ultimate advantages of more general types of training. In consequence, students from this kind of background have less specific orientations, and their greater preference for education at a *Lycée* reflects a perception of education as a long-run investment not immediately linked to specific short-run opportunities.

This specificity or diffuseness of educational ambitions is also reflected in students' attitudes toward the school they are now attending. An analysis of the reasons (or rationalizations) that they give for entering their present institution shows that technical and agricultural studies seem closely linked to specific vocational aspirations. Approximately 70 per cent of students in technical and agricultural schools viewed their education mainly in terms of the specific job to which it would lead. This type of response was given only by 30 per cent of individuals in academic schools; these students were more concerned

TABLE 28. Preferences of Male Students by Level of Acculturation (Percentages)

PREFERENCE	LEVEL OF ACCULTURATION	
	High	Low
Lycée or *Collège*	40.5	21.7
Technical schools (long and short)	43.1	32.8
Cours Normaux, Cours Complémentaires, and *Ecole Normale*	5.2	16.7
Agricultural schools	7.8	24.3
Others	3.4	4.5
Total	100.0	100.0
	(116)	(198)

with their schools' academic status and reputation. For example, 17 per cent of respondents in the long academic stream indicated that they entered their school because of its good standing, as against only 10 per cent of students in the short academic stream and 2 per cent of those in agricultural and technical institutions.[3]

In summary, we have attempted to show that secondary school students in the Ivory Coast are capable of making a clear estimate of the roles of alternative types of schools. In this sense assertions that different types of secondary education should enjoy parity of esteem and equal status are quite meaningless. Students are well aware that the various streams and cycles of study do not lead to equal occupational and academic opportunities. For them the crucial issue seems to be whether a particular type of school is terminal in nature or is effectively articulated with another cycle of study. Nor do they seem to be influenced in their choices by the extent to which their present education is linked to expanding opportunities in the bureaucracy and the economy in general. Social and ethnic background seems to have some effect on student preferences, but both these factors are perhaps less important than students' knowledge of how the system actually functions.

Academic Progress and the School Hierarchy

The diverse structure of secondary education in the Ivory Coast is reflected in different levels of demand for alternative types of schooling, the academic requirements of which vary considerably. An examination of rates of doubling in secondary classes is one indirect way of measuring the degree of rigor among the different types of postprimary schooling. Indeed one of the most striking characteristics of all French-type educational systems is the extent to which students are obliged either to repeat the same class for successive years until they have satisfactorily completed the appropriate requirements or else to drop out of school altogether. This practice prevails in all segments of the Ivory Coast system, but the rate varies markedly with the type of school.

Table 29 shows that the incidence of doubled classes averages well

3. Although this chapter does not examine the effect of geographical location on the status of a school, this factor seems of some importance. Thus students attending all schools located in Bingerville, just outside Abidjan, stressed the importance of the superior location of their institutions.

TABLE 29. Incidence of Doubling among Male Students by Stream and Cycle (Percentages) *

Past Record in Secondary School	STREAM				CYCLE		
	Agricultural	Technical	Short Academic	Long Academic	Low	Intermediate	High
Doubled	30.8	22.4	31.3	36.7	29.0	28.5	51.4
Did not double	69.2	77.6	68.7	63.3	71.0	71.5	48.6
Total	100.0	100.0	100.0	100.0	100.0	100.0	100.0
	(39)	(192)	(643)	(963)	(786)	(695)	(356)

* Totals exclude "No answer" category.

over 30 per cent for all students (and this excludes all doubling in primary school), but is markedly higher in the long academic system and in the senior cycles of study. In fact, these figures are higher than those derived from a previous study of the *Lycée,* in which the doubling rate was calculated as 10 per cent up to the B.E.P.C. level, rising to 30 per cent at the stage of the second *Baccalaureat.*[4] Although, it may be argued that the *Lycées* of the long academic system recruit the most academically talented population, their demands are such as to hold back students' progress. The obverse of this picture is that the promotion of younger cohorts of perhaps more talented students is similarly retarded, since they cannot obtain places in the academic system occupied by the "old guard" of repeaters. However, from the point of view of the academic student, the seriousness of doubling is dependent on the stage at which it occurs. If it takes place at or before the *troisième* or B.E.P.C. level, the chances of a student's being allowed to continue in that stream, or in school at all, are seriously diminished. But if doubling occurs at the *Baccalaureat* level it usually does not keep the student from repeating the examination until he finally passes it. As a result, over 80 per cent of all candidates for that examination ultimately receive their degree. Whatever the logic of this procedure, it seems to rest on the view that a previous heavy investment in a pupil's education *must* be justified by final success. (Whether students actually learn more as a result of this process would be difficult to assess, but at least they gain the qualification.)

Further, the amount of doubling seems to differ significantly between public and private academic institutions. At the level of the long B.E.P.C. examination only 18 per cent of private school students double one or more secondary classes, as against 32 per cent of public school pupils. At the *Baccalaureat* stage the contrast is even sharper; the percentage of doubling remains the same in the private schools but rises to 55 per cent in public ones. Paradoxically these significant differences could be due to either a relatively lax or an extremely rigorous policy on the part of private schools. Students could be promoted fairly automatically, without being obliged to repeat classes; or, on the other hand, academic inadequacy could lead not to doubling but to complete dismissal from the system. Clearly the present study cannot take into account the extent of actual dropping-out from the private system, but two reasons may be suggested to explain why

4. See UNESCO, *Première mission du groupe de planification . . . , op. cit.,* p. 60.

the private academic institutions tend to be more rigorous than some comparable public schools. First, insofar as private secondary schools compete with the public system, they must demonstrate that they offer at least as adequate a training. Traditionally the administration has not been altogether friendly to mission schools; hence, to survive and perhaps receive assistance, they must show parity of quality or even superiority in the education they offer. Second, students in private academic secondary schools have a somewhat better record of success in public examinations than do those in public schools. Here the inference is that a larger proportion of private school students are not allowed to continue in school long enough to take these examinations.[5]

What factors besides stream and cycle of study and who controls the school seem to be associated with the incidence of student doubling?[6] Certainly girls tend to double more frequently than boys (44 per cent as against 34 per cent) in spite of the fact that the girls come from more advantaged backgrounds and are rather more concentrated in the less demanding type of secondary school. However, other factors, such as social and ethnic background, lead to more interesting findings about doubling.

Two equally plausible but contradictory hypotheses can be entertained concerning the relationship between student background and the incidence of repeated classes. First, it can be argued that the more underrepresented groups in the system will tend to double more frequently, if they remain in the system at all. That is to say, students from rural or farming backgrounds, from illiterate homes, or from the more backward ethnic groups are likely to experience more difficulty with their studies and hence be obliged to double more often. Second, it can be suggested that students from these groups have been so rigidly selected and are so superior in terms of ability that they will do

5. In 1961 the rate of success in the *Baccalaureat* examinations was 65 per cent in the public schools and 80 per cent in the private schools. In the same year the private system had a 56 per cent record of successes in the B.E.P.C. examination, as against 53 per cent for the public schools.

6. It must also be noted that there are regional variations in rates of doubling. At the *Baccalaureat* level the public schools in Abidjan and Bouaké have slightly higher rates of doubling than do institutions in Bingerville and Dabou. Interestingly enough, students from the schools with the greatest record of doubling enjoy the highest level of success in the *Baccalaureat* examinations. The rate of doubling at the long B.E.P.C. level varies even more significantly by region, ranging from 15 per cent in the southwest to 38 per cent in Bouaké. In the short academic system regional differences are equally marked; in northern schools the doubling rate is only 24 per cent, as against 38 per cent in central and southern schools.

less doubling than their proportionally better represented counterparts.

Let us first consider these two propositions in relation to ethnicity. Among male students, rates of doubling do not vary significantly from ethnic group to ethnic group, with a mean rate of about 35 per cent for all peoples. Looking at the system as a whole, we find no evidence that students from the more backward minorities are obliged to double more often than other students from the better represented southeastern peoples. We can take this point a little further, since we have seen that rates of doubling vary between streams and cycles. How are these variations affected by ethnic representation? We might have suspected that the incidence of doubling for each ethnic group in the various cycles and streams of the postprimary system would be related to their overall representation in that system. And indeed Table 30

TABLE 30. Incidence of Doubling among Male Students, by Level of Ethnic Representation (Percentages)

ETHNIC SELECTIVITY INDEX	PERCENTAGE OF STUDENTS WHO DOUBLED BY STREAM AND CYCLE					
	Agricultural Schools	Lower Technical (C.A.P.)	Short Academic (B.E. and B.E.P.C.)	Long Academic (B.E.P.C.)	Long Technical	Long Academic (*Baccalaureat*)
Above 1.5	44.4	29.0	35.2	31.4	20.7	50.4
Below 1.5	28.1	15.5	30.4	27.6	36.7	54.9

shows that the repeating rate of overrepresented groups is higher than that of less well-represented peoples at the lower levels of the system, but the reverse occurs at higher levels.

What is the possible cause of this reversal? Initially it was shown that all groups that are proportionately well represented in the system tend to prefer those types of schools that have hitherto been high in prestige. These groups actually are slightly more represented in such schools. However, as we shall see in the following pages, the greater incidence of repeated classes among groups that are well represented in the system at its lower levels is a function of downward mobility from higher types of school. There are, therefore, two types of doubling within the system: doubling that occurs in the stream or cycle in which the student is now situated and doubling that has occurred previously in another type of school. In concrete terms, an individual may start his secondary school career in the long academic system, be forced to double a class, and then move to a *Cours Complémentaire* or a *Centre d'Apprentissage.*

This latter pattern is more frequent among the proportionally well-represented ethnic and social groups. The careers of students from less well-represented peoples are rather more regular; that is to say, these students display more limited mobility by entering the lower prestige streams in rather greater numbers and staying there. However, those who do reach the *Baccalaureat* level double a little more frequently in that cycle than do their better represented counterparts.

This sheds new light on the findings reported in the previous chapter. There a somewhat more static analysis demonstrated that the ethnic composition of the student body did not vary greatly between stream and cycle. Here our analysis provides a more dynamic picture. The present study does not include data relative to students in the *sixième,* or first year of secondary school. Yet on the basis of our interpretation we would argue that ethnic differentials will be more marked at the earliest stages of secondary school but will then tend to become progressively more blurred as placement on the basis of academic ability becomes more important. Agni students, for example, may be proportionally better represented than Mandefou students in the *sixième* class of the long academic system; three years later their initial advantages have been canceled out.

These observations tend to be generally confirmed by a similar analysis of the student body in terms of its social background. In other words, the greater proportional representation of a group, the higher will be its rate of repeating classes at the lower levels of the system.

Initially this hypothesis is not substantiated if students are considered in relation to urban origin or residence. There are no differences in rates of doubling between urban and rural children within the system as a whole, or even within its various subsegments. Indeed this substantiates an earlier observation—that although urban background may be of importance in influencing entry into the secondary system as a whole, it is only weakly associated with processes of internal allocation.

However, if we examine students in terms of their paternal occupational background, the first fact to emerge is that rates of doubling within the system as a whole are *higher* among students coming from superior circumstances. The offspring of professional and clerical workers double rather more frequently than do students coming from other occupational groups. When we compare students from diverse occupational backgrounds within the separate streams and cycles of the system, it is evident that this difference is totally accounted for by the high rate of doubling among students from higher socio-economic backgrounds who are at present in lower status institutions such as the *Centres d'Apprentissage.*

Level of paternal education is even more clearly associated with the incidence of repeating; in fact, rates of doubling in the system as a whole are directly related to the fathers' educational background. Thus the rate of doubling among students whose fathers never attended school is only 32 per cent, but this figure rises to 42 per cent among pupils whose fathers completed more than a primary school education. When stream and cycle of studies are taken into account, once again it becomes apparent that these differences in the rate of doubling are almost wholly concentrated in the short technical and short academic cycles. In the *Centres d'Apprentissage* 46 per cent of male individuals whose fathers had some education had doubled, as against only 26 per cent of the sons of uneducated fathers. The figures for the short academic stream are 33 per cent and 19 per cent, respectively.

Contrary to most expectations, the rate of doubling, where it does vary significantly, is positively correlated with socio-economic background. This evidence would suggest that doubling results from an interplay between the different academic requirements of the various parts of the secondary school system and the motivations and aspirations of the students. The better represented groups, whether we define them in terms of ethnic or of social characteristics, are likely to aim toward the more rewarding types of secondary education. However, their academic heterogeneity will lead a proportion of them to repeat classes and then move to institutions with lower prestige. As we have noted, doubling is often the first step in downward mobility in the system. Indeed one-third of the students who have been obliged to double secondary classes have also shifted schools, as against only one-quarter of the students who have never doubled.

A caveat must be made at this point. It is true that the rate of repeating increases as the socio-economic background of a student rises, and it is also true that doubling is associated with downward mobility in the system. Yet the present study cannot provide data concerning students who repeat a class and then drop out of the system altogether. It could be asserted justifiably that students from well-represented groups do double but remain in the system, although in a school with less prestige. Conversely, students from lower socio-economic backgrounds may double just as frequently but then leave secondary school. In other words, differential rates of repeating are merely an artifact of the present type of investigation. In a later chapter, which considers the characteristics of students who have already left secondary school, we shall present some evidence that students with lower socio-economic backgrounds may leave the system at earlier stages. This would certainly account for some part of the differential that we have noted here.

"Regular" and "Irregular" Progress within the System

Let us now take our investigation of mobility within the secondary schools a little further. Clearly, any educational system has a built-in process of normal upward movement as students progress through the usual sequence of grades. We are not concerned here with this regular process but rather with deviant patterns of mobility. Since secondary education in the Ivory Coast is hierarchically organized, it is possible for students to move from high-status to low-status schools as a result of academic inadequacy or even personal choice. An individual may commence his secondary school career in the long academic stream and end up either in the short stream, in an agricultural college, or in a *Centre d'Apprentissage*. Theoretically a hierarchy of this type implies that reversing such a movement is difficult, if not in some cases impossible. Students have little chance of moving from low-status to high-status streams, though in practice some of them do manage it despite formal regulations explicitly forbidding it.

Having indicated that rates of doubling vary between stream and cycle, we must see how far students have had "regular" or "irregular" school careers. Further, we can now indicate how certain segments of the system depend on other segments for their supply of students—the considerable role played by specific types of schools as feeder institutions for other schools.

Certain problems of definition do arise in typifying the secondary school careers of students. Clearly, students who change streams have irregular careers, and there is no problem in so classifying individuals who have moved from the academic to the technical and agricultural streams or vice versa. At the same time irregular careers can represent upward or downward mobility in the system. Movement from a short to a long course of study normally represents upward mobility; the reverse movement, downward mobility. In addition, changing one's stream is also a crucial factor, and crossing from the academic to the technical or agricultural cycles would suggest downward movement. The problem is to combine these two types of progress in the system and then decide whether a student's aggregate career has been up or down. Fortunately, in the overwhelming percentage of cases there is no great difficulty in determining the direction of movement. The number of difficult cases—as, for example, when a student moves from the short academic cycle to the long agricultural cycle—are so few as not to alter percentage distributions. Further, among students whose careers have been regular are those who have never changed their present stream and also a few whose movement has been slightly irregular but has involved no significant change in status. For example, there seemed little point in classifying individuals as having upward or downward careers if they merely changed from a *Cours Complémentaire* to a *Cours Normal.*

Table 31 demonstrates the considerable variability of student careers in the system. The academic schools, whether short or long, have a highly stable student body, and almost 90 per cent of their students began their careers in the type of school in which they are now situated. In fact only 10 per cent of students in the *Lycées* and *Collèges* commenced their secondary school work outside the long academic system. Overwhelmingly the academic schools recruit from their own ranks.

TABLE 31. Academic Careers of Students by Stream and Cycle (Percentages)

ACADEMIC CAREER	PRESENT STREAM					
	Technical		Academic		Agricultural	
	Short	Long	Short	Long	Short	Long
Regular	61.9	51.9	87.6	89.4	3.8	0.0
Downwardly mobile	35.1	17.3	11.7	0.0	77.0	69.2
Upwardly mobile	0.0	25.9	.3	10.2	15.4	30.8
No answer	3.0	4.9	.4	.4	3.8	0.0
Total	100.0	100.0	100.0	100.0	100.0	100.0
	(168)	(81)	(708)	(1,078)	(26)	(13)

By contrast, the technical schools show a much more diverse pattern of recruitment. The *Centres d'Apprentissage,* in particular, are dependent on a flow of students from other types of schools, 35 per cent of their enrollment being "rejects" from the short and long academic institutions. Students in the *Lycée Technique* are even more mobile, though the pattern here has different implications. This school tends to recruit students who have withdrawn from the high-prestige academic *Lycées;* but over a quarter of its student body is made up of upwardly mobile individuals from either the short academic system or the *Centres d'Apprentissage,* although the number of pupils from the latter type of school is very small indeed. The *Lycée Technique* is far more likely to recruit from the short academic schools. Paradoxically, an individual who commences his career in an academic institution has a better chance of pursuing higher technical studies than one who enters a lower technical school. In short, the *Lycée Technique* provides better opportunities for upward mobility than the long academic system, where only 10 per cent of students have been upwardly mobile.

Most students in agricultural institutions have irregular careers—in part as a result of the very newness of this segment of the secondary school system. Only one student now in an agricultural school went there directly after completing primary schooling, and the short agricultural schools recruit an overwhelming number of dropouts from the academic system. The *Collège d'Agriculture,* on the other hand, does provide opportunities for further study for some students whose careers would normally terminate at the end of the first cycle. Over 30 per cent of its student body are upwardly mobile, mostly from the short academic schools.

There is, therefore, a tendency for low-status schools to be manned to a great extent by dropouts from other institutions. Conversely, the incidence of upward mobility is less marked.[7] Whatever its extent, this process of internal reallocation of students introduces an element of flexibility into the system and provides alternatives for students who might otherwise drop out of school altogether. For a few it even gives

7. This process of upward mobility tends, as we might suspect, to favor students from underrepresented groups. To quote one example, the children of subsistence farmers provide only one-fifth of downwardly mobile individuals but one-third of all upwardly mobile students. In ethnic terms, the Malinke, more than any other group, seem to benefit from the process of student reallocation. They provide only 8 per cent of downwardly mobile pupils but over 15 per cent of the upwardly mobile cohort.

new opportunities that might not have been expected in view of their initial placement in the system.[8]

Since downward mobility is more frequent in the system, it is worthwhile to take a closer look at the ethnic and social characteristics of students who "spill over" from higher to lower status schools, if only to reinforce our earlier conclusions. The *Centres d'Apprentissage* provide a particularly useful category of school for this purpose, since a high proportion of their students have had irregular school careers.

First, we have suggested that the discrepancy between scholastic ambition and actual academic achievement is probably greater among students drawn from the more acculturated southern groups than among the less well-represented central and northern peoples. This would account for the fact that no less than 74 per cent of southern students now in the *Centres d'Apprentissage* have been downwardly mobile, as against only 45 per cent of central and northern students. This demonstrates that the higher incidence of repeated classes among students from highly represented ethnic groups who are at present in low-status schools is a result of their irregular pattern of entry into these schools from higher status institutions.

The same picture emerges if we consider the social background of students within the *Centres d'Apprentissage*. Only half of those with uneducated fathers had irregular careers, as compared with 80 per cent of those whose fathers had attended school. Similarly, 85 per cent of the children of professional and clerical workers in the *Centres d'Apprentissage* have been downwardly mobile, as against only 50 per cent of the children of farmers.

In the *Cours Complémentaires,* which enjoy a slightly higher status than the schools of the lower technical stream, the same pattern of association is apparent and is quite consistent; students with irregular careers tend to be drawn more frequently from southern groups and from families with superior social and educational backgrounds. However, the contrast between the backgrounds of regular and down-

8. The incidence of downward or upward mobility among students varies markedly between different parts of the country. In the southeastern and central portions of the Ivory Coast, 37 per cent of students in the short academic stream have had an irregular career, as against only 23 per cent of those in the same types of school in the more remote north and west. Although we devote our present discussion to movement between streams and cycles, it must not be forgotten that this involves considerable geographical mobility on the part of students. Even when students do not change their stream or cycle, they often move to similar schools in different locations. In fact, nearly 30 per cent of students in the long academic establishments have changed schools without changing their stream.

wardly mobile students is not so great as in the *Centres d'Apprentissage*. This is to be expected in view of the more intermediate position occupied by the *Cours Complémentaires* in the hierarchy.

To summarize, we have indicated that among students who remain in the system, the rate of doubling will be greater for those drawn from the most represented groups. On the other hand, among those from the least represented minorities the incidence of repeated classes and subsequent downward mobility is likely to be lower. These latter students demand less of the system, and once in a particular type of school they tend to stay there. By contrast, students from well-represented ethnic minorities or from higher social backgrounds may start out in a superior type of institution but will then show greater downward mobility. This is clearly evident when we compare our male highs and lows. No less than 42 per cent of the male highs have irregular downward careers, as against only 24 per cent of the lows.

Summary and Conclusions

The preceding three chapters on selection and allocation in secondary schooling have demonstrated three basic points: First, although there are inequalities of access into the system in terms of ethnicity and social background, the overall pattern of postprimary recruitment is relatively fluid. Second, this openness is still more marked when access to the various components of the secondary system is considered; social and ethnic background is an even less useful predictor of where a student will finally end up in the system than of whether he will enter it or not. Third, examination of the process of internal allocation in more dynamic terms shows that the relatively small difference in the backgrounds of students in different streams and cycles reflects a process of adjustment and internal mobility. Students with initial advantages in terms of access may begin in the higher status streams, but this is partially offset by their greater rate of subsequent downward mobility. In other words, the level of demand for different types of schooling varies more sharply along ethnic and social lines than does the actual distribution of students among different types of school. The influence of ethnic and social background upon student achievement and allocation declines continuously as one moves upward in the system.

Thus one can be struck by the ruthlessness of the system, in its weeding out and reallocation of students, and at the same time be equally impressed by the impartiality of the process in relation to students' ethnic or social background. The system knows no favorites except in terms of academic ability. It could be suggested that this situation is not solely a result of the examination system itself but also, in part, a result of the character of the secondary school teaching force. Nearly all the teachers are still French, and hence most of them tend to be remote from their students, with little real knowledge of their backgrounds. This fact is often bemoaned, yet it may have its advantages whenever teachers' judgments play a role in the assessment of students. If a teacher has some insight into his students' background, there is always a danger that particularistic factors will influence the processes of selection and allocation. That is, a teacher's decision about a student may be influenced by factors other than that student's actual academic performance. In most Ivory Coast schools, teachers' indifference to, and ignorance of, the background of their African students forces them to rely on formal academic achievement as the criterion of sucess or failure. This has certainly not been to the disadvantage of students from less favored social or ethnic groups.

Finally, there can be little doubt that the school hierarchy as it exists at present still gives primary place to the long academic stream, which provides direct access to university studies and to the most rewarding types of occupations.[9] Its preeminence persists in spite of the im-

9. We have seen that one of the major disadvantages of the *Cours Complémentaires* is that they lead nowhere in particular. Up to the academic year 1963, only the two top students of each *Cours Complémentaire* were allowed access to the second cycle *Lycée,* provided their grade average was high enough and sufficient places were available. However, in 1963 some attempt was made to give *Cours Complémentaires* students a better chance of entering *Baccalaureat* studies by making all students in both the short and long *troisième* sit for a common entrance examination to the second cycle. The aim was to open the doors of the upper cycle of the *Lycée* to talent from whatever quarter. This had the effect of enabling 49 students from the *Cours Complémentaires* to enter *Baccalaureat* classes, as opposed to an estimated maximum of 32 under previous regulations. If we bear in mind that there were more than 600 students in the *Cours Complémentaires* at the B.E.P.C. level at that time, then the increase was not dramatic. What was dramatic, however, was the fact that the examination was used to expel students from the schools altogether and return them to "civilian life" (as the officials put it). No less than 57 per cent of all students at the B.E.P.C. level in the public long and short streams were excluded from any further education. This action would appear to have resulted from the increased pressure placed on the *Baccalaureat* level of studies by growing enrollments at the earlier stage of secondary schooling. Certainly this was the most ruthless weeding out of students that has yet occurred in the system.

proved status of long technical studies and the creation of a technical *Baccalaureat.* For this very reason access to, and persistence in, the long academic stream is more difficult than anywhere else. In 1960, for example, more than 7,500 candidates presented themselves for entry into long academic institutions. Of these, over one-quarter were not even considered for admission to the *Lycées* in view of their age and were obliged to seek entrance to the *Cours Normaux.* Of the remaining group of applicants, only 26 per cent were admitted to the *Lycées.* Even when a student has entered the long academic stream, the chances of his being obliged to double or even of being dismissed are greater than anywhere else in the system. Nonetheless the most rewarding positions in the postprimary structure are still open to the talented individuals from most segments of society; at the same time the long academic system performs the important function of feeder institution to other types of schools.

Having seen how students are recruited into the system and allocated within it, we can now examine their own attitudes and values in greater detail. How do they see themselves in relation to their communities of origin, and how do they perceive their occupational futures in this rapidly changing society?

CHAPTER VI

Occupational Aspirations and Expectations

SECONDARY SCHOOL STUDENTS constitute a potential elite destined to occupy at least middle-echelon roles in Ivory Coast society. The most outstanding of them will proceed to higher studies and thence enter positions at the summit of the occupational structure. Although recruited on a wide basis, this potential elite has undergone an academic experience which automatically sets it apart from the mass. Given the immense importance of formal education in terms of access to high social status and new occupational opportunities, we may well ask whether the advanced schooling of the student leads to a change in his relationships with his native community. Or rather, does he perceive his status in that local milieu as unchanged by his educational experience?

Perceived Community Attitudes toward the Secondary School Student

The typical student believes that his own community's attitudes toward him have been modified as a result of his educational experience. Only a quarter of all students averred that they were treated by people near their homes in much the same way as any other young person, and believed they were not accorded any special status. A further two-fifths felt they were treated with special deference but at the same time regarded the attitudes of local people as positive and friendly. However, one-third of the total sample reported that deferential treatment was mingled with a degree of envy and ambivalence toward them.

One might expect community attitudes to vary according to the students' background; where schooling is very narrowly diffused, community reactions are likely to be more polarized. For example, people might either regard an educated individual with great deference and respect or, alternatively, view his presence as a threat to traditional modes of behavior and as a possible source of local conflict. Conversely, where schooling is widely diffused, community reaction might be expected to be less intense, with a greater indifference to the presence of students. Yet even where education is widespread, the nature of traditional organization itself may generate different types of response. Further, since traditional status and role vary markedly between the sexes, one might expect this to have considerable influence on local attitudes, toward the educated girl in particular.

To take this latter point first, it is rather surprising that no differences in response occur between girls and boys. In spite of the fact that the educated girl is an unusual phenomenon in the Ivory Coast, females do not perceive themselves as being exposed to any more unfavorable community reaction than their male counterparts, even when differences in the social background of the sexes are taken into account.

More surprising is the fact that perceived community attitudes do not vary significantly with other indices of social background. There are no differences, in fact, in response patterns where students are differentiated in terms of paternal occupational and educational background or urban-rural origin and residence. Even when male lows are compared with male highs, no significant variations in attitudes appear. Furthermore, no difference in the character of responses is manifest between distinct ethnic groups.

However, a rather significant pattern of responses emerges if we study the *interaction* between ethnicity and socio-economic background (Table 32). Here we compare the three largest ethnic groups in the sample, Agni, Baoulé, and Kru students, by level of

TABLE 32. *Perceived Community Attitudes toward Male Students, by Ethnicity and Level of Acculturation (Percentages)*

COMMUNITY ATTITUDES	ETHNICITY AND LEVEL OF ACCULTURATION					
	Agni		Baoulé		Kru	
	High *	Low †	High	Low	High	Low
Respect and friendliness	55.8	39.5	69.2	43.4	33.3	40.6
Respect and envy	15.4	33.6	19.2	32.6	46.2	36.1
Indifference	26.9	26.9	11.6	22.9	20.5	23.3
No answer	1.9	0.0	0.0	1.1	0.0	0.0
Total	100.0	100.0	100.0	100.0	100.0	100.0
	(52)	(134)	(26)	(175)	(39)	(219)

* Includes individuals who live in towns with a population of more than 10,000 and whose fathers have attended school.

† Includes individuals who live in towns or villages of less than 5,000 population and whose fathers have never attended school.

acculturation. Among Agni and Baoulé students there is a positive relationship between level of acculturation and the degree to which an individual sees his local community as reacting favorably to him. Conversely, the level of perceived envy rises among students from less acculturated backgrounds.

Kru students show an entirely different reaction. The perceived level of ambivalence and envy manifested toward them is generally higher than among the other two groups, and this negative reaction does not vary with social background. Indeed the more acculturated Kru students are even more likely to feel that people are jealous of them than are the less acculturated. This ethnic contrast, we would hazard a guess, is due in some measure to the highly competitive character of Kru society. There is some evidence to suggest that envy of the success of others is rather more evident in Kru societies than among some of the other major groupings of the Ivory Coast, and these data would tend to confirm some previous observations.[1] In summary, envy and jealousy of the educated few would seem to be widely diffused among the Kru, irrespective of the extent of actual chances to obtain secondary education. By contrast, in the case of the

1. See Denise Paulme, *Une société de Côte d'Ivoire: d'hier et aujourd'hui, les Bétés, op. cit.*, p. 193.

other two peoples, such attitudes occur more frequently among those subgroups where education is more narrowly diffused and where the chances of entering secondary school are indeed more limited.

Student Perceptions of the Functions of Education

As has been indicated, formal education probably involves the restructuring of relations between an individual and his own community, because the student's social status has been changed as a result of his attendance at secondary school. It still remains to see what value students themselves place upon education. One may assume reasonably enough that in societies with generally low standards of living, where education is important in allowing access to remunerative positions, people will appraise schooling in terms of its concrete and immediate rewards. Such rewards may involve increased personal prestige, higher income, access to positions of power and authority, or entry into occupations that are intrinsically satisfying and interesting. Although it is demonstrable that formal schooling heavily influences access to remunerative and high-prestige positions in the Ivory Coast, it is apparent that students do not view education solely in these terms (Table 33). They value education primarily as a means of enabling them to enter occupations which correspond in a general way to their personal tastes and inclinations. However, a little under 30 per cent of all students are more specific, valuing their educational experience in terms of income advantages and access to leadership roles. The frequent observation that Africans consider formal schooling as largely a

TABLE 33. Functions of Education as Perceived by Students (Percentages)

FUNCTION	MALE	FEMALE	TOTAL
To gain individual prestige	2.8	4.7	3.0
To obtain an interesting position	67.4	73.8	68.2
To acquire a good income	14.8	13.9	14.7
To exert power and leadership	14.3	7.6	13.5
No answer	0.7	0.0	0.6
Total	100.0	100.0	100.0
	(1,837)	(237)	(2,074)

prestige item appears to be largely without justification among this group; if we can rely upon the responses of students, mere prestige without other accompanying favorable circumstances is of no particular importance.

These responses do not differ along socio-economic or ethnic lines, but they do tend to vary with sex and type of secondary school attended. As we might expect, girls tend to be less concerned than boys with the role of education in enabling individuals to assume positions of leadership and authority. This reflects, in some measure, the limitations placed upon the status and potential roles of women in many contemporary African societies. More striking, however, are the differences between students in academic, technical, and agricultural institutions.

It has been noted previously that students in technical institutions tend to be more specific in their aspirations than those in academic institutions. This also leads them to stress the economic returns of schooling to a greater extent than students undergoing other types of training. One-fourth of the technical students see income as the most important advantage of education, as against only 13 per cent of students in the academic stream. Rather unexpectedly, perhaps, this tendency to stress the financial rewards of schooling increases as one moves up through the system; over one-fifth of students at the *Baccalaureat* level emphasize income factors, against a little over 10 per cent at the intermediate stages. We shall indicate in the following chapter some further evidence concerning student reactions to economic incentives—evidence which tends to confirm our belief that senior students and those in technical institutions tend to be more directly influenced by the financial attractions of the occupational structure. This could well be due to the fact that, in one sense, both these groups see themselves as closer to the actual job market than other students, and become increasingly preoccupied with the tangible rewards of their education.

Students were also given an opportunity to indicate freely whether they thought there were more important reasons for obtaining an education than those already discussed. Only 30 per cent of the sample made any further comment, and their responses were widely distributed over a variety of items. However, just over one-half stressed the importance of education as enabling a person to assist the nation in its development or to provide help to his kin. About 15 per cent of all students seem to be altruistically oriented, inclined to view education in terms of service and obligation rather than personal prestige, income, and power.[2]

The Educational Aspirations of Students

We have already indicated that the relationship between secondary school outputs and the expansion of opportunities in the labor market leads to a persistent and rapid rise in the educational qualifications deemed appropriate for particular types of job. Secondary education alone no longer provides automatic access to the highest positions in the occupational structure, and thus tends to be increasingly viewed as an intermediate stage leading toward higher studies. This explains why over 90 per cent of all pupils wish to proceed with further full-time schooling.

To be sure, the intensity of this desire does vary, in some degree, with the students' background. Our composite measure of acculturation tends to discriminate between levels of academic aspiration; 98 per cent of the highs wish to proceed with their studies, as against only 86 per cent of the lows. Similarly aspirations tend to vary with the type of institution attended by the student; just over 82 per cent of pupils in the lowest cycles of the system wish to continue, as against 97 per cent of those at the *Baccalaureat* level. This variation is also evident within the academic schools themselves, where only four-fifths of pupils at the short B.E.P.C. and B.E. level aspire to further studies, as contrasted with 94 per cent of those attending *Lycées* and *Collèges*.

Nonetheless, these differentials must not be exaggerated. Actually levels of academic aspiration are very high in every group—in marked contrast with experience, in Europe, where it has often been demonstrated that academic aspirations are closely correlated with the social background of students and the type of institution attended.[3]

Of course, although the overwhelming mass of students *hope* to proceed further with their schooling, their *expectations* of so doing

2. We use the term "altruistic" in this context, but it should be remembered that recognition of duties toward kin reflects obligations contracted by the educated person. Families may support their offspring in school, but they expect a return on the investment. The educated individual is aware of this limitation upon his autonomy.

3. For example, see J. Duquesne, *Les 16–24 ans* (Paris: Le Centurion, 1963), pp. 14–20, which indicates very sharp differentials between French young people from various social classes concerning secondary school attendance and attitudes toward schooling.

may be very different. However high a student's aspirations may be, he must realistically assess his chances of proceeding further in view of his academic abilities or status and his financial resources. One might anticipate a considerable gap between aspirations and actual expectations because of the limited number of places available in secondary or higher institutions. Yet the principal characteristic of these students is their highly unrealistic appraisal of their actual educational opportunities. Almost three-quarters of the sampled population not only hope to achieve a higher educational level but feel fairly certain of being able to do so. In fact only just over 7 per cent of the students stated that they had no chance for further education.

Realistic or not, these expectations show an interesting pattern of variation between distinct student subgroups. Each group tends to differ in its views concerning the major obstacles that might prevent continued schooling. Socio-economic background is consistently correlated with level of expectations. Thus 82 per cent of the children of managerial and clerical workers feel that they have at least a good chance of continuing, as against only 67 per cent of the offspring of subsistence farmers. In similar fashion, urban children are more optimistic than rural children; over 80 per cent of those living in the largest towns feel certain of continuing or feel they have a good chance of doing so, but this figure drops to 70 per cent for rural students. Furthermore, as we have seen so many times before, paternal level of education tends to be a rather stronger predictor of student responses; no less than 88 per cent of the children of fathers having a postprimary education feel that they have at least a good chance of continuing, as against 68 per cent of those whose fathers never at-

TABLE 34. Male Students' Self-estimated Chances of Continuing Their Education, by Level of Acculturation (Percentages)

SELF-ESTIMATION	LEVEL OF ACCULTURATION	
	High	Low
Certain of continuing	52.6	25.3
Good chance of continuing	35.3	40.9
Little chance of continuing	11.2	21.7
No chance of continuing	.9	11.1
No answer	0.0	1.0
Total	100.0	100.0
	(116)	(198)

tended school. As may be seen in Table 34, there are somewhat sharper differences between high and low male students, but not so great as might have been expected. Even students from the lowest socio-economic background are relatively optimistic about their academic future and consistently underestimate obstacles that will hinder their academic progress.

Table 35 indicates that lack of financial resources is seen by students as the most powerful obstacle to continuing their education—despite

TABLE 35. Student Perceptions of the Major Obstacles to Academic Progress (Percentages)

REASON	PERCENTAGE
Lack of money	44.1
Inadequate academic record	21.6
Parental opposition	8.1
Other	15.1
No answer	11.1
Total	100.0
	(2,074)

the fact that tuition is free and that, from the B.E.P.C. level upward, well over half of all students obtain bursaries and scholarships.[4] This suggests that the indirect costs of education to the families of students are still high in spite of increasing financial aid. On the other hand, it is striking that so few students are prepared to see their academic inadequacy as the principal obstacle to their future success. There can be little doubt that, as the system works at present, the shortage of places, combined with rigorous standards of academic achievement, remains the principal factor determining a student's continued education. Again, the demand for schooling is so high that it blinds students to the realities of the educational structure, leading them to inflate their expectations unrealistically and to ignore their own academic shortcomings.

Ethnic background tends to influence students' assessment of factors which might prevent their further study. Almost 15 per cent of the northern students were concerned about their parents' possible opposition to their continued education, as opposed to only 7 per cent of

4. However, some benefits to students have recently been curtailed, and they are now obliged to pay for books and clothing. It would be interesting to see whether this will have any effect on recruitment.

students from the more acculturated southern peoples. A similar rise in concern for potential parental opposition is seen in the responses of children from less educated homes; just over 10 per cent of those whose fathers had never been to school felt that such opposition might limit their opportunities for further study, as against only 3 per cent of students whose fathers had at least completed primary school.

However, social background primarily influences the relative importance students attach to academic achievement and financial resources as factors likely to affect their educational future. For example, urban children (29 per cent) are much more prone than their rural counterparts (19 per cent) to stress scholastic success as the main determinant of educational promotion. Conversely, almost one-half of the rural students are concerned about finance, as against only one-third of the urban students.[5] The difference is even more striking if we compare individuals by level of paternal education. The more educated his family, the more sensitive a student is to the importance of academic achievement and the less worried he is about financial problems. Almost half the children from uneducated homes are concerned about shortage of money, but only 20 per cent see their academic record as the main obstacle to their progress. On the other hand, though one-fifth of the children from the most educated environments are sensitive to financial obstacles, almost one-third of them are doubtful about their academic achievement.

In contrast to socio-economic background, religious affiliation has no influence on aspirations and expectations. In view of the supposed antagonism between Islam and modern Western secular schooling, one might expect that Moslem students would express less desire to continue their studies and would be faced with more parental opposition. This is not the case. Moslem students are just as eager to further their studies as Christians and just as confident of doing so. In fact, there is no indication that Moslem parents are any more opposed to their children's continued education than are Christian parents. This tends to suggest once again that the commonly alleged Moslem-Christian dichotomy is more often than not a reflection of differentials in socio-economic background and area of origin.

Of course, the previous academic record of students and the type of school in which they find themselves at present does exert some influence on their expectations. Table 36 illustrates that the further a

5. These attitudinal differences reflect real variations in the level of cash income between urban and rural areas.

TABLE 36. Students' Self-estimated Chances of Undertaking More Advanced Studies, by Stream and Cycle (Percentages)

SELF-ESTIMATED CHANCES	STREAM				CYCLE		
	Agricultural	Technical	Short Academic	Long Academic	Low	Intermediate	High
Certain of continuing	20.5	23.3	26.4	41.0	25.0	36.7	47.1
Good chance of continuing	41.0	36.3	37.0	40.6	36.7	39.9	41.8
Little chance of continuing	33.3	27.1	24.7	13.8	25.9	17.0	9.5
No chance of continuing	5.2	11.4	11.5	4.1	11.6	5.9	1.3
No answer	0.0	1.9	.4	.5	.9	.5	.3
Total	100.0	100.0	100.0	100.0	100.0	100.0	100.0
	(39)	(262)	(708)	(1,065)	(916)	(780)	(378)

student moves up through the secondary school system, the more optimistic he becomes about his chances for continued schooling. However, these expectations also vary with the particular stream in which students are situated. Students in the long academic stream feel that they have better chances for further education than their counterparts in short academic, technical, or agricultural institutions.

In spite of these differences academic expectations are invariably too high in relation to the real chances of continuing. Although students in the lower streams and cycles of the system display less optimism about their educational future, they are actually more unrealistic than are their counterparts attending more advanced institutions. To take an extreme case, no less than 54 per cent of all students at the *Centres d'Apprentissage* feel certain of, or feel that they have a very good chance of, pursuing their studies. In reality, their opportunities for any other type of further training are less than one in four. By contrast, over four-fifths of students at the *Baccalaureat* level are optimistic about their chances, and this optimism is almost entirely justified.

Academic standing also plays a modest role in influencing educational expectations. Of course, a past record of repeated classes is not a very good indicator of actual academic achievement, since we have seen that students in the high-prestige long academic stream actually double more frequently. Regardless of their present academic position, individuals who have a record of doubling are on the whole just as optimistic about their educational future as are those whose career has been more rapid and direct. Nevertheless doubling constitutes a powerful indicator of academic achievement when it occurs at the B.E.P.C. level, and a significant pattern emerges when we divide all individuals at this stage into "doublers" and "nondoublers." Over 80 per cent of the nondoublers expect to continue their education, as against 69 per cent of those who have repeated before entering the B.E.P.C. class. However, present academic performance seems to be more strongly correlated with levels of academic expectation. Half of the students who rank themselves in the top quarter of their present class feel absolutely certain of being able to pursue their studies further, as against less than one-fifth of those who place themselves in the lowest quarter.

All this evidence suggests that individuals do adjust their educational aspirations and expectations in terms of their socio-economic background, their present stage of studies, and their record of past and present academic achievement. Although these adjustments are fairly consistent and statistically significant, the degree of association is uniformly quite modest.

Students' relatively unrealistic hopes of continuing their schooling reflect the uniformly high value attached to any type of postprimary education. This situation provides a fundamental contrast with Western European societies. There, high educational aspirations have in the past been virtually restricted to the upper and middle classes, whereas lower class groups have frequently failed to take advantage of educational opportunities even when these have been available.[6] By contrast, Ivory Coast students from the least privileged social and ethnic backgrounds nourish educational hopes that are hardly any lower than those of students from the most advantaged groups. This relative uniformity of attitudes, we suggest, reflects two major sets of factors: first, the absence of a highly structured system of class subcultures, which might exercise a decisive influence on levels of educational motivation and achievement; second, the relative absence of ancillary mobility mechanisms outside formal schooling, which leads all groups within the society to give special salience to education as a means to occupational success and status achievement.

Student Preferences for Different Types of Further Education

If students tend to hold unduly optimistic expectations of their chances for further study, they are also misinformed about the nature of the educational offerings open to them. In its complexity the secondary school system of the Ivory Coast resembles a maze full of blind alleys and divergent routes which do not allow students to cross from one path to another. Small wonder, indeed, that individuals become confused about what courses of study are actually available.[7]

6. For recent examples, see J. Duquesne, *op. cit.*, and V. Isambert Jamati, "La Maturité sociale dans la France contemporaine," *Cahiers internationaux de sociologie,* Vol. 31 (1961), pp. 129–44.

7. In France, it is also to some extent true that students are often inadequately informed of academic and vocational opportunities. This has led the *Laboratoire de Psychologie Sociale* to undertake an investigation into the loss of talent caused by sheer misinformation. Further, the Ministry of Labor has been obliged to revise its procedures of disseminating information concerning the relation between training and job prospects. This kind of service is even more urgently needed in the Ivory Coast, but resources do not permit the development of existing facilities to an adequate level.

Candidates for the *Baccalaureat* have a clearer perception of their educational future than have other students. They have already surmounted the most formidable academic hurdles, and two-thirds of them expect to enter a university within two years. It is interesting to note, however, that contrary to a great deal of current opinion, this group is mainly oriented toward technical and scientific studies. No less than two-thirds of those who propose to prepare for the first university degree wish to do so in science or technology. Only one-third of university-bound students are interested in law, the humanities, or the social sciences. Not only this, but the latter group tends to be academically weaker; 55 per cent of them have been previously obliged to double secondary classes, as against 40 per cent of students who wish to enter scientific studies. This accords with the general French view that the natural and physical sciences are more demanding than are other academic fields. In later pages we shall draw attention again to this high level of interest in science and technology, but it should be noted here that students from the academic *Lycées* are even more oriented toward such fields than are their counterparts in the *Lycée Technique,* half of whom wish to study humanities, law, or social science—an interesting reversal of what might have been expected. However, one must remember that in spite of the rising status of this latter institution, its students are still academically weaker than are those in the academic *Lycées.* They may still prefer to choose the "softer" courses which were formerly monopolized by possessors of the academic *Baccalaureat.*

Apart from those *Baccalaureat* students who expect to enter the university, a further 15 per cent of the candidates at that level expect to fail this examination at their first attempt and have no further plans. Yet another opportunity presents itself for individuals who have completed the second cycle of secondary schooling. In recent years special vocational schools have been opened by various departments of government to prepare students for specific administrative and bureaucratic careers.[8] These institutions lie outside the formal educational system but have the advantage of providing automatic access to well-paid and secure positions within the administration. Some 14 per cent of present candidates for the *Baccalaureat* hope to enter such specialist institutions, where the certainty of employment compensates for the higher but less specific opportunities provided by university studies.

On the whole it can be concluded that students at the *Baccalaureat*

8. See Chapter II, Table 6.

level are reasonably familiar with the educational opportunities open to them, and their orientations are not unrealistic in view of their present status. The same cannot be said for candidates preparing for lower examinations. Exactly one-third of pupils in the short academic stream expect ultimately to prepare for the *Baccalaureat,* whereas in fact the short stream is largely designed to provide a terminal education to the B.E.P.C. level. In addition, about one-quarter of students in agricultural, technical, and short academic institutions hope to continue their education by entering the special government training programs to which we have referred. The limited scale of these programs and the competition from students with superior qualifications make this virtually impossible. To conclude, the students' high level of academic ambition tends to make them ignore administrative prerequisites for the continuation of their studies. They also overestimate their actual statistical chances of proceeding further.

The Content of Occupational Aspirations

Secondary school students do not tend to regard continuing education as an end in itself but in terms of the occupations to which it leads. Under these circumstances it is not surprising that high levels of academic ambition are paralleled by high levels of occupational aspiration. If people are merely asked what kind of career they would like to pursue, their answers are likely to range from a series of quite unrealistic goals to a relatively sober appraisal of existing opportunities. In the following pages we shall be concerned with the responses of students concerning what jobs they would prefer if they were *entirely free to choose.* Of course, such responses may bear little relation to the final occupational destination of students, but they serve two primary functions: First, they indicate the most desired occupations and provide evidence concerning the types of occupational "models" to which people have been most exposed. Second, they enable us to see to what extent vocational aspirations are linked to variations in social and ethnic background. Table 37 provides an initial profile of student aspirations by sector rather than by level. Each category, therefore, tends to be very heterogeneous in terms of occupational status.

The first notable feature in the table is the high interest of students in scientific and technological careers and, conversely, their lack of interest in administrative jobs, even very broadly defined. There are substantial reasons why aspirations should tend in the direction of science and technology. New opportunities in this field are becoming more and more available in both private industry and government. For example, heretofore higher technical positions with private companies in the Ivory Coast have not been available to Africans, but now employers are

TABLE 37. Occupational Aspirations of Sampled Students, by Sex (Percentages)

OCCUPATION	MALES	FEMALES	TOTAL
Teaching *	24.3	21.9	24.0
Scientific and technological †	23.8	.8	21.2
Medicine and nursing ‡	18.6	61.2	23.4
Agriculture **	14.1	1.3	12.6
Administration ††	12.3	11.0	12.2
Military and police ‡‡	3.5	0.0	3.1
Miscellaneous and no answer	3.4	3.8	3.5
Total	100.0	100.0	100.0
	(1,837)	(237)	(2,074)

* Includes teachers from the primary to the university level, plus a small group concerned with the social sciences.

† Includes research scientists, engineers, technicians, and skilled workers at all levels.

‡ Includes doctors, pharmacists, veterinarians, nurses, and social welfare workers.

** Includes agricultural engineers, technicians, demonstrators, but not farmers.

†† Includes all public and private cadres down to the clerical level, and law or politics.

‡‡ Includes both commissioned and noncommissioned categories.

realizing that this reluctance to hire African personnel may endanger the future of their enterprises.

Nor is the low level of interest in administrative jobs difficult to understand. During colonial times educated Africans aspired to clerical work because few alternatives were open to them. However, at present less than 4 per cent of the total sample wish to enter any form of clerical employment; most of those now wishing to enter administrative careers are interested in executive and managerial positions. This signifies a rise in the general level of aspirations associated with political independence, but at the same time it is precisely this kind of career which is becoming increasingly risky, especially within the public sector. Few observers of the contemporary African scene have failed to note the increasing politicization of upper- and middle-level administrative cadres and the movement away from the colonial tradition of a politically neutral administrative corps. Today, the scientist-technologist is much less likely to be exposed to direct political pressures than is his counterpart in general administration and law.

Indeed a legal career is increasingly parapolitical in its implications, and, not surprisingly, only just over 3 per cent of all secondary students are interested in this profession. We would hazard a guess that this pattern is in direct contrast to that prevailing in the colonial period, when the prestige of legal study was coupled with its role as a key to the highest administrative cadres. Also understandable is the extraordinarily low level of students' interest in politics as a career. Perhaps the picture was different on the eve of independence, when the uncertainty of political arrangements and the small number of educated individuals afforded apparently bright opportunities in the political sphere. However, since then political offices have been largely filled by previous cohorts who are not yet old enough to be replaced or to surrender their privileges—with the result that active political participation carries its occupational hazards. In these circumstances it is not unexpected that only 0.2 per cent of students are interested in careers in politics.

It can be seen, additionally, that a substantial proportion of male students do hope to enter some form of activity connected with agriculture. This is not to say that they want to become farmers; only 0.8 per cent wish to enter farming on their own account. Rather, they hope to become scientists and technicians working with the ever growing departments of government concerned with agricultural development. In fact, the proportion of students wishing to enter this type of occupation considerably exceeds the actual number engaged in agricultural studies in the sample. This reflects the typical metropolitan view that it is better not to specialize at the secondary level but to pursue more general studies which will ultimately enable specialization at a university or another higher institution.

Except for teaching, sex differences are quite marked, as we might expect. Female choices tend to reflect European stereotypes concerning the types of occupation appropriate for women. Just under 62 per cent of the girls hope to enter nursing or primary school teaching, with a further 8 per cent favoring clerical occupations. Only 19 per cent of the boys are interested in these three types of career.

Social Background, Academic Achievement, and Occupational Aspirations

Predictably, the occupational aspirations of students are influenced by their social backgrounds, though perhaps to a lesser extent in the Ivory Coast than in more developed areas. Rather than provide a series of separate tables, we have attempted to summarize the overall pattern of relationships in Table 38, through the use of positive and

TABLE 38. Influence of Socio-economic Background on Occupational Aspirations *

OCCUPATIONAL CHOICE	SIZE OF PLACE OF RESIDENCE	AREA OF RESIDENCE	LEVEL OF PATERNAL EDUCATION	PATERNAL OCCUPATION	LEVEL OF ACCULTURATION
Teaching	−−	0	−−	−−	−−
Scientific and technological	−	0	0	0	++
Medicine and nursing	++	−	+	+	0
Agriculture	−	−	−−	−−	−−
Administration	+	0	+	+	++
Military and police	−	−	−−	−	−

* Signs in the table have been derived from a matrix of correlations using gamma as a coefficient of correlation. A zero sign indicates values ranging between +.100 and −.100. A single positive or negative sign indicates values ranging between +.100 and +.250 or −.100 and −.250. A double positive or negative sign indicates values above +.250 or below −.250. For the complete matrix of correlations, see Appendix C to this volume.

It may be contended that all coefficients are on the low side, but it must be recognized that,i n contradistinction to some types of experimental and psychological research, one cannot expect to find surveys generating high correlation coefficients. Indeed a gamma coefficient of + or −.50 would constitute, in the normal course of events, a rather high level of positive or negative relationship.

negative symbols. Here the familiar indices of social background, place of residence, paternal occupation and education, and level of acculturation have been used, with the addition of another index based on area of present residence. In this instance students from the southeastern portion of the Ivory Coast have been classified as coming from the most acculturated zone, students from the center and west as coming from an intermediate zone, and students from the north as coming from the least acculturated area.

The use of positive and negative signs is a convenient way of indicating the extent and direction of the relationship between social background and occupational choice, but some additional explanation may be necessary. A minus sign indicates a moderate or strong inverse relationship between the choice of a particular career and the level of social background of a student. In other words, students from less acculturated backgrounds are more likely to choose a certain occupation. A plus sign indicates a positive association, implying that students from superior backgrounds are more likely to choose a given career. A zero indicates little or no relationship.

It is evident that the choice of a teaching career is significantly influenced by social background and tends to be chosen more frequently by individuals from rural, illiterate farming backgrounds. In fact, the level of choice for teaching is twice as high among the children of farmers as it is among the offspring of professional and clerical workers. This finding confirms virtually all the evidence derived from other societies concerning teaching as a career. It constitutes almost invariably a first step in the process of upward mobility for less privileged groups, but its importance declines among individuals with higher social status.

Preference for agriculture follows the same pattern and more often characterizes the responses of children with a rural background, particularly those from the north. This occupation enables the individual to acquire a stable income and status within the modern occupational hierarchy without removing him from a familiar social and economic environment. It would be no exaggeration to suggest that such a choice satisfies both the need for traditional affiliation and occupational achievement. Furthermore, one must bear in mind that the schoolteacher and the agricultural demonstrator are the two primary modern-type occupational models that are presented to the rural child. By contrast, urban children with higher socio-economic backgrounds have more models available to them.

The same observation could be made with respect to the higher level of choices among the less acculturated students for careers in the military and police. Perhaps to the rural child these are also more visible than other occupations and still carry an aura of prestige dating from the colonial period.

Thus teaching, agriculture, and the military or police are more frequently chosen by less acculturated pupils. Careers in the medical profession and administration (whether in government or private concerns) are more often the choice of individuals from more acculturated backgrounds. Aspirations to enter the scientific and technological field, on the other hand, are only very loosely associated with a student's background. Perhaps the very newness of this type of career, plus the growing prestige of science and technology in general, is what leads most students to regard this occupation as more open than others.[9]

Table 39 also indicates that present academic standing does have

TABLE 39. Influence of Academic Achievement on Occupational Aspirations *

OCCUPATIONAL CHOICE	PRESENT CYCLE OF STUDY	SELF-ASSESSMENT OF PRESENT ACADEMIC STATUS	SELF-ESTIMATE OF CHANCES OF CONTINUING EDUCATION
Teaching	– –	–	–
Scientific and technological	0	+	+
Medicine and nursing	0	0	0
Agriculture	0	0	0
Administration	+	0	+
Military and police	–	–	– –

* For an explanation of signs in this table see footnote to Table 38. For the complete matrix of correlations see Appendix D to this volume.

some influence on occupational aspirations, though its effect is somewhat less marked than that of social background. To clarify the interpretation of the table, it must be noted that a relation is defined as positive (+ sign) when a particular occupation is chosen more frequently by the more successful students as defined by their higher cycle of studies, their higher self-assessment of their present academic achievement, and their greater confidence in their ability to continue with their education. A negative sign indicates that an occupation is more frequently chosen by the less successful students as measured by the same cluster of items.

This table is particularly illuminating when compared with the pattern shown by Table 38. The influence of academic status on choice

9. It may be noted, however, that although the relation between the choice of science and technology and most indices of social background is usually slight, there seems to be a much closer relation when the combined index of acculturation is used. This is largely an artifact of the correlation technique employed; a very small number of cases in one category can tend to change a pattern of relationship in a direction opposite to that usually observed.

of teaching as a career parallels the influence of socio-economic background. It is consistently the poorer students, as well as those from the most limited social backgrounds, who choose teaching. The police and the military are also most frequently chosen by the weakest students, exactly paralleling the findings concerning social background. On the other hand, higher social background and more substantial academic achievement tend to reinforce each other with respect to the choice of administrative and executive occupations. There can be no doubt that individuals aspiring to this type of career are a socially and academically more select group than those aspiring to teaching and to the police or the military.

In some cases social background and present academic standing do not tend to operate in the same direction. Choices of careers in medicine and agriculture are markedly associated with social background, but present academic achievement seems to play little or no role in influencing these aspirations. A more significant fact is that although the choice of a career in science and technology is loosely linked to social background, it is more closely associated with a higher assessment of academic achievement. This reinforces a previous observation concerning the openness of careers in that area: Social background is no obstacle to access to these new and exacting types of occupation, but academic ineptitude certainly is.

Before leaving this discussion of the content of aspirations, let us examine the reasons (or rationalizations) that students give for their preferences. There are some interesting variations here. Persons oriented toward medical careers proffer the most altruistic reasons for their choice, and some two-thirds stress service to the nation or their community as being the most influential factor in determining their decision. These altruistic motivations also characterize about 40 per cent of those pupils hoping to become teachers. However, the latter also differ from other groups insofar as they are more likely to stress opportunities for further study and the advantages of entering a job which provides longer vacations. Students proposing to enter scientific and technological careers are significantly differentiated from the others by their higher stress upon two principal sets of factors: About one-third of them stress existing job opportunities and the relatively high level of income to be achieved, while almost 40 per cent emphasize the intrinsically satisfying nature of the job as well as their own special academic gifts and abilities. In the case of students choosing agriculture or administration, the pattern of choices is much more diffused, with no emphasis on one particular category of responses.

This differentiation of occupational attitudes would imply that it is not possible to explain the choices of African students by employing a few motivational categories. In fact, one might suggest that their occupational psychology is no less complex than that of their counterparts in more developed countries.

The Level of Occupational Aspirations

So far we have discussed student aspirations in terms of their area of choice, but we have not dealt with the *level* of student ambitions. Researchers concerned with the nature of occupational choice often combine these two dimensions, but a separate analysis does enable us to see to what extent they tend to co-vary.

Thus we have produced a dichotomy of high and low levels of aspiration which roughly corresponds to the French distinction between *Cadres Supérieurs* and *Cadres Moyens.* The first group, therefore, includes managerial or professional workers, medical doctors, university or secondary school teachers, and industrial, civil, or agricultural engineers. The second category comprises clerical workers, nurses, primary school teachers, and industrial or agricultural technicians or skilled artisans. We decided to retain choices for careers in the military or police as a separate category, since it proved difficult, in practice, to distinguish between levels.

Postprimary students do regard themselves as a potential elite, and 60 per cent of them aspire to jobs in the *Cadres Supérieurs* (Table 40). However, this table also indicates sharp sex differences. Girls are

TABLE 40. Level of Occupational Aspiration, by Sex (Percentages)

LEVEL	MALES	FEMALES	TOTAL
High	64.3	24.5	59.7
Low	28.8	71.7	33.7
Military and police	3.5	0.0	3.1
Miscellaneous and no answer	3.4	3.8	3.5
Total	100.0	100.0	100.0
	(1,837)	(237)	(2,074)

far less ambitious, in spite of their superior socio-economic background. The more marginal position of females in the educational system as well as in the labor market tends to depress their level of aspiration.

Taken separately, individual socio-economic variables, such as size of place of birth or residence, area of residence, or paternal characteristics, do not affect levels of aspiration in any significant manner. This was at first rather surprising in view of the fact that in Western countries paternal characteristics particularly have always seemed so crucial in determining how high individuals hope to rise on the occupational scale. This negative finding stresses once more the fluidity of the status structure in the Ivory Coast and the apparent homogenizing influence of the secondary schools on the attitudes of their students. However, if we use the combined index of acculturation and compare our male highs and lows, a clearer relationship appears between level of occupational choice and level of acculturation (Table 41). To this extent the variation at the extremes may suggest a growing crystallization of the status structure, which is slowly leading to a tighter relationship between social background and levels of aspiration.

TABLE 41. Level of Aspiration of Male Students, by Level of Acculturation (Percentages)

LEVEL OF ASPIRATION	LEVEL OF ACCULTURATION	
	High	Low
High	81.9	56.6
Low	9.5	39.9
Military and police	3.4	2.5
Miscellaneous and no answer	5.2	1.0
Total	100.0	100.0
	(116)	(198)

Generally differences in ethnic background are not associated with significant variations in levels of occupational aspiration, although interesting differences do occur between Agni, Baoulé, and Kru students when some control of socio-economic background is effected (Table 42). Among the first two groups level of aspiration rises with level of acculturation. By contrast, although average levels of aspiration are much the same among the Kru, differences by level of acculturation are of far less magnitude. We have already seen that Kru students coming from acculturated environments seem to arouse just as much envy as those coming from less favored environments. We can now view the other side of the coin and see that high levels of ambition are uniformly distributed among more or less acculturated subsegments of that society. This would seem to provide additional evidence concerning the highly competitive nature of Kru society.

It has sometimes been asserted that a student's religious affiliation may have some impact on his need for achievement, which in turn may

TABLE 42. Level of Occupational Aspiration, by Level of Acculturation, in Three Ethnic Groups (Percentages)

LEVEL OF OCCUPATIONAL ASPIRATION	ETHNICITY					
	Agni		Baoulé		Kru	
	High *	Low †	High	Low	High	Low
High	76.9	62.7	76.9	57.7	66.7	59.8
Low	13.5	33.6	11.5	37.1	28.2	32.0
Military and police	3.8	2.2	3.8	4.0	2.6	5.5
Miscellaneous and no answer	5.8	1.5	7.7	1.2	2.6	2.7
Total	100.0	100.0	99.9	100.0	100.0	100.0
	(52)	(134)	(26)	(175)	(39)	(219)

* Includes individuals who live in towns with a population of over 10,000 and whose fathers have attended school.

† Includes individuals who live in towns and villages with a population of under 5,000 and whose fathers have never attended school.

manifest itself in the level of his occupational aspiration. More specifically it could be contended that Moslems might show lower levels of aspiration than Christians. But no evidence for these views can be observed in our samples. In particular, there is no significant variation between Moslems and Christians when socio-economic background is held constant.

There can be little doubt that in those societies where investigations have been undertaken the immediate family environment does play a crucial role in determining levels of aspiration and need for achievement. Such conclusions have been based on detailed examinations of patterns of family interaction and child-rearing practices. Certainly the present study does not pretend to provide any insight into patterns of socialization, and what data we have is based on students' reports. Still, one could hypothesize that students who perceive that their parents have relatively high academic expectations for them might display a higher level of occupational aspiration. Yet this is not the case. Our figures show no differences in this respect between individuals reporting high and those reporting low parental pressures for educational achievement.

A similar observation can be made when we consider family structure. It has been suggested that children reared in polygynous households are likely to exhibit a lower need for achievement than those brought up in monogamous families. This may well be true, but it is not demonstrable that such differentials are reflected in the occupational aspirations of our students. In fact, there is no difference whatever in the level of ambition of students reared in polygynous and those reared in monogamous families. Wider studies of child populations would very likely indicate substantial variations, but our study shows that the common experience of a secondary education tends to homogenize levels of ambition and to attenuate the influence of socio-economic and cultural background.

The critical influence of academic experience is, indeed, observable in Table 43, where it is clear that the further a student goes in the system, the higher is his level of aspiration; individuals within the long academic streams are characterized by higher levels of occupational ambition. This finding may not seem surprising until one recalls that students were given the opportunity to designate occupations *absolutely freely*. On this basis we originally expected that levels of aspiration would be more closely linked to socio-economic and cultural background, in view of the differentiated occupational models which this background provides. Alternatively it was hypothesized that answers to this question would reveal little relationship between level of aspiration and academic status. This latter assumption proved to be incorrect. A student's level of aspiration is not "detached" from his actual position in a given stream and cycle of the system.

The significance of academic standing for vocational aspirations is also evident if we look at students in terms of their record of doubling classes. If we remember that overall rates of doubling are not necessarily good indicators of actual academic status, it would seem more appropriate to look only at students in the long academic stream who are preparing for the B.E.P.C. examination. Among those who have

TABLE 43. Level of Occupational Aspiration, by Stream and Cycle of Studies (Percentages)

LEVEL OF ASPIRATION	STREAM				CYCLE		
	Agricultural	Technical	Short Academic	Long Academic	Low	Intermediate	High
High	43.6	37.0	50.2	72.3	44.4	64.2	87.6
Low	48.7	58.8	41.9	21.5	48.4	29.0	7.9
Military and police	0.0	0.8	4.5	2.8	3.5	3.2	1.9
Miscellaneous and no answer	7.7	3.4	3.4	3.4	3.7	3.6	2.6
Total	100.0	100.0	100.0	100.0	100.0	100.0	100.0
	(39)	(262)	(708)	(1,065)	(916)	(780)	(378)

not doubled before reaching this stage, almost three-quarters have high levels of aspiration, but this figure drops to 58 per cent of students who have a previous record of doubling.

Perception of present academic achievement is an even better predictor of level of aspiration. Two-thirds of students who rank themselves in the top quarter of their present class have high ambitions, against only 44 per cent of those who place themselves in the bottom quarter. In similar fashion, levels of academic expectation strongly influence occupational aspirations. Almost three-quarters of students who feel certain of continuing with their studies have high occupational hopes, as against only one-third who feel they have little or no hope of continuing. These findings suggest that academic record is a more potent predictor of levels of occupational aspiration than is socio-economic or cultural background.

Occupational Expectations

So far we have been largely concerned with the level of student aspirations, without taking into account the realities of the academic structure, the limitations of the labor market itself, and the possible obstacles to occupational mobility generated by the present status structure in the Ivory Coast. First, whatever their aspirations, we know that the overwhelming majority of students will not proceed beyond their present stage of studies and will be "dumped" onto the labor market. Second, although new types of occupation are becoming increasingly available, the overall rate of growth in all levels of employment opportunities in the modern sector is not great. This low rate of growth is characteristic of those sectors of the economy where students who have completed secondary school might expect to find employment. One often hears that rapid Africanization produces new opportunities for educated individuals in the Ivory Coast, but it is also true that the number of French personnel employed at middle levels has increased rather than diminished since independence. Their continued presence, whether justified or not, has proved to be a source of frustration to new educated cadres. In view of these limited occupational opportunities, it can be seen that as the secondary school system expands, the level of jobs available to persons with a given educational background may decline rapidly.[10] Further, however optimistic stu-

10. Conversely, of course, the costs to the nation of the services performed by individuals will increase.

dents may be about their future, undoubtedly ethnic, socio-economic, and cultural factors do limit the fulfillment of their aspirations. Thus some preference is often given to individuals from certain ethnic backgrounds, and family influence can facilitate or impede access to various jobs.

Students were therefore asked what kind of job they would be likely to obtain *in fact* if they were unable to continue with their studies beyond their present level. This was a reasonable question, since the vast majority would certainly not be able to continue their education. In effect, although students may have high aspirations, they also have

TABLE 44. Occupational Expectations of Sampled Students, by Sex (Percentages)

OCCUPATION	MALES	FEMALES	TOTAL
Teaching	57.6	48.5	56.6
Scientific and technological	7.1	0.0	6.3
Medicine and nursing	3.8	32.9	7.1
Agriculture	3.1	0.0	2.7
Administration	18.1	14.4	17.6
Military and police	5.5	0.0	4.9
Miscellaneous and no answer	4.8	4.2	4.8
Total	100.0	100.0	100.0
	(1,837)	(237)	(2,074)

a very shrewd estimation of the occupational worth of their present level of education, which reflects itself in a totally different profile of responses.

Although some 60 per cent of our students have high levels of occupational aspiration, only just over 2 per cent of them, at their present level of attainment, actually expect to join the *Cadres Supérieurs*. They reconcile themselves to much more modest types of occupation and at the same time shift their area of choice, as seen in Table 44. A comparison of this table with Table 37 is, therefore, most revealing.

It is apparent that teaching (notably in primary schools) increases its number of potential recruits, as do administration and the police and military. In the case of administration, the increase is almost entirely due to students who expect to enter low-level clerical work. Significant declines are apparent in medicine and nursing, agriculture, and the scientific and technological occupations.

The reasons for these shifts are not difficult to discover. For most students the labor market offers few alternatives to primary school teaching or clerical work. In fact almost three-quarters of students of both sexes expect to enter these two occupations. Significantly enough, there are no differences between boys and girls at this level except that girls have an alternative not open to boys—nursing, as indicated in Table 44. Hence boys have to make a much more drastic adjustment between their aspirations and their expectations. They manifest a high level of interest in scientific and technological occupations, but in view of present market conditions and their own level of education, there is little likelihood that such careers will be open to them. The swing away from science and technology is dramatically illustrated by the fact that only 13 per cent of those with aspirations in this area expect to enter it at a lower level; the rest have changed their field completely. The same phenomenon is apparent in agriculture and in medicine, where only 7 per cent and 11 per cent, respectively, of those aspiring to enter these fields would remain in them in subordinate jobs. This indicates a lower level of real commitment to these occupations, except at the highest levels. In other words, one either starts at the top or doesn't bother to start at all.

Shifts are much less apparent in the fields of education and administration; all students who aspired to enter the primary schools as teachers still expect to do so, and no less than three-quarters of those who wished to enter university or secondary school teaching are prepared to downgrade their expectations and become primary school teachers. This greater degree of commitment also characterizes individuals who originally aspired to higher administrative positions; over one-third of them favor clerical work.

In summary, therefore, relatively high and diffuse levels of aspiration become constricted and are downgraded toward the only two occupations that are in practice available and acceptable to individuals at these educational levels. Even if it is true that individuals with superior social backgrounds or from certain ethnic groups do have actual occupational advantages, this fact is not perceived by students. In other words, there are no differences whatever in *levels* of expectation of students coming from distinct socio-economic or ethnic groups. The only observable difference is in *area* of expectation. Male highs are far more likely to expect to enter clerical work than male lows (29 per cent against 13 per cent), whereas the latter more often expect to enter primary school teaching (68 per cent, as contrasted with 43 per cent of the highs). This finding confirms our previous observations concerning the extreme importance of teaching as a career among individuals from lower socio-economic categories.

Although we expected to find a stronger relationship between occupational aspirations and socio-economic background than proved to be the case, we did expect a fairly close relationship between vocational expectations and present academic situation. These predictions were based on the assumption that aspirations would be a function of the models available to students, while expectations would be related to their perceptions of current occupational conditions and their view of the worth of their current education. The latter assumption at least seems justified, and present stream of study is a reasonably good predictor of occupational expectations.

For example, three-quarters of the students in the industrial or clerical sections of the *Centres d'Apprentissage* and *Lycée Technique* expect to enter middle-level industrial or clerical employment, and an identical proportion of students in the short academic stream expect to become primary school teachers. The relation between expectations and the educational stream in which students are at present situated is, however, much lower among students in agricultural schools or long academic institutions. Less than one-half of agricultural students expect to enter agriculture if they cannot carry their studies further—once again an indication that such a career is worthwhile only if one can start at a reasonably high level. The expectations of long academic students tend to be very diffuse: A little over one-half of them expect to become primary school teachers, while another fifth expect to do clerical work. The traditional role of the long academic institutions as feeders to further education probably accounts for this greater diffuseness of student expectations.

Three salient features emerge from a study of student expectations when viewed in relation to their present cycle of studies. First, the expectation of entering the teaching profession declines consistently as we move up in the system; about 60 per cent of the students in the lower cycle expect to enter this occupation, but the figure declines to 45 per cent among senior students. Expectations of careers in science and technology follow a similar pattern, dropping from 9 per cent at the lowest levels to 3 per cent among more advanced students. This suggests that although more senior students are drawn toward scientific and technological work at higher levels, they are not very interested in lower level opportunities within this general area. Rather, they are much more likely to choose clerical occupations, and about one-third of them expect to enter this type of job, as against only 13 per cent of junior students.

These brief remarks point to one general conclusion: Students' job expectations are unaffected by their socio-economic background but are related to their perceptions of the labor market and to their assessment of the occupational worth of their present level of education. For example, primary school teaching is not viewed as an intrinsically desirable occupation—evidenced by the decline in the proportion of students who expect to enter it as they move up the educational ladder.

Some General Conclusions

No one acquainted with contemporary Africa can fail to be impressed by the great value placed on formal education by the mass of the population. Even groups who up to a few years ago were indifferent or even hostile to schooling now wish their children to be educated. Schooling carries with it powerful emotional connotations, which are manifested in the deference most Africans pay to the educated individual. Three-quarters of the students in our Ivory Coast study consider themselves worthy of respect because of their educational attainments. To be sure, within some ethnic groups and among less educated minorities, they also perceive this deference as often mingled with envy and concealed hostility. But the important thing is that, whether a group views the educated person with positive or negative feelings, they rarely view him with indifference. Most groups realize the growing significance of schooling as a determinant of social and economic status.

This crucial role of education, perceived by the students themselves, accounts for the remarkably high level of their academic aspirations and expectations. We have attempted to show that social and cultural background and academic achievement do play some role in influencing the individual's perception of his academic future. However, this influence is rather limited, and the student born in humble circumstances does not view his future very differently from the student who comes from what might be termed an elite family background. Of course, surveys cannot demonstrate cause-and-effect relationships, but our present findings appear to provide a plausible reason for believing that secondary school attendance has a homogenizing effect on the attitudes of students, tending to attenuate differences in socio-economic and cultural background. This fact seemed to be equally evident in our study of recruitment patterns.

Of course, high levels of academic aspiration really reflect high levels of occupational aspiration, since schooling is not valued as an end in itself but in terms of the job opportunities to which it leads. To be sure, subgroups do show some differences in this respect, but we have seen that the interplay of socio-economic and strictly academic factors is very complex when we consider *areas* of occupational aspirations. In the choice of teaching as a career, both by inferior students and those from more limited social backgrounds, these two sets of factors work closely together. Despite the recent expansion of the primary school teaching force, few places are available at the top of the teaching hierarchy, and strict rules of seniority prevail; hence there are not many opportunities for quick promotion. Thus, although many students choose teaching, they tend to be drawn largely from the less talented and less acculturated groups.

The choice of administrative careers provides a contrasting picture. Fewer students favor this field than favor teaching, but they are likely to come from superior backgrounds and to attain somewhat higher levels of academic achievement. These students are mainly interested in top-level posts in the public or private sector, which may offer enhanced opportunities in view of the possible Africanization of upper-echelon positions and the creation of new occupational categories. Obviously such posts are particularly important in the power structure of the contemporary Ivory Coast, but openings are still scarce in spite of recent changes which have tended to increase opportunities and offer new channels for mobility.

Teaching and administrative careers constitute two occupational extremes in which both social and academic factors reinforce each other. This crystallization is not so apparent in choices of agricultural and medical careers. Here family background has a crucial influence on aspirations, and school achievement very little. Like aspiring teachers, prospective agriculturalists tend to be drawn more often from less advantaged groups, while medical careers are rather more favored by students from superior backgrounds.

Of all career choices, those in the scientific and technological field are the most interesting. These are new occupations which have only recently developed in the Ivory Coast and about which students and their families probably know very little. The prestige of these careers is manifested by the large number of students who choose them. Strikingly, these choices have no relation to socio-economic status but are associated more with academic achievement.

Of course, it cannot be argued that the relation between occupational aspirations and social or cultural background is anywhere overwhelmingly strong. Even if we take teaching as an example, only 26 per cent of male lows would choose this career, as against 10 per cent of male highs. This is the largest single percentage difference that occurs in the whole analysis of the relation between occupational aspirations and social background. The plain fact is that though differences do occur among groups, they are not great.

Nonetheless there is some merit in assessing the relative influence of social background or present academic situation on aspirations to enter certain occupational clusters. In a very general way we can talk of specific ascriptive or achievement orientations which underlie aspirations. Medicine represents the ascriptive polarity, since social background seems to be more important here than academic achievement. Conversely, science and technology tend more to represent an achievement-oriented polarity, since academic standing seems to play a larger role here than social background.

Finally, the emphasis on academic achievement and the great importance attributed to education per se is most evident in the pattern of student expectations. Socio-economic factors seem to have very little to do with selection of occupations except when the choice is between teaching and clerical work. By and large, students' estimates of their opportunities are a function of their position in the academic hierarchy.

So far this analysis of occupational choice has dealt only with the content and level of aspirations and expectations. In the following pages we shall attempt to see what relation exists between students' choices and their perception of the occupational hierarchy of the Ivory Coast. We also need to undertake a far more detailed examination of the factors which determine job desirability. Finally, in view of the probable importance of innovative behavior in processes of economic development, we propose to see to what extent students are characterized by what might be loosely termed as "entrepreneurial" and "bureaucratic" orientations.

CHAPTER VII

Student Attitudes toward the Occupational Structure

THE ECONOMIC DEVELOPMENT of the Ivory Coast has implied the growth of new-type roles and the consequent emergence of an occupational hierarchy more complex than the relatively undifferentiated structures of traditional societies. In addition, comparative research in industrialized societies has pointed to a relatively invariant scale of occupations based on differential prestige, and it is important to see how far the perceptions of Ivory Coast students parallel these general findings.[1] A priori, one would expect a marked similarity between African and Western occupational rankings for the simple reason that the development of the occupational hierarchy in the Ivory Coast has been a result of Western contact. The presence of Europeans as a reference group has largely determined African perceptions of which jobs carry more prestige.

Prestige and Income Rankings of Occupations

Table 45 indicates the prestige rankings given by students to twenty-five occupations generally familiar to the people of the Ivory

1. A. Inkeles and P. Rossi, "National Comparisons of Occupational Prestige," *American Journal of Sociology*, XI, pp. 329–39.

TABLE 45. *Prestige Rankings of Twenty-Five Occupations, by Sex*

OCCUPATION	MALES			FEMALES		
	Score	Rank	S.D.	Score	Rank	S.D.
Engineer	1.23	1	.50	1.24	2	.45
University professor	1.26	2	.52	1.15	1	.39
Doctor	1.45	3	.62	1.52	4	.61
Lawyer	1.82	4	.84	1.40	3	.62
Secondary school teacher (*Lycée*)	1.87	5	.60	1.75	5	.59
Secondary school teacher (*Collège*)	2.14	6	.66	1.99	7	.74
Clergyman	2.25	7	1.22	1.88	6	1.06
Radio announcer	2.55	8	.78	2.45	8	.82
Bank clerk	2.80	9.5	.80	2.84	13	.78
Primary school teacher	2.80	9.5	.76	2.53	9	.79
Electrician	2.85	11	.86	2.64	10	.98
Hospital nurse	2.97	12	.71	2.96	15	.75
Chief	3.01	13	1.15	2.65	11.5	1.13
Government clerk	3.04	14	.79	2.88	14	.75
Policeman	3.05	15	.98	2.65	11.5	.91
Cash-crop farmer	3.11	16	.98	3.14	17	.97
Auto mechanic	3.16	17	.88	3.37	18.5	.82
Transport proprietor	3.42	18	.90	3.37	18.5	.87
Soldier	3.53	19	.96	2.98	16	1.05
Carpenter	3.87	20	.78	3.74	20	.76
Salesman	4.05	21	.80	3.91	21	.77
Agricultural laborer	4.10	22	.85	4.00	22	.79
Peddler	4.69	23	.60	4.53	23	.68
Minstrel	4.72	24	.62	4.58	24	.79
Street cleaner	4.79	25	.60	4.81	25	.51

Coast, ranging from the professions to unskilled labor. For the most part, these are modern-type jobs, but we have deliberately included two traditional occupations: minstrel (*griot*) and chief.[2] The inclusion of chief raises certain problems. Strictly speaking, chiefs do not receive official remuneration for their services and frequently derive the bulk of their income from other activities. Further, the significance of their office varies a great deal.[3] In spite of these anomalies, it is still desira-

2. The traditional role of minstrel has been particularly important among the Mande peoples, where the minstrel group formed a particular subcaste. However, such performers in one form or another also exist outside the Mande areas in the southern Ivory Coast.

3. First, a distinction can be made between societies with an elaborate chief hierarchy and others where the office of chief did not exist beyond the level of the village headman. The Agni and Bété provide examples of these two types. Further, even where the office of chief existed, it varied greatly in terms of area of jurisdic-

ble to include this office, if only to indicate in a rough way how a traditional occupation ranks with the new-type occupations now available to educated cadres.

Clearly the profile shown in the table is highly consistent with findings in other societies. Professional and semiprofessional roles are at the top, followed by white-collar and skilled technical occupations and finally by unskilled jobs. It is interesting to note, however, that the one traditional occupation to which access is very restricted and which demands long training, that of minstrel, is classed along with unskilled labor. Moreover, the office of chief occupies only a median position on the scale, about the same as government clerk.

When one turns to the other occupations, certain interesting features emerge. It is notable, for example, that boys view the occupation of engineer as carrying the greatest prestige, while even the less technical role of electrician commands a relatively high rating—above government clerk, for example. In spite of oft-repeated assertions that only white-collar jobs command prestige in West Africa, the evidence in Table 45 suggests that occupational ratings are rather similar to those that a group of Western students might provide (although it must be stressed that the data give no indication of the relative distance between occupations on the scale).

One striking feature is that the cash-crop farmer is a long way from the bottom of the scale. It has often been assumed that this occupation is accorded very low status in most African territories, and this in turn is said to account for the lack of interest in that career among educated minorities. True, farming is not high on the list, but it does rank above other occupations which one might have expected to rate higher. To be sure, few students wish to enter farming as a career, but their reluctance cannot be attributed solely to the prestige rank of farming itself.

In general, one can see that the occupational aspirations of students discussed in the preceding chapter tend to follow the profile of occupational rankings and are clustered in the top half of the scale. However, exceptions exist. Law, for example, commands high prestige but is chosen by few students as a career for reasons already indicated.

There is, moreover, a high level of consistency between occupational ratings by sex (the rank-order correlation between male and female

---

tion and extent of authority. However, most people know what chiefship involves, since the colonial administration perpetuated the traditional institution and even introduced it into areas where it was formerly unknown.

ratings is 0.98), and such divergences as occur were predictable. Boys tend to rank some technical occupations rather higher than do girls, while girls ascribe a trifle more prestige to authority figures such as policemen, chiefs, or soldiers. This consistency is equally apparent among all subgroups of the student population. Ethnic background, for instance, seems to have no influence on occupational ratings, with one exception: The office of chief is more highly ranked by the northern Malinke and the Agni than by other groups. Among the Agni, of course—in spite of the fact that they have been longer exposed to European influence than other peoples—the chiefship had already developed in its most complex and hierarchical form.[4]

Socio-economic status, as measured by paternal level of occupation and education, similarly generates no contrasts in occupational rankings. Neither do these rankings vary between students at different educational levels or in different types of educational stream. The picture is, therefore, remarkably consistent, and the pattern highly stable.

However, between different occupations there is a measure of variability in the standard deviation of scores. Students' responses show a marked tendency to be more homogeneous at the upper and (to a lesser extent) the lower ends of the scale. In some cases there appears to be a greater crystallization of notions about occupational status, but this is notably absent in regard to clergyman, chief, and farmer, where a far greater dispersion of scores indicates a greater heterogeneity of responses and a lack of consensus on the ranking of these jobs. This uncertainty to some extent reflects the objective heterogeneity of the occupations themselves. Chiefs vary greatly in status and prestige, depending on their position in the chiefship hierarchy and the nature of the traditional organization. Similarly, although the mean status of farmers is not high, a small number do control larger plantations and enjoy markedly high levels of prestige because of their wealth.[5]

4. The prestige ranking of chief is much lower in the Ivory Coast than in Ghana, where a similar occupational scale was administered to secondary school students in 1961. This difference is even more striking if one bears in mind the substantial overlapping of ethnic groups between the two countries. This finding lends some substance to the view that the more consistent policies of indirect rule pursued by the British in Ghana have enabled the chiefs to retain considerable prestige, even after independence. This is in spite of the fact that during the past decade every effort has been made to diminish their authority and status.

5. There is a great deal of variation in the size of holdings and level of income of farmers in the Ivory Coast. See Margueritte Dupire, "Planteurs autochtones et étrangers en Basse Côte d'Ivoire Orientale," *Etudes éburnéennes,* VIII (Abidjan:

This brings us to a crucial question: To what extent do occupational status rankings tend to reflect perceived differences in levels of income? Very often one gains the impression from previous writers on West African education that African school graduates have tended to enter white-collar jobs even when income opportunities have been superior in other fields of activity. In other words, African students become clerks because of the prestige attending that occupation, though they could probably earn far more by becoming trained artisans. Whether this has been objectively true in West Africa is very doubtful. Historically, in fact, clerical workers tended to be paid more than many technical workers, simply because the demand for clerical personnel was relatively higher in colonial times.[6]

Apart from the fact that this well-worn argument about the white-collar preferences of Africans does not fit historical realities, it is equally apparent from Tables 45 and 46 that there is a strong relationship between students' prestige and income rankings. Indeed the rank-order correlation for each sex is on the order of 0.85. This is remarkably high and considerably greater than correlations of a similar nature produced by research in other societies.[7]

An examination of particular occupations which exhibit deviations between prestige and perceived income is quite revealing. The difference between occupational status and income for the clergy is a familiar phenomenon; so is the gap between chiefship prestige and income. Primary school teaching and nursing are also jobs whose prestige markedly exceeds perceived wealth. The reverse, however, is true for certain manual occupations. Neither mechanics nor electricians appear to enjoy a prestige commensurate with their supposed levels of income. This is even more the case with farmers. We have

---

Centre IFAN, 1960). In more general terms there probably has been a close association between wealth and status in West Africa. Nonetheless a distinction must be made between those societies where wealth followed access to political office and those where initially acquired wealth could be used to enhance status. Further, some societies exhibited both modes of mobility.

6. In an Abidjan survey of some 700 Ivory Coast workers conducted by the present writers, it was evident that the salaries of clerical workers were uniformly higher than those of technical and industrial workers. Moreover, their rate of promotion was much more rapid.

7. For example, the correlation between occupational prestige and perceived income is considerably higher in the Ivory Coast than in either Japan or the United States. See Charles E. Ramsey and Robert J. Smith, "Japanese and American Perceptions of Occupations," *American Journal of Sociology,* Vol. LXV, No. 5 (March 1960), pp. 475–82.

TABLE 46. Income Rankings of Twenty-Five Occupations, by Sex

OCCUPATION	MALES			FEMALES		
	Score	Rank	S.D.	Score	Rank	S.D.
Engineer	1.23	1	.47	1.22	2	.44
University professor	1.40	2	.60	1.18	1	.40
Doctor	1.63	3	.64	1.62	4	.58
Lawyer	1.79	4	.70	1.37	3	.55
Secondary school teacher (*Lycée*)	2.04	5	.60	1.85	5	.55
Secondary school teacher (*Collège*)	2.24	6	.62	2.06	6	.67
Clergyman	3.97	21	1.13	3.70	21	1.28
Radio announcer	2.55	7	.64	2.45	7	.71
Bank clerk	2.71	9	.72	2.77	10	.68
Primary school teacher	3.04	13	.49	2.88	12	.49
Electrician	2.71	8	.74	2.49	8	.80
Hospital nurse	3.10	15	.52	3.10	18	.49
Chief	3.67	19.5	1.01	3.04	16	1.11
Government clerk	3.08	14	.60	2.92	13	.57
Policeman	3.18	16	.64	2.84	11	.65
Cash-crop farmer	2.82	10.5	1.00	2.57	9	.89
Auto mechanic	2.82	10.5	.76	3.00	15	.77
Transport proprietor	2.88	12	.98	2.96	14	.98
Soldier	3.46	17	.76	3.06	17	.83
Carpenter	3.63	18	.74	3.56	20	.67
Salesman	3.67	19.5	.85	3.53	19	.78
Agricultural laborer	4.01	22	.76	3.85	22	.80
Peddler	4.51	23	.69	4.28	23	.73
Minstrel	4.69	25	.63	4.53	24	.74
Street cleaner	4.65	24	.67	4.74	25	.56

already noted that they enjoy a rather higher status than has often been suggested, but it is still below their purported earnings. The same can be said of transport proprietors, in whose area of activity African entrepreneurs have been particularly active. Thus there is a tendency for certain manual occupations, farming, and certain kinds of business activity to be limited in prestige despite fairly high rankings in terms of income.

Clearly, these discrepancies are analogous to those which occur in Western nations; still, our evidence points to the fact that income operates as an important determinant of occupational prestige in the Ivory Coast. Although correlations do not in themselves provide evidence of a causal relationship, the assumption that income largely determines occupational prestige seems logically far more tenable than a view which implies that income is merely a reflection of the prestige of a particular occupation. Levels of income are usually in some measure a corollary of the market demand for various types of skill.

What we suggest here, therefore, is that in the long run students' perceptions of the status of an occupation, and perhaps its desirability, are likely to be influenced by market conditions and the actual level of demand for different types of skill. Later we shall explore in greater detail some of the complex factors which influence occupational choice. Here we would argue that in a very rough fashion students' aspirations are likely to conform to the realities of the occupational structure, since a rise in the demand for particular skills will manifest itself in raised levels of income and prestige for the occupational categories involved. We concede the fact that Africans are highly concerned with the status of various occupations, yet this notion of prestige does not exist in a vacuum. It is firmly rooted in very clear-cut conceptions of income and material wealth. In this respect Africans differ very little from most Westerners.

The Occupational Preferences of Students

We can take the whole problem of occupational choice a little further. So far we have examined the *free* responses of students in terms of their aspirations and expectations. How do they react when asked to choose from a restricted list of occupations, all of which demand a high level of skill and a varying degree of formal education? Further, how do they choose between occupations of a bureaucratic or traditional professional type and those which are basically technological or entrepreneurial in character? In order to provide some answer to these questions, students were presented with a list of eight occupations (these differed for boys and girls) and were asked to list their first three choices in rank order. Mean scores were computed for each occupation on the basis of three points for a first choice, two points for a second, and one for a third choice.

Table 47 shows the male pattern of responses to this kind of question. Once again the overwhelmingly preferred occupation is that of engineer. We may note further the very low level of preference for the law. There is a tendency to display less interest in the entrepreneurial-type occupations, though even here that of factory owner ranks above university professor, in spite of the latter's very high position in the scale of occupational prestige. This lack of interest in university teaching might be accounted for by the fact that up to now such posts have been so completely monopolized by Europeans that they do not yet appear as a possible area of aspiration to Africans themselves.

The internal variations in preferences among subgroups of the student population are also significant. There is, for example, a definite association between occupational preference and the type of studies being pursued. This is particularly marked with respect to entrepreneurial, as opposed to the nontechnical professional or bureaucratic,

TABLE 47. *Vocational Preferences of Male Students*

OCCUPATION	MEAN SCORE	RANK
Engineer	1.81	1
Doctor	1.08	2
Lycée professor	0.83	3
Factory owner	0.67	4
University professor	0.54	5
Plantation owner or manager	0.37	6
Businessman or merchant	0.31	7
Lawyer	0.23	8

occupations. With the exception of engineer, which is uniformly ranked high, and plantation owner, which is uniformly ranked low, there are marked differences between the preferences of technical students and those of students in other types of institution. Factory owner and businessman are ranked fourth and seventh respectively by most individuals, but are placed second and third by students in technical schools. Correspondingly, the latter tend to give significantly lower scores and rankings to the educational, medical, and legal professions.

Technical students especially favor technological and entrepreneurial occupations, but it must be added that the most highly educated group of students in our sample, those preparing for the first and second classical or modern *Baccalaureat*, score and rank technological and entrepreneurial occupations more highly than do any others in the whole academic secondary school system. Since more students in this group might have been expected to choose bureaucratic careers than in any other group, the fact that they are not really so favorably disposed to such occupations is highly significant.

Similar preferences tend to be more frequent among the more highly acculturated segments of the student body. We have already seen that when occupational aspirations were analyzed in terms of open-ended responses, there were no clear associations between socio-economic origins and preferences for scientific and technological careers. By contrast, such associations do emerge when subgroups are confronted by a restricted cluster of occupations, some of which involve technological skills and an element of risk (Table 48). The

TABLE 48. Male Vocational Preferences, by Level of Acculturation

OCCUPATION	LEVEL OF ACCULTURATION			
	High		Low	
	Mean Score	Rank	Mean Score	Rank
Engineer	2.05	1	1.85	1
Factory owner	1.08	2	0.49	5
Doctor	0.77	3	1.25	2
Lycée professor	0.53	4	1.04	3
University professor	0.48	5	0.52	4
Businessman or merchant	0.43	6	0.25	7
Plantation owner or manager	0.35	7	0.42	6
Lawyer	0.29	8	0.18	8

most acculturated individuals give significantly higher scores and ranks to such careers as factory owner, engineer, and businessman, while the less acculturated lean more toward the older established professions. The essential point here is the degree to which the most highly acculturated groups tend toward activities which are new, in the sense that they have only recently come within the purview of Africans, and which are more innovative and entrepreneurial in character.

This represents an interesting shift from what has historically been the pattern of relationship between education and entrepreneurial and business activity in the Ivory Coast. Business enterprise on any scale has, of course, been overwhelmingly in European hands, although Africans have been active in small-scale trading. Yet, most of the African entrepreneurs have been drawn from the uneducated or poorly educated segments of the population. In the past the more highly acculturated minorities with substantial levels of schooling were almost inevitably recruited into the ranks of the bureaucracy. Our evidence here would suggest that this pattern may well be changing, even if slowly. Students with urban backgrounds, coming from educated families, are more likely to perceive new opportunities created by economic development and perhaps may be better prepared to reevaluate the desirability of different occupations. Conversely, the image of the successful man and the high-prestige occupation held by the less acculturated students is more likely to be based upon stereotypes formed in the earlier period of colonial rule. Clearly these students have had less opportunity to perceive the development of new-type occupations.

Girls' preferences present a simpler and more homogeneous picture than do those of boys (Table 49), because they are drawn from a

TABLE 49. Vocational Preferences of Female Students

OCCUPATION	MEAN SCORE	RANK
Midwife	1.53	1
Social worker	1.40	2
College professor	0.94	3
Primary school teacher	0.86	4
Secretary	0.51	5
Beautician	0.44	6
Assistant in a fashionable store	0.18	7
Businesswoman	0.07	8

narrower segment of society and also because occupational outlets for educated girls are much more restricted than for boys. Up to the present, virtually the only jobs available to girls have been in nursing or midwifery, primary school teaching, or minor clerical activities. Social work and secondary school teaching within the short academic system are, in fact, new careers that are becoming increasingly open to women. In addition, work in the larger stores and beauty parlors of Abidjan is for the first time becoming available to educated girls. Needless to say, African women have been traditionally active in small-scale trading and to a degree in large-scale wholesale and retail activities, but generally this has been carried on mostly by illiterates.

It is evident that girls as a whole are oriented toward those quasi-professional jobs that have usually been regarded as appropriate for them. However, clerical and secretarial work, which in the Ivory Coast is becoming increasingly regarded as a woman's job, is not highly favored by the girls themselves. Yet in spite of the homogeneity of the female sample, there are slight differences in preference if social background is taken into account. The most acculturated girls, in contrast to the remainder, tend to prefer social worker (one of the new jobs) to midwife, traditionally the occupation of highest prestige.[8] They also rank beautician higher than secretarial work, unlike the majority of girls, and tend to give slightly lower mean scores to all teaching positions. On the other hand, their mean score for businesswoman is higher than that of the less acculturated majority.

These differences, though slight, indicate that female choices tend to move in a direction similar to those of males. The preference for teaching and nursing is less evident among the more acculturated girl students, who show a greater willingness to enter new-type occupations and seem less preoccupied with basically governmental types of employment. Indeed the data suggest that the greatest response to new employment opportunities is likely to occur among students of both sexes coming from large urban centers and having a rather superior family background. It is, therefore, the less acculturated students whose responses tend to be more stereotyped, favoring those occupations that have been available in the past.

Preferences for Government and Private Employment

Notwithstanding our preceding observations, it is still true that students tend to be oriented toward bureaucratic careers. This is illustrated in Table 50 by the overwhelming preference for government employment shown by both sexes. Such an orientation is understandable, since the administration has provided, and still provides, a high proportion of employment opportunities. Indeed during the colo-

TABLE 50. Employer Preferences of Students, by Sex (Percentages)

PREFERRED EMPLOYER	MALES	FEMALES
Government	80.5	85.2
Private industry or commerce	10.7	5.1
Self	7.8	8.9
No answer	1.0	.8
Total	100.0	100.0
	(1,837)	(237)

8. The small number of girls made it impossible to compare highs and lows in the same manner as for boys. In this case girls whose fathers had had more than a full primary education were compared with those whose fathers had never been to school.

nial period undoubtedly conditions in government employment were more favorable than those prevailing in the private sector. However, in recent years there has been a partial reversal of this situation, and in many respects jobs with large commercial companies offer better conditions than work in the administration.[9] This is true not only with respect to income but also with respect to promotion opportunities in European-controlled private firms.

In fact, a greater preference for private employment or self-employment distinguishes students in the technical schools and those at the level of the *Baccalaureat*. Only 67 per cent of students in these two categories are oriented to government employment, against 86 per cent of all others.

In view of past colonial history, it is tempting to assume that preferences for public, as opposed to private, employment might be associated with ethnicity. Certain ethnic groups have indeed been heavily represented in particular types of activity. The Malinke have been involved in private trade (this is evident in the background of our Malinke students), and the Agni have been conspicuous in the ranks of the public bureaucracy. Yet the occupational traditions associated with various minorities do not appear in students' responses, with one notable exception: Among the Kru preference for careers with government is somewhat higher than among the other major peoples and, furthermore, is not affected by socio-economic status. However, for all other groups in the sample it is social background rather than ethnicity which influences preferences for a particular type of employment. Only 70 per cent of male highs favor government service, against 85 per cent of male lows. This difference, though not substantial, points to a significant trend. Yet such a difference is not apparent among girls from varying social backgrounds. Since the occupational opportunities of girls are more limited, they consistently tend to favor government employment. In this respect they might be compared with male lows, whose perception of occupational opportunities is also more circumscribed. In effect, the more differentiated one's view of occupational outlets becomes, the more likely one is to favor employment in the private sector.

9. It is understandable that the larger European-controlled companies are very anxious not to be labeled as "neocolonial exploiters." As a result, they are increasingly scrupulous in obeying regulations concerning conditions of employment and are also making considerable efforts to recruit Africans for higher positions. Conversely, positions in the administration are increasingly subject to political manipulation.

We suggest that these findings reinforce the tentative conclusions expressed in previous pages. The students who come from rural, illiterate families and who have succeeded in entering secondary school are not those most oriented to new-type occupations in the private sector of the economy. Precisely the reverse is the case. It is the children of the best educated and urbanized parents (the majority of them employed by the administration) who are most aware of new opportunities in the private sector and whose conceptions of the character of the occupational structure are most likely to change. We would argue that this minority can be expected to make a somewhat greater contribution to the economic future of the Ivory Coast, provided the labor market offers them adequate opportunities and outlets. Yet, as we shall see, the orientation of this minority is associated with another feature that is perhaps less desirable in the context of present development.

Preferences for Urban and Rural Employment

Historically, maximum economic growth and the accompanying enlargement of occupational opportunities have been associated with the development of large urban centers. Correspondingly, the students who complete their schooling have tended to drift toward these centers in pursuit of employment and opportunity for advancement. In consequence, although only 21 per cent of our students at present reside in the largest towns, Abidjan and Bouaké, almost 54 per cent hope to work there after completion of their studies. Only 15 per cent of them express any wish to work in the smaller villages, whether or not these are their home communities.[10] The degree of preference for urban residence and employment is not significantly related to the students' sex, but it is highly associated with socio-economic background.

In summary, the most highly acculturated students, who tend to be more flexible in many of their career preferences, are at the same time those least oriented to employment opportunities outside the big towns. There is a consistent relationship between level of paternal

10. This pattern of preference is equally apparent in a number of other surveys conducted in West Africa. For example, see Remi Clignet, "Education et aspirations professionnelles," *Tiers Monde,* Vol. V, No. 17 (January–March 1964), pp. 61–82.

occupation, education, or urban residence and preference for employment in the largest cities. This relationship is exemplified in Table 51, where we once again contrast the two extreme subgroups of our male sample. The highs are overwhelmingly oriented to employment in only two major urban centers, as against just over one-third of the lows. However, even among the latter group, well over one-third wish to work in Abidjan and Bouaké, and less than one-quarter in rural areas.

This preference for urban as opposed to rural employment is shown very clearly when the courses being pursued by students are considered. Technical students are markedly oriented to employment in the largest towns. No less than 72 per cent would prefer to work in Abidjan and Bouaké, as against 52 per cent of the students in academic studies and less than 10 per cent of those in agricultural schools.[11]

TABLE 51. Male Student Preferences for Urban or Rural Employment, by Level of Acculturation (Percentages)

EMPLOYMENT PREFERENCE	LEVEL OF ACCULTURATION	
	High	Low
Abidjan and Bouaké	74.1	37.4
Smaller towns	6.9	21.2
Villages (below 5,000)	5.2	22.7
No preference	13.8	18.2
No answer	0.0	0.5
Total	100.0	100.0
	(116)	(198)

A more vital question concerns the relationship between occupational aspirations and willingness to work in either urban or rural areas. Students' awareness that certain types of job are more likely to be available within the largest towns leads those aspiring to enter technological, scientific, and administrative careers to express a marked preference for urban employment. However, if government is committed to lessening the gap in social and economic development between town and country, three types of occupation are particularly vital to the rural districts: teaching, nursing and medical services, and agricultural assistance. It is evident that people who wish to enter these activities are more inclined to prefer working in the less developed areas (Table 52). Granted this, the individuals who would

11. Thus in technical, academic, and agricultural schools there is a relationship between place of origin and preference for urban or rural employment.

TABLE 52. Preference for Urban or Rural Employment, by Occupational Aspiration (Percentages)

EMPLOYMENT	TEACHING	SCIENTIFIC AND TECHNOLOGICAL	MEDICINE AND NURSING	AGRICULTURE	ADMINISTRATIVE	MILITARY AND POLICE	MISCELLANEOUS AND NO ANSWER
Abidjan and Bouaké	44.4	59.7	51.4	45.0	73.1	59.4	53.5
Smaller towns	14.9	13.0	14.0	17.6	8.3	17.2	11.3
Villages (below 5,000)	26.9	8.4	16.3	14.9	6.7	6.2	21.1
No preferences	12.8	18.7	18.1	22.1	11.9	17.2	14.1
No answer	1.0	.2	.2	.4	0.0	0.0	0.0
Total	100.0	100.0	100.0	100.0	100.0	100.0	100.0
	(498)	(439)	(486)	(262)	(253)	(64)	(71)

choose to work outside Abidjan or Bouaké or who express no preference amount to only 55 per cent of those intending to teach, 48 per cent of aspirants to medical occupations, and only 55 per cent of those hoping to work in agricultural occupations. Yet almost 90 per cent of the Ivory Coast population lives in small towns and villages![12]

The preference for urban employment reflects a real conflict between community needs, as defined by government policy, and individual needs and aspirations. Students' preferences reflect a realistic appreciation of the greater opportunities and more congenial environment offered by the city. Yet if, as manpower specialists sometimes suggest, an adequate feedback of trained personnel into the rural areas is necessary for general development, then it is equally clear that there must be special inducements to attract and retain such personnel. At present the system works in exactly the opposite direction; special allowances are given to workers in Abidjan, on the doubtful assumption that the cost of living is higher in the towns.[13] In short, one cannot but conclude that the kind of person most needed in the rural areas is the kind least likely to work there.

Factors Influencing Job Desirability

So far we have considered the nature of occupational preferences as these affect the choice of occupation and the location of employment. This cluster of responses can be partly explained by an analysis of the factors that students themselves regard as being important in occupational choice.

Obviously jobs differ in the advantages or benefits they offer, and it is important to see what particular factors weigh heavily in the minds of students when they are faced with a range of job alternatives. Five factors seemed to us especially important to consider: the prestige, the security of tenure, the current income and promotion opportunities afforded by a particular occupation, and the congenial nature of the

12. Of couse it is unlikely that fully qualified doctors would be expected to reside in smaller communities. In functional terms they can work more efficiently when concentrated in medium-sized centers. However, less qualified nurses are needed in smaller towns and villages, and it is notable that individuals aspiring to enter this occupation are no more oriented to rural work than are doctors.

13. This assumption is not correct unless it implies that the educated African living in rural areas is prepared to live in a substantially traditional manner. In practice, if he wishes to live in a partly European fashion, even at a very modest level, his cost of living is much higher than in the towns.

job itself. Using the method of paired comparisons, we assigned a rank order and scale value to each of these items in terms of expressed student preferences.[14]

Overwhelmingly, security and stability of job tenure was the factor deemed by students most crucial in choosing between occupations. Next in order came occupational prestige, congeniality of employment, and current income. The actual difference in scale values between these three items was quite small, but all occupied a position a long way below job security on the scale. Last, and with a value considerably less than that of all other items, came opportunities for promotion and advancement.[15]

Few of these students can be considered risk takers. Of course the findings do not imply that individuals attach no importance to income or promotion opportunities, but rather that, when faced with a choice, they will normally opt for security and stability of employment. The evidence indicates a degree of rigidity in the occupational values of individuals who see their future in terms of a continuation of present occupational status rather than as providing a spectrum of new opportunities.

Furthermore, although the various ethnic and socio-economic subgroups of students do not differ in their rank-ordering of items, they do vary significantly in the scale values they accord to some of these items. Male highs score income factors more highly than do the lows and, as suggested earlier, seem to display a greater degree of flexibility. There are also some slight but revealing differences between students when they are classified by preferred type of occupation. We have already noted that the incidence of choice for employment in the private sector increases with a rise in socio-economic status. In turn this preference is associated with a significantly higher value assigned to income factors in the present scale. Pay is more important for all individuals preferring to enter the private sector but is more crucial for those wishing to enter the larger companies than for those choosing self-employment.

In fact, the group of individuals who would prefer jobs with the larger commercial concerns offer the greatest contrasts with the bulk

14. For the method pursued, see Allen L. Edwards, *Techniques of Attitude Scale Construction* (New York: Appleton-Century-Crofts, 1957), pp. 40–46.

15. Actual mean scale values were 0.000 for opportunities for promotion and advancement; 0.487 for income; 0.517 for congenial conditions of employment; 0.551 for prestige; and 1.000 for security and stability.

of the student population. Not only do they evaluate current income relatively more highly than does any other group, but they also give a significantly higher scale value to promotion opportunities. Conversely, they accord a markedly lower scale value to occupation prestige and the congeniality of the work. Above all, although they rank security and stability first (as does every other group), they assign this item a lower scale value.

These differences, it must be stressed, are relatively minor. Nevertheless they support the view that a preference for private employment reflects a greater willingness to sacrifice security and high prestige for increased income-earning opportunities and greater chances for promotion. The individuals preferring employment with the larger commercial concerns are also to be contrasted with the minority who prefer self-employment. Offhand it might have been assumed that the latter would constitute the most divergent minority, but actually persons choosing self-employment, in spite of their previously noted stress on income factors, approximate much more closely the general profile. The probable reason is that a substantial proportion are oriented to independent careers in the high-status professions, such as medicine, law, or engineering; they are not, in fact, oriented toward business-type careers.

The Conditions of Occupational Success

We can now shift from a discussion of the factors which may influence choices of different occupations to an examination of what students believe to be the prerequisites for achievement within a job, once they have entered it. In short, do they believe that their success will largely depend upon their academic achievement or intelligence, upon their actual performance on the job, or, alternatively, upon their possession of the right contacts and social skills in manipulating others? [16]

Table 53 shows that individuals of both sexes consider achievement and hard work (that is, job proficiency) to be far more important to occupational success than all other factors, and accord much less

16. Traditionally, in West Africa, mobility often depended to a degree upon a person's willingness to attach himself to more powerful individuals and in turn collect a group of followers dependent upon him. Personal manipulation thus played a crucial role in mobility processes.

importance to intelligence and education. Individuals make a rather sharp distinction between academic and work experience, and only 9 per cent of all students regard schooling alone as being the major factor in determining their advancement. At first sight this finding may seem paradoxical in the light of our stress on the importance attached to education. However, students may emphasize it as essential for *access* to employment but may not regard it as crucial to success in their jobs. In other words, formal education may be a necessary

TABLE 53. Factors Considered Important in Occupational Success, by Sex (Percentages)

FACTOR	MALES	FEMALES	TOTAL
Job proficiency and hard work	65.3	78.9	66.8
Intelligence and a good education	24.1	13.5	22.9
Age and seniority on the job	4.3	2.5	4.1
Social skills and personal contacts	5.5	2.1	5.1
No answer	.8	3.0	1.1
Total	100.0	100.0	100.0
	(1,837)	(237)	(2,074)

condition for obtaining a rewarding occupation, but it is not a sufficient qualification for doing well in it.

In view of what is known about conditions of bureaucratic employment in the Ivory Coast and the significance of particularistic ties in the traditional societies of the area, we expected that students would strongly believe in the importance of age, seniority, and social skills or contacts as influencing occupational success. What is surprising is their lack of sensitivity to the role of particularistic ties as contrasted with their high level of commitment to achievement criteria. This idealistic view is likely to change when students are actually employed, since there is very little doubt that family or ethnic ties do favor or impede occupational success in the contemporary Ivory Coast.

However, students do vary in the relative weight they give to these various factors. Groups that might be said to be disadvantaged in terms of occupational access give rather distinctive responses. Thus girls, whose educational and occupational opportunities are more limited than those of boys, attach less importance to intelligence and education. The same response patterns characterize male lows, whose opportunities are likewise limited. Only 18 per cent stress education and intelligence, as against 27 per cent of male highs. In addition to sex and social background, academic experience per se tends to determine future educational opportunities and hence to influence students' notions of what leads to job success. For example, 28 per cent of those who rank themselves in the top quarter of their class underscore the role of education and intelligence, as opposed to 16 per cent of those in the lowest quarter. But over three-quarters of these poorer students emphasize job proficiency, as against less than two-thirds of the best students. Similarly, the more certain a student feels about continuing his schooling, the more likely he is to emphasize education and intelligence, while downgrading the importance of efficiency on the job (Table 54). In summary, whatever factors may obstruct their educational progress, those who can expect little additional schooling systematically place less emphasis on the role of education or intellectual ability in influencing occupational achievement.

This does not prevent these disadvantaged groups from differing in the stress they place on other factors which can compensate for their educational limitations. Girls attach great importance to job proficiency but, in contrast to all male students, accord less significance to seniority and social contacts; their responses probably reflect the fact that they are far less in a position to take advantage of these conditions in the labor market. At present women are far less likely to gain seniority than men, and even if they have this or other advantages, they are not likely to be successful in competition with men unless they can demonstrate definite superiority on the job.

The pattern followed by disadvantaged males to compensate for their probable educational deficiencies is somewhat different. Like girls, they tend to stress job proficiency as against education, but they also attach more significance to seniority and social contacts or skills than do other male students. Over 12 per cent of male lows lay emphasis on these two sets of factors, as against only 6 per cent of male highs. Table 54 also indicates a slight but consistent increase in the importance attributed to particularistic factors as students become less certain of their academic future.

In spite of these interesting variations between subgroups, the preceding discussion has indicated that African students see their future success in employment as largely dependent upon their personal achievements, whether these are viewed in educational or occupational terms. "What you *do* is more important than who you are, or whom you know."

TABLE 54. Factors Considered Important in Occupational Success, by Self-estimate of Chances of Continuing Full-time Education (Percentages)

FACTOR	CERTAIN OF CONTINUING	A GOOD CHANCE OF CONTINUING	LITTLE CHANCE OF CONTINUING	CERTAIN NOT TO CONTINUE	NO ANSWER	TOTAL
Job proficiency and hard work	64.8	67.3	67.5	75.2	30.8	66.9
Intelligence and a good education	25.5	23.1	21.2	12.7	46.1	22.9
Age and seniority on the job	3.2	4.1	4.4	7.0	7.7	4.1
Social skills and personal contacts	4.9	5.0	5.9	3.8	7.7	5.0
No answer	1.6	.5	1.8	1.3	7.7	1.1
Total	100.0	100.0	100.0	100.0	100.0	100.0
	(693)	(805)	(406)	(157)	(13)	(2,074)

This attitude mainly reflects an adjustment to existing employment opportunities within the present occupational structure. Students almost invariably see themselves as employees working in situations where conditions of employment are clearly defined. They rarely view themselves as self-employed, and when they do, this is generally in terms of professional careers rather than entrepreneurial or business roles. Yet we would argue that a great deal of development in African countries rests not merely upon persons' fitting themselves into existing slots in the occupational structure but also upon their creating new opportunities through their own activities.[17] If this view is substantially correct, what factors might explain the widespread reluctance even to envisage innovatory or entrepreneurial careers?

We have already mentioned some of the historical reasons which have made educated persons reluctant to enter business. Further, the present government makes little effort to facilitate the emergence of an African private sector whose activities extend beyond small-scale trading. The entrepreneur receives small encouragement, and for this reason is less likely to be drawn from the ranks of the more educated.

Additionally, an analysis of the attitudes of students does throw a little more light on their lack of interest in business enterprise. We have already seen what factors students regard as important in getting ahead in existing types of employment. We can now see the attributes they view as significant when it comes to creating a new enterprise (Table 55).

TABLE 55. Orientations Underlying Attitudes toward Starting a Business (Percentages)

ORIENTATION	MALES	FEMALES	TOTAL
Achievement oriented	27.5	20.2	26.6
Ascriptively oriented	71.8	78.5	72.6
No answer	.7	1.3	.8
Total	100.0	100.0	100.0
	(1,837)	(237)	(2,074)

17. Perhaps one of the underlying weaknesses of the purely manpower approach to problems of development is that it considers only the supply of skills as these relate to the expanding needs of the existing occupational structure. This approach does not take into account the possible creation of new opportunities and hence alternative uses of manpower.

In this table we have grouped together such factors as academic achievement, job proficiency, and hard work and labeled them "achievement orientations," in the sense that these responses stress the role of personal effort in business success. By contrast, responses which emphasize the importance of wealth, family connections, and ethnic affiliation we have termed "ascriptive orientations." It is evident that the students' view of the qualities necessary to start a business is totally at variance with their attitudes concerning success in the existing labor market. They attach overwhelming importance to initial advantages rather than personal achievement. Forty-four per cent stress initial wealth alone, and 13 per cent family or ethnic ties. In contrast with many Western stereotypes, the image of the self-made man is not apparent here; rather, the students believe, a man starting a business builds upon initial advantages.

However, there is a consistent relationship between the emphasis placed on achievement and students' social background or academic status. Almost one-third of male lows stress achievement, as against 17 per cent of male highs. Similarly, the emphasis on achievement declines as one moves upward to more advanced students in the postprimary system or from the academic to the technical stream.

These findings might at first seem to be at variance with our earlier observation that the preference for employment in the private sector is greater among senior students and those with superior social backgrounds. We have also indicated that the latter groups place greater stress on achievement in occupational success. Why this reversal of attitudes when proprietary business enterprise is considered? We suspect that this differential pattern of response is largely an artifact of the varying images that students have of business activity itself. The more acculturated individuals, particularly those at senior levels and in the technical schools, are more likely to see business in terms of a large-scale, European-type model, which in fact requires considerable initial investment and appropriate contacts. Other students probably have a model of business activity that corresponds more closely to the stereotype of the small-scale African entrepreneur, whose limited success is contingent more upon his personal shrewdness than upon his financial assets. To be sure, this tentative inference requires further substantiation, but the contrasts upon which it is based are so consistent and of such magnitude that they cannot be attributed to chance variation.

Student Attitudes toward the Use of Money

Although groups of students differ in their ideas of what is important in starting a business, it is quite apparent that adequate financial assets are viewed as the single most important contribution to initial success. This raises the crucial question of what students believe to be the most productive use of financial assets. Clearly, money can be viewed largely as a means to increased current consumption or as capital which can be invested in a variety of productive enterprises. Table 56 shows the pattern of responses when students are asked what major use they would make of a windfall of 1,000,000 francs (approximately 4,000 dollars).

One thing is clear enough: Africans are not likely to dissipate their resources in increased spending on consumer items. The data also confirm previous observations that investment in housing is extraordinarily important.[18] Of course, housing itself can be regarded as a durable consumer item, but about one-quarter of the students who made this choice indicated that they would rent for profit. In general, this reaction reflects a typical West African pattern in which the

TABLE 56. Student Attitudes Concerning the Use of 1,000,000 Francs C.F.A. (Percentages)

USE	MALES	FEMALES	TOTAL
Build a house	41.3	35.9	40.6
Investment in land or agriculture	4.8	1.3	4.4
Investment in commerce or industry	7.1	2.1	6.6
Deposit in savings account	11.3	22.8	12.6
Investment in further education	13.0	6.7	12.3
Discharge of family obligations and gifts	13.6	24.0	14.8
Expenditure on consumer goods	5.2	5.1	5.2
Other	3.4	2.1	3.2
No answer	.3	0.0	.3
Total	100.0	100.0	100.0
	(1,837)	(237)	(2,074)

18. See also *Enquête nutrition, niveau de vie, subdivision de Bongouanou, 1955–1956* (Abidjan: Service de la Statistique, 1958), p. 64, and *Condition de vie de l'enfant africain et délinquance juvénile* (Paris: Centre International de l'Enfance, 1959), pp. 43–44 and 93.

individual wishes to build a house in his home community but may not live in it for a considerable period. The property is frequently rented out until the owner wishes to take up residence himself, often upon retirement. About 10 per cent of the students would favor investment in commercial, industrial, or agricultural activities, just a little less than those who would invest in savings accounts.[19] Investments in further education or discharge of familial obligations also constitute significant categories of response.

In spite of the fact that traditionally women have been more active in trade and commerce in the Ivory Coast, it is clear that educated girls are less risk oriented than are boys.[20] They are more likely to make safe investments in which returns are regular and guaranteed, and they also stress the importance of traditional family obligations. Although the socio-economic background of girls is higher than that of boys, girls are much less interested in pursuing further education; in this case sex is more important than social background in influencing educational aspirations.

In similar fashion the responses of the less acculturated male students tend to resemble those of females in some, but not all, respects. Male lows are a little less oriented to educational investment than male highs (13 per cent against 18 per cent), and they are less likely to invest in commercial, industrial, or agricultural enterprises (6 per cent against 7 per cent). By contrast, they emphasize safe forms of investment in housing or savings accounts (55 per cent against 42 per cent) and, like the girls, attach more importance to the fulfillment of family obligations (17 per cent compared with 10 per cent).

Ethnic background does have a measure of influence on the relative stress placed on different forms of investment, irrespective of social background. The Agni, the group most represented in the secondary school system and historically most affected by European influence, are more likely to favor investment in further education than are either the Kru or the Baoulé. The latter are distinctive in their preference for

19. Actually, the use of savings accounts is very limited, even among the urban population. In 1963 no less than 79 per cent of all savings accounts in one of the major Abidjan banks were held by government employees. Only 10 per cent were held by independent artisans, traders, or farmers, and 11 per cent by wage earners.

20. Although West African women have been important in trade and business, they have also been much more conservative in their methods and less willing to innovate than male traders. See Margaret Katzin, "The Role of the Small Entrepreneur," in Melville J. Herskovits and Mitchell Harwitz, *Economic Transition in Africa* (Evanston: Northwestern University Press, 1964), p. 189.

expenditure on housing, while the Kru are differentiated by a significantly greater emphasis on agricultural, commercial, and industrial investment or savings.

In short, the findings suggest that the less chance a subgroup may have of actually continuing its education, the less emphasis it will place upon educational investment. This is true for girls and in general for male students from the less represented ethnic or socio-economic groups. With the notable exception of the Kru, girls and male students from less acculturated groups tend to be conservative in their perceived use of money and to stress either expenditure on housing, savings accounts, or fulfillment of family obligations. These contrasts in the ways people wish to invest income should not obscure the principal conclusion that students are investment- and not consumption-oriented.

Summary and Conclusions

The prestige and income rankings given to various occupations in the Ivory Coast are not unique to that area. What is remarkable about this kind of investigation, which has been conducted in a number of countries, is the high consistency of the findings. Occupational prestige is very similar in different countries and, furthermore, seems to change little over short time spans.[21] Additionally, in the Ivory Coast there are no differences in the rankings given to occupations by various socio-economic and ethnic subgroups in the student population. This stability of rankings can be explained by the diffusion of Western models into Africa, though it can be argued that, irrespective of Western influence, this picture of stability is likely to appear wherever modern-type systems of social stratification, based largely on occupational criteria, emerge. However, the high correlation between occupational prestige and perceived income makes the Ivory Coast picture somewhat different from that in other areas; more, perhaps, than in many industrialized societies, wealth and prestige are indissolubly linked.

There is, moreover, a general relationship between students' occupational aspirations and the occupational hierarchy, with individual

21. In the case of the United States, for example, a recent article has pointed out that the structure of occupational prestige has been remarkably stable over time. Robert W. Hodge, Paul M. Siegel, and Peter H. Rossi, "Occupational Prestige in the United States, 1925–63," *American Journal of Sociology,* Vol. LXX, No. 3 (November 1964), pp. 286–302.

choices being largely concentrated in the upper sector. What is significant is that occupations such as transport proprietor or cash-crop farmer, which are accorded much lower levels of prestige than of income, are also seldom chosen by students. Their reluctance to enter careers like business or commercial farming, which involve a degree of financial risk and where success is dependent to some extent on innovation, reflects an overall preoccupation with security and stability. This concern is further manifest in preferences for employment in government or in large-scale enterprises and a high level of commitment to urban residence and employment. It is hardly an exaggeration to say that this is also evident in the heavy emphasis placed upon investment in physical property. Perhaps the stress on security is understandable when one considers that most African societies adjusted to the harsh conditions of existence by developing institutions which guaranteed survival rather than the rapid accumulation of wealth.[22] Colonial overrule did little to alter this situation, since it created an attitude of dependency on the part of Africans toward the colonial elite.[23] Even more, it gave rise to the notion that bureaucratic careers were by far the most desirable form of employment and that a stable bureaucracy was the most efficient form of organization. The African was hardly ever presented with the image of the individual entrepreneur.

To be sure, the relative emphasis on security varies with socioeconomic and academic status. We have seen that some groups of students, notably those with more favorable family circumstances and those with higher levels of secondary education, do lay more stress on promotion and income opportunities. They also tend to react less negatively to employment in the private sector and to rank some kinds of business activity more highly than do other students. Further, they are more likely than others to perceive the advantages of investment in industrial or commercial enterprises. On the other hand, this same minority is rather more oriented to urban employment and emphasizes the significance of ascriptive factors in the creation of proprietary business enterprises.

22. To be sure, marked differences in wealth did often exist between sections of the population, but generally such wealth was disbursed among followers and kin. This provided a minimal insurance policy for group survival but did not lead to capital accumulation that could in turn generate more development.

23. Perhaps the greatest evil of colonialism was the state of psychological dependence that it created among Africans vis à vis their colonial masters. See O. Mannoni, *Prospero and Caliban: The Psychology of Colonization* (New York: Frederick A. Praeger, 1964). In many formerly French territories, independence does not seem to have altered this pattern of relationship.

While these variations are consistent, they are not great; entrepreneurial attitudes do not appear to be dominant among the majority of students. In recent years great importance has been attached to the significant role that individual entrepreneurs can play in economic growth. It is possible to argue that even with adequate physical resources and sufficient supplies of skilled manpower, development may not take place without the presence of a small but effective minority of innovators. A good deal of current research has suggested very convincingly that innovators are likely to score very highly in terms of achievement motivation.

It has not been our task here to explore these more fundamental psychological characteristics of individuals, and it could well be that various socio-economic and ethnic groups in the Ivory Coast would show significant differences in levels of achievement motivation. Our present purpose has been rather limited, confined to the examination of a more superficial set of attitudes vis à vis alternative employment opportunities. From this viewpoint students tend to perceive their future in terms of an existing structure of opportunities more than in terms of creating new ones.

Of course, preference for secure bureaucratic employment in the larger towns is a perfectly rational reaction to current conditions in the Ivory Coast. However, this situation creates problems of its own. The drift of the educated into the towns widens the gap between urban and rural areas. The latter lag behind in development, and their people feel they are not receiving a fair share of resources and personnel. Furthermore, the concentration of educated cadres in the public bureaucracy and in the very largest private companies means that some sectors of the economy, notably medium- and small-scale entrepreneurial activities or commercial agriculture, are deprived of adequate supplies of educated manpower. It also implies that the aspirations of individuals to enter careers in the public bureaucracy or large-scale private activities will be frustrated, since opportunities here are limited.

CHAPTER VIII

The Career Patterns of Former Students

OUR ANALYSIS of the occupational attitudes of secondary school students has given us only a partial picture of the articulation between the secondary schools and the social and occupational structure of the contemporary Ivory Coast. So far we have dealt only with the subjective appraisals that students make of occupational opportunities, but we have not seen how educated individuals actually flow into the labor market. This actual relationship between secondary schooling and occupation can be ascertained through two principal modes of investigation. The first is to use national census data, which may provide information on the association between various levels of education and the occupations of the adult population. However, the Ivory Coast, like most African countries, does not have sufficiently good census material to permit this kind of operation.

A second approach is to follow up earlier cohorts of secondary school pupils and attempt to obtain information about their present activities. Such a technique is fraught with considerable difficulties in areas where school records are ill kept or nonexistent, but even a partial picture of the occupational activities of individuals who have already left secondary school would be useful. Therefore, in spite of the problems involved, the present writers decided to undertake such a follow-up study, while recognizing that no adequate representative sample could be obtained.[1]

Biases in the Survey

Initially we decided to confine the investigation to students who had been enrolled in the final year of the various cycles of the secondary system from 1958 to 1962. Actually school records were so inadequate that it was impossible to obtain more than an approximate number of students enrolled in these classes over the five-year period. Not only that, but the incidence of doubling necessarily led to an overcount of the size of the student body during this period. Against this possible source of overestimation must be set the fact that dropouts between the first and second cycle of studies would lead to an underestimate of enrollments. At best the figures can be regarded as only rough estimates (Table 57).

Additionally the only way of contacting ex-students was to obtain their names and addresses from school principals and then try to reach them by means of a mailed-out questionnaire.[2] This procedure is extremely risky in areas where people are not accustomed to responding to such types of inquiry and where postal services leave a good deal to be desired.

Schools differed greatly in the degree to which they were able to provide information about their previous students—a fact explainable in part by a high rate of turnover in administrative personnel, which frequently resulted in inadequate keeping of records. This failure to maintain contact with former students was particularly striking in the *Cours Normaux,* even though the majority of the graduates became teachers and hence should have remained in close contact with their former training institutions. Agricultural schools, which also prepare for rather specific occupations, were able to provide much more ade-

1. A study now in preparation by R. Clignet and M. J. Bowman will give further insights into the relation between education and occupational recruitment in the Ivory Coast. The findings will be based on interviews with a sample of several hundred workers employed by a number of major companies operating in the area.

2. For a copy of the questionnaire used, see Appendix E.

TABLE 57. Representativeness of a Sample of Previous Cohorts of Secondary Pupils

CHARACTERISTICS OF THE SAMPLE	ACADEMIC PUBLIC LONG SCHOOLS		ACADEMIC PRIVATE LONG SCHOOLS		SHORT ACADEMIC SCHOOLS	
	B.E.P.C.	*Baccalaureat*	B.E.P.C.	*Baccalaureat*	*Cours Complémentaries*	*Cours Normaux Publics*
Estimated total enrollment,* 1958–1962	1,970	1,600	295	120	659	800
Number of questionnaires mailed out	340	123	171	0	127	178
Mailed-out questionnaires as a percentage of estimated enrollments	17.0	8.0	58.0	0	19.0	22.0
Number of questionnaires returned	43	21	63	0	40	45
Rate of response to mailed-out questionnaires	12.6	9.9	36.8	. .	30.7	25.3

* Includes independent private candidates and individuals pursuing correspondence courses.

quate information. Private institutions controlled by religious organizations maintained reasonably adequate records, which reflected their continuing interest in the welfare of their ex-students. This interest was also characteristic of the smaller, less established public institutions, such as the new *Cours Complémentaires.* The largest and best established schools, on the other hand, seemed to have great difficulty in keeping any satisfactory form of student records.[3]

In view of the fragmentary and uneven information available, we decided to mail our questionnaires to all students whose name and full address could be obtained. Table 57 illustrates the considerable variation in the sampling ratios for the various types of secondary school. On one hand, it was possible to locate the addresses of over two-thirds of ex-students of the *Lycée Technique* and the agricultural schools. On the other, addresses could be secured for only 17 per cent of former long B.E.P.C. candidates and only 8 per cent of ex-*Baccalaureat* students.

Another source of bias resulted from very uneven rates of return to the mailed-out questionnaires. Once again Table 57 shows that the percentage of responses varied from 64 per cent for ex-students of private *Cours Normaux* down to 9.9 per cent for former *Baccalaureat* candidates in the public schools. Returns were also biased toward later cohorts of students; only one-third of the final responses came from those who had been enrolled in 1960 or earlier, though since that time the system has not grown so rapidly as to account for this underrepresentation. Given all these biases, a total response of 419 cases, or 27 per cent of mail-outs, was surprisingly high.

In spite of the lack of representativeness of the sample, respondents were similar to present students with respect to three major traits. Their sex distribution was almost identical, girls representing slightly more than 10 per cent of the respondents in both cases. Further, there was no difference in the ethnic composition of current students and those in the present sample, or in their socio-economic characteristics; 66 per cent of the former students were the offspring of farmers, as against 65.7 per cent of the current students. At the other end of the scale 15.5 per cent of earlier cohorts had fathers engaged in professional, clerical, or managerial occupations, as against 18.5 per cent of present students. Thus, in spite of the biases apparent in the response,

3. This did not necessarily reflect a lack of desire to do so, but under present circumstances the larger institutions do not have the administrative facilities to maintain adequate contact with former students.

there is reason to believe that as good a sample as possible was obtained under very unsatisfactory field conditions.[4]

A Comparison between Former Students Engaged in the Labor Force and Those Still Undergoing Full-time Education

The 419 cases which comprised the final return included both individuals who had already entered the labor force and others who were still continuing their studies. Since the initial sample was drawn from the available lists of students who were actually enrolled in specific classes from 1958 to 1962, there was no way of knowing how many actually continued their schooling. Of the total number of respondents, 36 per cent were still in school; the remainder were in the labor force.

We have previously noted that opportunities to continue one's education vary considerably with stream and cycle and that some courses are specifically designed to be terminal. This is amply illustrated in Table 58, where it is apparent that the level of persistence in studies is

TABLE 58. Proportion of Former Students Still Continuing Their Education, by Type of Course Previously Attended (Percentages)

PREVIOUS COURSE	PERCENTAGE STILL IN FULL-TIME EDUCATION
3me *Cours Complémentaires*	57.6 (23)
3me *Cours Normaux*	23.1 (24)
3me academic long	45.3 (48)
Baccalaureat classes	95.2 (20)
Centres d'Apprentissage	21.5 (17)
Lycée Technique	42.9 (3)
Agricultural schools	0.0 (—)
Unknown	72.7 (16)
Total	36.0 (151)

4. It should be recognized that other sources of bias in the response could not be controlled. For example, it is possible that former students who responded were those who had been more successful in gaining employment or continuing their studies. Normally, interviews with a random sample of nonrespondents might have indicated possible sources of bias, but this was quite impossible under Ivory Coast conditions.

highly variable, ranging from 95 per cent of those candidates formerly preparing for the *Baccalaureat* down to zero for former students of the agricultural schools. Individuals trained in specifically vocational institutions—technical, teaching, and agricultural—do not often proceed further. It is surprising, however, that a substantial proportion of the former students in the *Cours Complémentaires* are still in school, since this is basically a terminal type of institution. Apart from a few who are actually doubling classes, the majority of these manage to filter into the *Lycée Technique* or the agricultural schools, and some even enter the academic *Lycée*. Thus the *Cours Complémentaires* are not such "closed" institutions as are other schools in the lower secondary system.

Actually two other factors also seem to be systematically related to persistence in further studies. The first of these is ethnicity (Table 59). Here it is quite clear that students from the less acculturated peoples in the central and northern areas do not continue their studies as frequently as do those from such groups as the southern Agni or Lagoon peoples. Part of this variation might be attributed to a relationship between ethnicity and the particular stream or cycle which a student entered. Lack of an adequate number of cases does not enable us to test this proposition directly, but we have pointed out in a previous chapter that the relationship between stream or cycle and ethnic background is loose. In fact, the chances of continuing one's schooling seem to be closely associated with the relative representation of an ethnic group in the *entire* secondary school system. In other words, the higher the selectivity index for an ethnic group (see Chapter III, Table 8), the more likely it is that a higher proportion of that group will continue with its studies.

Undoubtedly part of this variation in persistence can be attributed to differences in socio-economic background. Among the total group of former students who are still continuing their education, just over 23 per cent are the offspring of professional, managerial, and clerical workers, and 37 per cent are the children of farmers. Conversely, of those individuals who are now in full-time employment, only about 11 per cent come from the higher occupational groups, as against 71 per cent who come from farming backgrounds.

We can refine this analysis a little further by removing the possible effect of stream and cycle, which could confuse the relationship between persistence in schooling and socio-economic background. This procedure could be used with former students of the *troisième* aca-

TABLE 59. Persistence in School, by Ethnic Background (Percentages)

PRESENT STATUS	AGNI	LAGOON CLUSTER	BAOULE	MANDEFOU	KRU	MALINKE	SENOUFO-LOBI	AFRICAN FOREIGNERS	TOTAL
Still in school	40.1	40.4	31.1	23.3	41.9	30.3	23.1	51.5	36.0
	(30)	(19)	(28)	(7)	(31)	(10)	(9)	(17)	(151)
In labor force	59.9	59.6	68.9	76.7	58.1	69.7	76.9	48.5	64.0
	(43)	(28)	(62)	(23)	(43)	(23)	(30)	(16)	(268)
Total	100.0	100.0	100.0	100.0	100.0	100.0	100.0	100.0	100.0
	(73)	(47)	(90)	(30)	(74)	(33)	(39)	(33)	(419)

demic long stream, where a sufficient number of cases was distributed in such a manner as to provide an opportunity for further examination. Of students who had been in that class during the period 1958–62, we have seen that over 45 per cent were still studying. Of this latter group 57 per cent came from the largest towns (Abidjan and Bouaké); of the employed group only 37 per cent were from these urban centers. Similarly, 17 per cent of the continuing students were from professional, managerial, and clerical families, as against only 6 per cent of the employed group. These findings, fragmentary though they may be, point to a significant relationship between socio-economic background and persistence in schooling, even where stream and cycle are held constant. However, one must remember that persistence in school is largely a function of achievement in public examinations, and we have no information concerning student academic success in this respect. If these data were available, we might expect a measure of correlation between paternal status and academic results. This would largely explain differential rates of persistence in schooling, since we have seen that aspirations to continue do not vary significantly between various subgroups.

Characteristics of Former Students Who Are Still in School

Although our primary concern in this chapter is to see what kinds of occupations people enter when they finish secondary school, there is considerable value in first observing how students progress from one stage of their studies to another. This provides a longitudinal, if fragmentary, picture which complements the analysis of internal mobility presented in Chapter V. It tends to validate many of our previous observations concerning the aspirations and values of students.

Table 60 shows the considerable attraction and importance of the *Baccalaureat;* almost 38 per cent of all continuing students are preparing for this examination in the *Lycées* and *Ecoles Normales* in spite of the fact that many of them were formerly in streams that are theoretically terminal. It can also be noted that students who had been enrolled in the two cycles of the long academic stream tend to be dispersed more evenly over various types of further schooling than do those in either the *Cours Normaux* or the technical stream. This amplifies our earlier statements concerning the relative diffuseness or specificity of various types of secondary instruction.

No less than 8 per cent of these continuing students are pursuing their education overseas, mostly in technical fields and at the university level. Virtually all of them are in France, and, however limited the size of this sample may be, it does indicate the considerable attraction of metropolitan education. The courses being pursued are usually available in the Ivory Coast itself, but the status conferred by a metropolitan education rather than a local one is still considerable.[5] Quite apart from the specific vocational skills that overseas training provides, study in France carries high prestige. The obverse of this is that training in other overseas countries is of little advantage, because qualifications acquired elsewhere are not recognized in France.[6]

TABLE 60. Present Academic Status, by Level of Previous Studies (Percentages)

PRESENT SCHOOLING (1963)	PREVIOUS SCHOOLING 1958–1962					
	3me Cours Complémentaires	*3me Cours Normaux*	*3me Long*	Technical *	*Baccaiaureat*	Total †
Vocational and technical training ‡	56.5 (13)	20.8 (5)	41.6 (20)	84.1 (17)	15.0 (3)	43.0 (58)
Baccalaureat	34.8 (8)	75.0 (18)	43.8 (21)	0.0 (..)	20.0 (4)	37.8 (51)
University	0.0 (..)	0.0 (..)	8.3 (4)	5.3 (1)	60.0 (12)	12.6 (17)
Other and no answer	8.7 (2)	4.2 (1)	6.3 (3)	10.6 (2)	5.0 (1)	6.6 (9)
Total	100.0 (23)	100.0 (24)	100.0 (48)	100.0 (20)	100.0 (20)	100.0 (135)

* Includes both short and long technical cycles.
† Excludes 16 cases where position in previous school was not clear.
‡ Largely includes programs where the *Baccalaureat* is not required for admission. Such courses include nursing, technical, commercial, and administrative training. However, three cases do involve vocational training at the post-*Baccalaureat* level.

5. See also J. P. N'Diaye, *Enquête sur les étudiants noirs en France,* (Paris: Editions Réalités Africaines, 1962), passim.

6. American qualifications in particular are rarely recognized by the French government. It follows that senior personnel in the Ivory Coast, all of whom have had some training in France, adopt a similar view. Under such conditions Ivory Coast students rarely accept offers to study in other countries if they are given similar opportunities in France.

A further point concerns the high rate of examination failure among certain types of student. Of all individuals enrolled in the *Cours Complémentaires* or the technical schools between 1958 and 1962 who are still studying, no less than 43 per cent had been unable to acquire any further qualification beyond their old primary-school-leaving certificate (C.E.P.). By contrast, in 1963 only 6 per cent of students in the *Cours Normaux* and *Lycées* had not finally gained the qualifications for which they had been preparing in 1958–62. What this signifies is that persistence in studies is not necessarily a sign of progress or advancement in the system. Some students are, in fact, entering other types of course in the hope that they will do better than they have done previously; only about three-quarters of the students have passed any examination during the period under review. In some cases, retardation in studies does occur because of financial difficulties, and about 14 per cent of all continuing students have been obliged, at some time or other, to interrupt their education temporarily and go to work as primary school teachers or as clerks.

Finally, we should expect these students to be quite similar, in their educational and occupational attitudes, to the much larger group of current students whom we have examined in previous chapters. After all, those who are continuing their education are merely another sample of that student body obtained in a different manner, though in some cases they are in classes not represented in the larger group. Regardless of their small numbers, the individuals discussed here do display characteristics identical with those of the larger student body. Their academic and vocational aspirations are just as high and vary internally by present stream and cycle in much the same way. They also show the same preference for public employment in the larger towns, and once again there is a significant relationship between desire for private employment and seniority in the educational system. These findings merely confirm the data available for the larger student body.

Characteristics of Former Students Who Have Entered the Labor Force

We now turn to our main task, to see what really happens to students who are obliged to terminate their secondary studies at one stage or another and take paid employment. Of course, students normally make every effort to continue their education as long as possible, but only 20 per cent of those now employed were able to satisfy this aspiration before going to work.[7] Whether students continue their education a little further or not, the important thing is to learn how many of them finally enter the labor force with some form of secondary qualification. Table 61 shows that about three-quarters of the students left school

TABLE 61. Percentage of Former Students Who Gained a Postprimary Qualification before Entering the Labor Force (Percentages)

TYPE OF SECONDARY SCHOOL ATTENDED	PERCENTAGE GAINING A FORMAL POSTPRIMARY QUALIFICATION
3me academic long	75.4 (43)
3me *Cours Complémentaires*	82.4 (14)
3me *Cours Normaux*	76.6 (59)
Centres d'Apprentissage	61.5 (40)
Agricultural schools	95.0 (38)
Total	75.8 (194)

with one sort of secondary school certificate or another. The rate of final success in the academic system does not vary much from this average, but it is distinctly higher among individuals from agricultural schools and markedly lower among those from the *Centres d'Apprentissage*. The situation among the latter group of students needs further comment. First, we have seen in previous pages that C.A.P. candidates are often dropouts from academic institutions, and it is here evident that some cannot even meet the standards of the vocational system. Further, the requirements of the C.A.P. examination are quite rigorous, since its practical sections are supervised by representatives of private industrial or commercial firms, who are understandably reluctant to award diplomas to weak candidates when occupational opportunities are limited.

Having obtained some qualification or other, the majority of students are absorbed into the public sector when they leave school. No less than 71 per cent of all former students now in the labor force are

7. Students from the vocational and agricultural schools rarely continue their education by transferring into the academic stream. Less than 5 per cent of them did this; the majority merely continue to add to their present qualifications in their former area of study.

employed by the government. A further 11 per cent are working with missions, usually as primary school teachers, while only 5 per cent have been hired by private firms. Even among clerical and technical personnel trained in the *Centres d'Apprentissage,* the figure rises only to 25 per cent. Such a massive concentration of workers in the public sector reflects the pattern of preferences for such employment to which we have earlier drawn attention. This has some consequences for private companies which support the *Centres d'Apprentissage* through a compulsory tax.[8] The original rationale for the tax was to provide skilled labor for the private sector, yet firms are obviously not in a position to profit from their compulsory contribution. In effect, private industry is indirectly subsidizing the government's recruitment of personnel.

Let us now see what kinds of careers students enter. Table 62 shows that primary school teaching absorbs the largest proportion of secondary school graduates.[9] This percentage corresponds closely to the expectations of the 1963 classes. We must add, however, that the lower rates of return from students who were in the academic streams in 1958–62 pull down the percentage of those who are in teaching or clerical work. Conversely, the higher rate of returns from former agricultural students inflates the percentage of persons in agriculture; the actual figure is certainly lower than this.

Granted these limitations, the table still shows differentials in the tightness of fit between educational and occupational experience. The agricultural schools and *Cours Normaux* are closely related to specific occupations, and the overwhelming bulk of their students enter the careers for which they have been prepared. Here employment is predetermined and automatic, since the government is both the instructor and the employer. The other vocational training programs which lead to the C.A.P. may provide specific skills, but they do not guarantee automatic employment. Thus at least 30 per cent of the students from these institutions are not in the occupational "slot" for which they have been trained. Furthermore, over one-fifth of them are unemployed.[10] Many of these persons are competing for jobs with

8. This tax is computed on the basis of the total annual wage bill of private companies.

9. The teaching profession is the major employer of educated personnel in all developing areas. In the course of development, however, the proportion of educated individuals absorbed into the teaching force should decline as new opportunities present themselves.

10. This conclusion is confirmed by earlier data gathered by the Manpower

TABLE 62. Occupational Destinations of Former Students, by Type of School Previously Attended (Percentages)

PRESENT OCCUPATION	TYPE OF SCHOOL PREVIOUSLY ATTENDED					
	3me Academic Long	3me *Cours Complémentaires*	3me *Cours Normaux*	*Centres d'Apprentissage*	Agricultural Schools	Total
Clerical	10.5	17.6	1.3	20.0	2.5	9.4
Industrial	7.0	0.0	0.0	26.2	0.0	8.2
Teaching	56.1	70.6	88.3	9.2	0.0	46.1
Agriculture *	5.3	0.0	2.6	4.6	95.0	18.0
Military service †	7.0	0.0	2.6	13.8	2.5	6.3
Miscellaneous	5.3	5.9	0.0	4.6	0.0	2.7
Unemployed	8.8	5.9	5.2	21.5	0.0	9.3
Total	100.0	100.0	100.0	99.9	100.0	100.0
	(57)	(17)	(77)	(65)	(40)	(256)

* All individuals in this category are agricultural demonstrators or technicians working for the administration. None is a farmer.
† These individuals have been compulsorily drafted into military service.

graduates of the long academic stream, who are well placed and a large number of whom are employed in teaching, clerical work, and even agriculture and industry. Very few of them are jobless.

This raises the whole question of the relative merits of specific vocational training as against general academic instruction. In recent years there has been a tendency to stress the importance of vocational education and to suggest that unemployment is higher among graduates of the academic schools because of their lack of specific skills. Our limited data would suggest that people holding this view may be mistaken. The person with a general education seems to be more flexible and finds employment in a wider range of occupations, even when he has not been specifically trained for them. The vocationally trained individual is more likely to have trouble getting a job unless his employment is already guaranteed, as in the case of graduates of the *Cours Normaux* or agricultural schools.

The very nature of the vocational student's education makes it difficult for him to move easily into those sectors of the labor market that offer the greatest opportunities. There is often a time gap between changes in the structure of that market and corresponding adjustments in the offerings of the *Centres d'Apprentissage*. These institutions are just as liable to inertia as any other schools in the educational system and often turn out persons trained in skills for which there is no demand. An example of this occurred recently in the Ivory Coast. In spite of warnings given by the employment service of the Ministry of Labor in December 1962 that the building industry could no longer absorb additional trained labor, the *Centres d'Apprentissage* still continued to produce masons, carpenters, and other skilled construction workers through 1963.[11] Further, it is difficult for vocational schools not only to adjust to variations of demand by the labor market but also to alter their curriculum content to meet the specific needs of local industry. The program of studies is largely metropolitan in nature and

---

Office of the Ivory Coast government and obtained through a survey of former pupils of the *Centres d'Apprentissage* who had entered the labor force between 1955 and 1960. Of 112 respondents, almost 45 per cent were not employed in the occupation for which they had been trained, while a further 12 per cent were unemployed.

11. Letter from the director of the Manpower Office to the director of Technical Education (December 3, 1962). It can be argued that a reserve of skilled manpower is essential to meet a nation's future needs even if current demand is limited. However, this is no great consolation to the graduates of vocational training centers. It can also be questioned whether a specifically trained reserve group is preferable to a group possessing more general skills.

is either below or above the level of the technological training required by Ivory Coast conditions.[12]

Thus the *Centres d'Apprentissage* furnish a substantial proportion of the unemployed, who constitute 9 per cent of the total group in the labor force. Such a proportion seems rather high in view of the somewhat advanced training of the respondents. To be sure, this figure does not necessarily represent a pocket of chronic unemployment, since some unemployed persons are in the process of changing jobs and others have only recently entered the labor market. Nevertheless it suggests that students from these schools do have problems in gaining immediate employment. Just over 3 per cent of the individuals who left school in the period from 1958 to 1960 have never had jobs, and the proportion rises to 11 per cent among students who finished their education in 1961 and 1962.[13]

If we include persons who have never been employed and also those who have held jobs but are at present unemployed, there is a tendency for aggregate unemployment to diminish over time. Five per cent of the students who left school before 1961 were out of work in 1963, as against 11 per cent of the 1961 and 1962 cohorts. These figures imply that although individuals are ultimately absorbed into the labor force, they do have trouble entering it.

This conclusion is amply supported by the responses of the former students themselves. Whereas the majority found suitable employment easily, a little under 40 per cent indicated that they had had some or a great deal of difficulty getting a job (Table 63). As we might expect, the proportion of individuals experiencing such difficulty is considerably lower among the graduates of agricultural schools and the *Cours Normaux,* which virtually guarantee employ-

12. Some of the older business firms in the Ivory Coast have been reluctant to utilize new techniques and continue to rely on a supply of relatively unskilled manpower. The rudimentary nature of their technology implies that graduates of the vocational centers are overtrained and possess skills inappropriate to the needs of these companies. By contrast, some of the newest firms have invested heavily in advanced technology, which makes them far less dependent on local manpower. Not only are their demands quantitatively limited, but the *Centres d'Apprentissage* do not produce workers who meet their qualitative requirements.

13. It is very common in West Africa for students to take a "rest" after the completion of their studies before beginning an active search for employment. This normally lasts about three months. However, the 11 per cent of students who left school in 1961 and 1962 and never got jobs have been without work for at least one year.

ment for their students. Conversely, the figure is distinctly higher among persons from the *Centres d'Apprentissage.*

Another indication of the problem of adjustment to the labor market is provided by the rates of job turnover among former students. Frequent changes of occupation or employer can be associated with a rapidly expanding economy where new opportunities lead to a highly mobile labor force; they can also reflect a dissatisfaction with existing prospects, even when alternative opportunities are limited. This latter

TABLE 63. Percentage of Former Students Who Indicated Difficulty in Obtaining Suitable Employment, by Type of School Previously Attended

PREVIOUS TYPE OF SCHOOL	PERCENTAGE INDICATING DIFFICULTY
3me academic long	43.9 (25)
3me Cours Complémentaires	47.1 (8)
3me Cours Normaux	24.7 (19)
Centres d'Apprentissage	55.3 (36)
Agricultural schools	30.0 (12)
Total	39.1 (100)

situation is likely to prevail in the Ivory Coast, where the number of secondary school graduates has been increasing more rapidly than have aggregate job opportunities. Later cohorts of school-leavers find that the occupational "plums" have already been preempted by the earlier groups. They find it harder to get jobs, as we have seen, and their rate of job turnover is actually higher; over 11 per cent of students in the classes of 1961 and 1962 have held more than one position, as against only 6 per cent of those who left school before 1961. This in itself is not a direct indication of dissatisfaction, but limited evidence suggests that the dissatisfaction does indeed exist. In fact, 42 per cent of later cohorts, as against 33 per cent of the earlier group, indicate that they are dissatisfied with their present occupation. We do not wish to insist on the validity of these findings, since they are based on a very limited sample, but at least the direction of the differences would support our tentative argument that higher turnover of later cohorts is associated with increased job dissatisfaction.

Almost 40 per cent of all school-leavers are generally dissatisfied with their current employment. The level of dissatisfaction varies significantly among different educational groups. It is lowest among workers from agricultural schools and the *Cours Normaux* but significantly higher among those from other types of institution. The level of satisfaction also varies between occupational groups. Clerical workers appear the least happy; over half of them say they are dissatisfied.

Of course, we should expect occupational dissatisfaction to be related in some degree to a desire to change one's present job. This is, in a measure, borne out in Table 64, which shows that teachers and agricultural demonstrators are less eager to leave their present jobs than are clerical workers.

The kinds of alternative jobs that workers would prefer to enter are listed in Table 65. Here, paradoxically, in spite of the fact that clerical

TABLE 64. Percentage of Former Students Who Wish to Change Their Present Occupation, by Current Type of Employment

CURRENT TYPE OF EMPLOYMENT	PERCENTAGE WISHING TO CHANGE
Clerical	66.7 (18)
Industrial	43.5 (10)
Teaching	34.5 (41)
Agriculture	29.8 (14)
Miscellaneous	0.0 (..)
Total	37.1 (83)

TABLE 65. Preferences of Workers Expressing a Wish to Change Their Current Occupation (Percentages)

PREFERENCES	PERCENTAGE	
Clerical	31.3	(26)
Industrial	13.3	(11)
Teaching	10.8	(9)
Agricultural	12.0	(10)
Nursing and medical technology	8.4	(7)
Other	16.9	(14)
Further schooling	7.2	(6)
Total	99.9	(83)

employment is associated with a high level of dissatisfaction, it is most in demand as an alternative. This is largely because workers in other fields tend to exaggerate the benefits of clerical employment and at the same time to desire higher types of job within this category than are actually held by any clerical workers in the sample.[14]

We can now go a little further and discover what principal factors apparently affect the general level of job satisfaction or dissatisfaction.[15] The most important single element influencing general job satisfaction is congenial relationships with fellow workers—a factor stressed by 27 per cent of the employees. Just over 23 per cent emphasized stability and security, and 17 per cent underscored the social prestige of the occupation itself. On the other hand, pay and promotion opportunities were hardly mentioned as causes for satisfaction. By contrast, in listing principal reasons for dissatisfaction with current employment, over 37 per cent of the workers mentioned the difficulty of the job as a major source of discontent; another 23 per cent stressed low pay; and a further 16 per cent, the distance of the place of work from their home community.

It is apparent that current workers are rather similar to students in their emphasis upon the importance of stability, occupational prestige, and congenial working conditions. To be sure, the groups differ in their rank-ordering of items, but both attach little importance to pay or promotion as a source of job satisfaction. Workers do regard inadequate pay as a substantial reason for discontent, but this item is considerably less significant than job difficulty. The almost total indifference to promotion opportunities is most striking; only 4 per cent of all workers mention this as a factor influencing either satisfaction or dissatisfaction with the job.

Of course, employees might be expected to give some emphasis to inadequate pay as a source of discontent, but in reality there is little variation in levels of income between different occupational subgroups. The mean salary for all workers is 27,000 francs C.F.A. per

14. Clerical workers in the sample are confined for the most part to routine duties such as typing and bookkeeping. However, those respondents choosing clerical employment are really looking for skilled clerical posts, such as head clerk, comptometer operator, or, in other words, posts carrying greater responsibility.

15. Our conclusions are derived from only 108 responses in this case, owing to a high rate of inadequate responses. Employees were asked to indicate the most important *single* cause of satisfaction or dissatisfaction with their job, but a substantial number made multiple responses. These were eliminated from the final count.

month, but this drops to 24,000 francs for clerical and industrial workers and rises to more than 28,000 francs for teachers and agricultural demonstrators.[16] Additionally, there is no systematic relationship between monthly income and occupational dissatisfaction.[17]

Even if chances for promotion are not assigned much importance by the responding employees, it is interesting to see what they believe to be the crucial determinants of job success. We can then compare these responses with those of current students in order to ascertain how far individual attitudes appear to be modified by actual job experience.[18] We appreciate that the employees' responses are small in number and must be accepted with reservations; still, they diverge from students' answers in a significant and understandable manner. We expected that the workers would tend to emphasize seniority and social contacts more than the students do, since the workers have had experience with the realities of bureaucratic employment in the Ivory Coast. Table 66

TABLE 66. Factors Considered Important in Occupational Success (Percentages)

FACTOR	CURRENT STUDENTS (1963)	CURRENT * EMPLOYEES
Job proficiency and hard work	66.9	36.0
Intelligence and a good education	22.9	42.4
Age and seniority on the job	4.1	10.4
Social skills and personal contacts	5.0	11.2
No answer	1.1	0.0
Total	100.0	100.0
	(2,074)	(125)

* Only 125 cases have been included from employee returns. This is due to the high percentage of responses that were spoiled because of failure to follow instructions. Respondents gave multiple answers where only one was required.

16. At an exchange rate of 245 francs C.F.A. to the dollar, average income equals $110 per month. Mean incomes for the different occupational groups thus vary between $97 and $114.

17. Employees were divided into two segments: those with incomes above and those with incomes below the median. There was no significant difference in levels of expressed satisfaction between the two groups.

18. A truly systematic study of the impact of job experience upon occupational attitudes would necessarily involve careful longitudinal studies of selected groups of individuals. In the present case this was not possible, but it is reasonable to assume that the two groups compared are quite similar in terms of significant characteristics.

bears out this expectation. It also shows that the workers attach much less importance to job proficiency than do the students—a fact not so clearly foreseen. It could be suggested on an *ex post facto* basis that if employees deemphasize hard work and job proficiency it is because they have learned that in the bureaucratic situation actual achievement receives less than a fair measure of recognition.[19] Their greater emphasis upon intelligence and education reflects the fact that promotion is more likely to depend on the acquisition of additional formal qualifications. There is little doubt that regulations governing promotion in the public service are largely concerned with such qualifications rather than with effectiveness on the job. Promotion occurs as a series of steps; to move from one level to another the employee must acquire further "pieces of paper."

For this reason it is not surprising that many workers make an effort to continue their education after entering the labor force. About half of the employed respondents are pursuing part-time courses, successful completion of which may enable them to enter a higher category of employment.[20] Of this group a little less than half are financed by their employers; the rest are paying their own educational costs. Whether individuals have a chance for further education at their employers' expense appears to be determined by their occupation. Teachers are probably the best served of any occupational group; 44 per cent of them are undergoing further part-time instruction under government auspices. Just over one-quarter of clerical workers receive similar assistance from their employers. By contrast, only 4 per cent of industrial workers and 6 per cent of agricultural demonstrators receive such aid. Persons in these two latter groups, however, compensate for the lack of employer support by paying for their own part-time studies; well over one-third of them are doing so. The number of individuals who are continuing their training in one way or another is impressive —evidence of the extreme importance of formal qualifications as a condition for occupational advancement in the Ivory Coast.

Does the extent to which employees are eager to continue their part-time studies indicate that the schools have failed to equip students for

19. Particularly in the bureaucracies of the former colonial territories, it becomes difficult to make adequate assessments of job proficiency. It is far easier to judge a person in terms of his formal qualifications, even though his performance may be mediocre.

20. It should not be necessary to point out that this group of individuals pursuing part-time education was not included in earlier tables concerning students still continuing their education.

the kind of life they will lead after completing their formal education? Of course, it is idle to expect any school to prepare students fully for their working life, but just over three-quarters of workers felt that their schools could have done a better job of enabling them to adjust to the realities of their postacademic careers.

Employees were given an opportunity to explain what they perceived to be the major shortcomings of their schooling.[21] A substantial proportion of responses, amounting to 18 per cent, were largely concerned with inadequacies in the internal organization of the schools themselves. This general heading included miscellaneous complaints about financial difficulties, overcrowding, and inefficient teaching. However, responses in this category were not related to the shortcomings of the schools in terms of their impact on the student's future career. Furthermore, over 34 per cent of all responses were concerned with the lack of opportunity to continue full-time schooling, and there was a general reaction among former students that, in some way or other, they had been cheated of their rightful opportunities for further study.[22]

More relevant to the vocational question were the other categories of response. Just over one-fifth of respondents complained of the rigidity of the secondary school structure, which did not permit individuals to move freely in the system according to their vocational inclinations. Further, these answers stressed that the schools provided inadequate vocational information—a shortcoming that led some persons to observe that adequate guidance could have prevented their training for work not in demand by the labor market. As one former student put it: [23]

Il s'agissait tout simplement que des professeurs bien experimentés, connaissent bien leurs élèves et leurs capacités, nous guident et nous orientent.

21. Former students were encouraged to write short essay-type answers discussing their attitudes toward their former school experience. These responses were then subjected to a content analysis. Over three-quarters of all respondents indicated that they felt their schools could have done a better job to prepare them for their present life, and a little over half of these made extended comments. In this case the distribution of responses has been made on the basis of individual comments, and the percentages include multiple responses.

22. There was little recognition by former students that their academic records had anything to do with the cessation of their studies. Rather, most of them indicated that it was the obligation of government to provide each individual with as much education as he personally wanted.

23. We retain the following quotations in their original form, if only to indicate the inadequate command of the language exhibited by students.

J'ai perdu mon temps après le B.E.P.C., ne sachant au juste quelle branches choisir. Beaucoup de camarades sont restés comme moi et nous n'avons obtenu qu'échecs.

(We need teachers who are well trained and know their way around, so that they can provide us with adequate guidance and counseling. I have wasted a good deal of time after graduating from the B.E.P.C. class because I did not know what to do. A lot of my classmates were in the same situation and have experienced failure after failure.)

Another 20 per cent of responses were specifically concerned with the inadequacies of the curricula of the schools themselves. However, these comments were of two kinds. Either students were concerned with lack of direct preparation for particular careers or, less frequently, they emphasized the overspecialization of certain forms of vocational curriculum. To give a typical example of the former type of comment: [24]

Après le B.E.P.C., les bonnes soeurs savaient que toutes celles qui ont signé un engagement doivent enseigner aussitôt après le B.E.P.C. Et elles ne nous ont pas fait une seule fois un cours de pédagogie.

(The nuns did not ignore the fact that we were under obligation to teach after having obtained our B.E.P.C. Yet they did not teach us one single hour of pedagogy.)

Alternatively, an individual who had achieved an intermediate position in the agricultural administration noted: [25]

Il y avait certaines lacunes dans le programme de l'école que j'ai quitté au dernier moment: prédominance de l'enseignement technique (agronomie) au détriment des cours de droit, d'économie, et de philosophie.

(There were some gaps in the curriculum of the school from which I graduated. We got too many hours of agronomy and not enough hours of law, economy, and philosophy.)

A final category of responses, amounting to some 6 per cent of all cases, displayed an extremely disenchanted attitude concerning the supposed vocational rewards of schooling. Persons within this category expressed grave doubts that their education had led them anywhere or provided them with any real form of opportunity. One

24. This does not constitute any criticism of the institutions run by religious bodies. The same comments were forthcoming from the former students of public institutions.

25. This employee held a high-level post in one of the ministries, a post that required qualities rather broader than those a highly specific agricultural training might develop.

individual, at present unemployed, who had completed his C.A.P. qualification as a skilled artisan, observed:

Même tu es beau instruit que tu es sans emploi, tu n'es rien du tout . . . je parcours dans toutes les entreprises administratives aussi que dans les privés, on me refuse; même dans tous les bureaux. Je voudrais savoir pourquoi nous delivre-t-on le diplôme donc!

(However you are educated, you are bound to be unemployed and to remain a bum. I spend all day long visiting public and private employers, and they tell me that there is no job for me. I would like to know why we are permitted to graduate under these conditions.)

What is significant in this comment, as in so many others, is the misguided belief that possession of a formal qualification automatically guarantees employment. In other words, it is assumed that the nexus between the school and the labor market is complete, and the higher the diploma, the better the available post. Of course, this is a distorted view of what really happens, and it is clear that in more recent years there is less likelihood of fairly automatic employment for secondary school graduates than during the earlier colonial period.[26]

Summary and Conclusions

We feel obliged to repeat that the data presented in this chapter are fragmentary and partial and can be regarded as only suggestive of certain trends. A more adequate study would have involved the mobilization of research resources quite beyond those available to us. Nonetheless we must point out the extreme importance of careful follow-up studies of school-leavers in the new African nations, so as to provide systematic empirical material which will assist educational planners. At present much so-called educational planning is based upon completely inadequate data on the articulation between educational systems and the occupational structure. What we have described here is no more than a tentative effort in this direction. At the

26. Earlier colonial administrators made every effort to ensure that the schools turned out individuals with specific skills who could be employed immediately in the tasks for which they had been trained. See Eugène Guernier, *Civilisations et doctrines d'enseignement* (Paris: Librarie Felix Alcan, 1936), p. 37, and the comments of Albert Charton, former Inspector General of Education in French West Africa, in W. Bryant Mumford, *Africans Learn to be French* (London: Evans Brothers, n.d.), p. 113.

same time we have attempted to point out some of the possible sources of error that can arise from the interpretation of our materials.

In earlier chapters we have drawn attention to the great desire of secondary school students to continue their education, a desire only slightly modified by social background. However, their actual expectations of continuing are sharply influenced by socio-economic and ethnic affiliations as well as by the stream or cycle of studies they have followed. The present chapter has provided supplementary material which indicates that educational careers are in fact influenced by such variables. How does this relate to our earlier remarks that social and ethnic background is not a good predictor of the particular stream or cycle a person will enter? Certainly the total picture of the present student body shows little difference in the social composition of the population at various stages of secondary education. Yet our data suggest that the individual who drops out of the system is likely to come from certain less acculturated ethnic groups and from an inferior social background. This conclusion, however, is based on very limited materials and, furthermore, the two sets of students have been drawn from different cohorts. Thus it might be argued either that the social composition of the two groups is very different or, that the greater size of the system in 1963 has diminished the significance of social factors influencing selectivity. We are in no position to make a judgment on these points.

Turning to the labor market itself, one can see the overwhelming importance of public employment, which absorbs the majority of the graduates of secondary schools. No wonder the classes of 1963 show such a massive predilection for government service! Yet the demands of government and private industry, taken together, are not unlimited. To be sure, teachers in particular (as in most developing areas) have no trouble getting employment, but this is not true of all job seekers. Some have been unable to find jobs, and some have difficulty adjusting to the labor market. So it is not surprising that students still in school attach considerable importance to security of employment and that employees themselves emphasize it as a crucial factor in job satisfaction.

The persons who seem to have the greatest difficulty in finding or holding a job are those from the *Centres d'Apprentissage*. This raises the whole question of the relative utility of specific vocational training as against more general education. After all, former students from the academic system are more fortunate than their vocationally trained counterparts; they usually find employment, even if they are not too satisfied with it. Hence it is disturbing that so much current commentary on education in the new African states tends to underestimate the value of an academic or general education and sees vocational training as a kind of panacea. This may be reasonable so long as jobs are guaranteed; certainly there is no problem with teachers and agricultural demonstrators. There is a very real problem, however, when it is impossible to estimate with any accuracy what the demand for other types of skilled workers will be. Highly specific training *in the schools* may make it more difficult for an individual to adapt to the changing conditions of the labor market. We would go so far as to say that employers would prefer generally educated personnel who are flexible and can be trained to meet requirements on the job rather than persons whose education is too specific to facilitate flexibility and whose general educational background is deficient.[27]

Individuals who have trouble finding employment or whose present work conditions are unsatisfactory tend to regard further full-time education as a solution to their problems. There is some truth in this assumption, since employment in the public sector does place a premium on formal qualifications. However, in no society is the relationship between education and occupation so tight that individuals are justified in seeing education as an automatic guarantee of occupational success. In essence, educated persons still attach far too much importance to the schooling they have received.

27. By stressing the value of a general education we do not imply that students should read more Racine and Corneille, but that at present their education does not provide them with an adequate mastery of French, mathematics, and general science.

CHAPTER IX

Some Concluding Observations

PERHAPS OF ALL "IMPORTED" INSTITUTIONS in contemporary Africa the school has struck the deepest roots. To be sure, in many areas people were suspicious of the early efforts of missions and government to create a minimal system of formal education and were reluctant to send their children to school. Even today in parts of Africa the school is regarded as an alien institution. Yet this attitude is rapidly disappearing. One of the most striking features of the last decade has been the growth of a mass demand for education, which has often far outstripped the ability of governments or voluntary agencies to supply it. It is on the school that the mass of the African peoples place their highest hopes and aspirations for their children. It is also on the school that African governments rely in great measure for the rapid spread of modernization and accelerated economic growth.

Unfortunately this African preoccupation with education has not led to any substantial volume of scholarly research on how the schools actually function in Africa and what part they are playing in development. Perhaps more is known about traditional lineage organization in Africa than about an institution which is playing a major role in the transformation of African societies.

Current studies of African education frequently attempt to examine quantitatively how groups in different parts of the educational system can be adjusted to meet expected demands for skilled personnel on the basis of current manpower estimates. Whether available data are adequate for the purpose of making reasonable forecasts is beyond the scope of our present discussion. We may note, however, that most estimates are likely to be wildly inaccurate, even if African governments were in any position to carry out the planning required. Further, this approach leads to a greatly oversimplified view of the relationship between the occupational structures of African nations and their educational systems. If the schools are to assume the major responsibility for training skilled individuals, there is still a general reluctance to realize what this type of planning involves on the part of the state: far greater control of the quantity and content of schooling and far greater power in the direction of labor than any African government is likely to be able to have at its disposal. Even within total-command economies, the adaptation of educational systems to government-defined economic priorities has been extremely difficult, and no present African regime is so stable that it can directly bend the schools to its immediate purposes. Educational development in Africa has an autonomous quality, and any government which attempts direct qualitative and quantitative control of the schools may well find itself in conflict with the aspirations of the mass of the population. The plain fact is that although educational systems continue to grow very rapidly, the numerous plans made for the transformation of the schools have been largely ineffective.

A second focus of current controversy concerns the question of the Africanization of schools and their adaptation to African cultural traditions and society. One has an intuitive sympathy for some of these views, stemming as they do from the present climate of African nationalism and an understandable desire for that cultural self-respect which colonialism did much to erode. Yet an air of unreality and a peculiar mixture of sense and nonsense attend the whole discussion. Few persons would deny the need for the Africanization of schools in the sense that curricula should contain more African content. Indeed it would be desirable for those Africans who have been actively demanding Africanization of content to bend their immediate efforts to the development of new curricula and the preparation of new texts. Unfortunately most books ostensibly prepared to conform to African requirements are still written by Europeans.

However, the implications of the Africanization controversy go far deeper than this, and at bottom there is a vague notion that somehow the schools can be wholly integrated with African culture. This is a delusion which avoids the basic issue: If modernization and economic development are major goals, then a price will have to be paid in the destruction of certain cherished cultural traditions. The school in Africa is inevitably an agent of change. Through its role as a creator of new elites, through its diffusion of new ideas and skills, through its increasingly important function as a criterion of economic and social status, it inevitably erodes the foundations of traditional society and culture. Schools in Africa can never become agencies of simple cultural transmission facilitating consensus and stability, whether the content of instruction is African or European. In this sense the whole issue of adaptation is spurious. Even if one were sure what the term "adaptation" really means (and this point is rarely raised explicitly), it would be equally clear that in any changing society an educational system might be adapted to one institutional complex but not to another.

What we suggest here is that this kind of controversy tends to overlook the real educational issues confronting the new states. In colloquial terms, the school has come to stay, and its curricula will remain primarily Western. Our task is to see how it actually operates and what are its functional relationships with other aspects of the contemporary social and economic order of the African states. For example, only systematic studies of African educational systems and their clientele can enable us to avoid both the oversimplified approach of the manpower planner and the rather more diffuse and prescriptive statements of the educational ideologues. We can now turn to examine the implications of the findings of this study for both further research and planning.

Secondary Education and Social Mobility

Few observers of the African scene have failed to notice the extraordinarily humble origin of many contemporary leaders in politics and other realms of behavior. In reading the biographies of many of these individuals, one notes that the local mission or government school seems to have played a salient part in facilitating their upward mobility. Further, in those areas where adequate primary schooling is available, entry to secondary school is often crucial to later success.

Of course, all this does not imply that aggregate rates of mobility in African societies are high; quite the reverse is true. Only a tiny proportion of individuals will achieve any degree of upward mobility in view of the relatively small number of places available at the top and middle levels of the occupational structure. In many African nations contemporary economic growth has been relatively slow, with the result that occupational opportunities are limited—apart from those generated by the Africanization of formerly European-held positions (a feature not so evident in the Ivory Coast). Yet despite limited occupational outlets and the small size of the secondary school systems in most African countries, present-day elites are drawn from a very broad base. It can never be argued that they are self-recruiting and that their membership is restricted to a predetermined group.

In earlier chapters we have attempted to show that, in the Ivory Coast at least, the secondary schools have been extremely effective in facilitating occupational mobility and potential elite membership. Of course, studies of this nature are always subject to two kinds of interpretation, depending on the "ideological stance" of the investigator. Initially one can argue in terms of the *relative* chances that different subgroups within the population will have of entering secondary school. In this case it can be said that patterns of inequality are very marked in the Ivory Coast. A southern Agni is about ten times more likely to enter some form of secondary education than a northern Senoufo. The chances of the child of a managerial or clerical worker are about eleven times greater than those of the offspring of a farmer. Those of boys and girls in the great towns of Abidjan or Bouaké are three times greater than those of children in small communities.

Thus one can build up a picture of glaring inequality of opportunity, much of which has resulted from earlier patterns of colonial penetration and development. This is quite apart from the question of sex differentials and the fact that among girls inequalities are even more marked. Yet we would argue that anyone concerned with the role that schools play in facilitating mobility is misled by this kind of analysis. For it is evident that in *absolute* terms, recruitment patterns are still extremely open. Of Ivory Coast secondary school students (excluding African foreigners), almost 70 per cent do not come from the more advanced Agni and Lagoon peoples, over two-thirds are the children of farmers, and well over one-half come from the smallest towns and villages.

Further, the influence of ethnic and social background actually tends to diminish as students move up through the educational system. We had expected (in view of much Western evidence) that there would be differences in the ethnic and social composition of the student body at the *troisième* and *Baccalaureat* levels, while the different streams in the system would cater to distinctive clienteles. But though slight variations are apparent they are not large enough to be significant for processes of elite recruitment.

Indeed internal movement of students between cycles and streams within the system seems generally to smooth out differentials. The doubling of classes, with consequent downward mobility, more characteristic of students with superior social backgrounds, enables others to remain within sectors higher in prestige. To be sure, cross-sectional studies like the present one have severe limitations. Inclusion of students within *sixième* classes would have given a clearer picture, while a longitudinal investigation would have shown whether dropping out of the system is significantly associated with ethnic and social background.

Notwithstanding these deficiencies, one major finding concerning recruitment is that the characteristics of students in different levels and streams do not vary greatly. Once within the system, the rural farm child's chances of entering the higher prestige streams are not overwhelmingly different from those of his urban counterpart with a superior social background.

All this, of course, applies to only about 2 per cent of Ivory Coast children, the proportion who enter secondary school. But it suggests that openness of access and allocation is possible even when the size of the secondary school system is very small. Therefore our rejoinder to those critics who have so vociferously condemned French-type systems as "elitist" in orientation is that they are sometimes equivocal in their use of the term "elitist." If they imply that schools actually check mobility and confine secondary education to a socially exclusive minority, then this contention is totally untrue. On the other hand, if they imply that only a relatively small proportion of the child population enters secondary school, then they are obviously right. Quite clearly, even where African leadership is genuinely committed to the mass diffusion of education at the primary and secondary level, sheer limitation of financial and teaching resources makes any short-run expansion of secondary education very difficult.

In view of the peaked nature of the occupational structure of the Ivory Coast, it follows that only very few Africans will achieve elite status or enter high-level occupations; the important thing is that access to these positions remains relatively open. We would argue that the crucial issue in the new African states is not whether the number of persons occupying high- and middle-level occupations remains small, but whether people perceive that they or their offspring have some chance of gaining such positions. Men may be prepared to accept glaring economic and social inequalities so long as they believe that the existing arrangement is "just" or that they have an opportunity to improve their lot. Indeed it might be suggested that a significant difference between Western societies and contemporary Africa is that in some Western nations the "lower orders," until very recently, accepted their subordinate status. In Africa relative deprivation will be tolerable only if there is a visible chance for mobility.

The schools have certainly provided such opportunity. Will they continue to do so? Will the doors to secondary schools remain open and opportunities increase, or will places become increasingly monopolized by the offspring of existing elites?

This touches upon a more fundamental question: What kinds of social structure are emerging in contemporary Africa? It is almost inevitable that income, education, and occupation should become increasingly important as determinants of individual status. Does this imply the gradual emergence of social classes as we of the West understand this term? Some observers (including many Africans) have suggested that the persistence of lineage and affinal ties, which tend to cut across potential lines of stratification, has militated against the emergence of class subcultures. The resulting open and fluid society is reflected in patterns of recruitment into secondary education and in a relatively weak association between students' attitudes and values and their socio-economic background. In other words, objective inequalities in wealth, status, and education have so far not been paralleled by marked cultural differentiation along class lines.

Alternatively, the fluid character of contemporary African societies may be perceived as transitional. One might therefore expect increased social differentiation, with a corresponding emergence of rigid horizontal strata. This trend, it can be argued, will be particularly marked if rates of economic growth and the consequent expansion of opportunities are low. Under these circumstances existing elites will attempt to perpetuate themselves while at the same time cultural differences between the higher occupational groups and the mass of the people will become sharper. This development will be correlated with a corresponding deemphasis of lineage and affinal ties and higher level of endogamy between occupational groups. Thus over time we would see the emergence of a much more crystallized and rigid class structure. The secondary schools would become correspondingly less effective as a mobility mechanism, reflecting in greater measure the rigidities of the class structure and becoming more and more the preserve of privileged minorities. Not only this, but social differentiation of students in a multistream system would be likely to increase.

The prediction of future trends in African systems of social differentiation is a risky undertaking. Undoubtedly they will be heavily influenced by economic development, and a quickening in the tempo of economic growth will maintain or enhance opportunities for mobility. In Western societies where rapid development is still going on there has been no indication of a decrease in mobility opportunities or an increase in rigidification of the status structure. But at present contemporary Africa (including the Ivory Coast) faces rather gloomy prospects for rapid economic growth in the foreseeable future. Many development schemes depend on primary products whose world prices are subject to drastic variations.

On the other hand, the expansion of secondary schooling might also keep existing jobs open to talented persons from various segments of society. As the number of secondary school places increases, almost certainly the absolute representation of different subgroups will also expand. However, it does not follow that relative representation will change very much. For example, it is well documented in the case of England that the expansion of secondary grammar and higher education has had little effect on the opportunities of lower class people to enter these types of institution.[1] One must not expect, therefore, that merely enlarging the secondary school enterprise in African countries will lead to radical shifts in the character of the student population.

In this connection it is worthwhile comparing the Ivory Coast with neighboring Ghana. Both countries are extraordinarily prosperous by West African standards, yet Ghana is certainly the more highly developed of the two. Its occupational structure is more complex and broader at the summit and at intermediate levels. Even more striking, educational development in Ghana is at a far higher level. In 1963 that country, with a population about twice that of the Ivory Coast, had

1. See, for example, the Committee on Higher Education, *Higher Education*, Appendix II, "The Demand for Places in Higher Education" (London: H.M.S.O., 1963), p. 52.

eleven times as many students in some form of postprimary school, excluding those in higher education. To be sure, about four-fifths of them were in four-year middle schools, but these institutions are, generally speaking, not too different from the *Cours Complémentaires*. Further, Ghana had 20,000 students just in secondary schools roughly equivalent to the *Lycées*—as many as there were in the whole postprimary system of the Ivory Coast.

These striking differences, however, cannot be attributed to the fact that the pattern of recruitment in Ghana is much more open than in the Ivory Coast.[2] When a comparison was made between male students in the fifth forms of Ghanaian secondary schools and those at roughly the same level in the first *Baccalaureat* classes in the Ivory Coast, differences were smaller than expected. Both systems were very open, though understandably more Ghanaian students came from urban areas and from educated families; this was inevitable in view of Ghana's higher level of development. But when differences in the characteristics of the general population were taken into account, the picture was rather similar.

In ethnic terms a student from the southern part of the Ivory Coast has between two and three times the chance of entering the *Baccalaureat* class as has a student from the north or the central area. The proportionate chances are almost identical in Ghana. Indeed a northern Ghanaian boy has even less chance of reaching the fifth form of a secondary school than has his Ivory Coast counterpart. Even more striking, rural-urban differentials are still greater in Ghana than they are in the Ivory Coast. A student living in Abidjan or Bouaké has about the same chance of entering the *Baccalaureat* class as a boy from a community with a population of less than 5,000. By contrast, a Ghanaian student living in one of the larger towns (including Accra, Kumasi, and Sckondi-Takoradi) has about fourteen times the chance of reaching the fifth form of secondary school as has a rural child.[3] The

2. For a fuller discussion of the findings mentioned here, see Remi Clignet and Philip Foster, "Potential Elites in Ghana and the Ivory Coast: A Preliminary Comparison," *American Journal of Sociology*, Vol. LXX, No. 3 (November 1964), pp. 349–62. The complete results of the Ghanaian survey are to be found in Philip Foster, *Education and Social Change in Ghana* (Chicago: University of Chicago Press, 1965).

3. Actually these figures are a trifle misleading, since we are not suggesting that there is no relationship between urban residence and recruitment into the *Baccalaureat* classes in the Ivory Coast. However, there is a peculiar downswing in the relationship when the largest towns are considered. In fact, an Ivory Coast child living in a medium-sized town with a population between 10,000 and 50,000 has

only case in which the Ivory Coast shows a sharper pattern of inequality than Ghana is in level of paternal occupation. In Ghana the child of a professional, higher technical, or managerial worker has over twenty-eight times the chance of entering a fifth form as has the offspring of a farmer. In the Ivory Coast the comparable figure is thirty-two. It could hardly be claimed that this difference is significant.

In summary, although the secondary school enterprise in the Ivory Coast is so much smaller in scope than that in Ghana, it is remarkable that recruitment ratios in the two countries are not very different. In other words, as educational systems expand, there is no reason to believe that differentials in opportunities will rapidly diminish. To be sure, comparisons between Ghana and the Ivory Coast are risky (as indeed are all comparisons). Only studies over time will tell us whether openness or rigidity will characterize recruitment patterns in the new African states. Nonetheless Western precedent leads us to believe that recruitment patterns will exhibit a degree of "stickiness" in the years to come.

Despite these caveats it is still clear that schools in both Ghana and the Ivory Coast succeed very well in drawing their clientele from a broad spectrum of the population. In one sense the openness of the system is a function of the socio-economic environment in which the schools operate. It could be postulated that whether or not recruitment patterns remain open will largely depend upon what happens outside the schools rather than on specific educational policies concerning entry to secondary education. There is much to be said for this view. However, the structure of the educational system can in some measure enhance or diminish talented students' opportunities to advance. No one can fail to be impressed by the current volume of literature which argues against early selection for secondary education combined with relatively rigid tracking of students. In Western Europe there is growing pressure to delay the selection of students for specific types of secondary education by creating a longer common secondary school experience. In some places (Sweden, for example) such pressure has led to an outright demand for comprehensive forms of secondary schooling.

---

about six times the chance of entering a *Baccalaureat* class as does a child from a village with a population of below 5,000. By contrast, in Ghana the relationship is quite linear; the larger the town, the greater the chances of entry. All this does not alter the fact that entry into the fifth form in Ghana is more closely associated with urban residence than is entry into the *Baccalaureat* class in the Ivory Coast.

The 1959 educational reforms in France reflect this preoccupation with loosening up the system of secondary schooling. The creation of a common *Cycle d'Observation* for all children up to the age of thirteen as well as attempts to create greater opportunities for students to change their course of study are moves in that direction.

We could argue that this kind of development is equally important in the Ivory Coast if an open policy is to be pursued and maximum use made of talent. Indeed the Ivory Coast has been experimenting with the development of a *Cycle d'Observation*, and, as we have noted, there is a good deal more informal movement of students within the system than is sometimes supposed. Although the secondary school system is likely to remain small in size for some time to come, there is no reason why a period of *common* secondary schooling for selected students should not precede specialized study, to enable a more effective final allocation of students. Beyond this, it can be asked whether the present system of multiple tracking performs any function other than to enhance the rigidity of the system. In practical terms, is there any real rationale in the separation of the *Cours Normaux* from the *Cours Complémentaires* or the lower long academic system? Can a substantial case be made for the development of a highly specialized lower vocational cycle—a cycle which thus far, as we have observed, has not effectively carried out the functions ascribed to it?

Of course, arguments in favor of more general secondary education, later selection, and less tracking run counter to a great deal of current observation concerning African educational policy. It is frequently argued that because of manpower needs the new states cannot afford the luxury of deferred selection and general studies. Efficient use of available talent, it is urged, presupposes early allocation of individuals and development of more highly specialized types of secondary schooling directly related to manpower needs. On the contrary, we would argue that this is just the kind of development that the African states cannot afford. Under such systems the chances of misallocating students are vastly increased, the rigidities of the structure are reinforced, and there is greater danger of mismatching secondary school training with the skills actually in demand. It would be unfortunate indeed if the Ivory Coast or other African countries simply duplicated earlier secondary education structures that most European nations are now striving to change. In view of the overwhelming importance of keeping access to secondary education open and minimizing social and ethnic differentials between low- and high-status types of schooling, every effort should be made to keep the structure of secondary education as loose as possible.

Student Attitudes and Aspirations

Perhaps one of the greatest unknowns in the calculations of educational and manpower planners in the new states concerns the attitudes and dispositions of the students. Human beings are not merely pegs that can be moved at will to meet expected shortages of certain types of manpower. Usually they have notions of the kinds of occupation they wish to enter and are able in some measure to indicate the factors that influence their choice. Indeed their occupational decisions are often based on rational appraisals of actual opportunities and benefits. Unless there is compulsory labor drafting, recruitment into certain types of occupation considered necessary for national development requires that individuals see these jobs as offering advantages over other alternatives. Occupational attitude becomes, therefore, one of the major parameters within which educational and manpower planners must work.

A striking feature of the aspirations of secondary students in the Ivory Coast is how loosely linked they are to social or ethnic background. To be sure, the use of a combined index of acculturation does discriminate between groups, but sex quite obviously remains a stronger predictor of aspirations than does any other variable. The fact is that nearly all students have high vocational and educational aspirations, quite incommensurate with their actual chances of continuing their studies. Of course, levels of aspiration tend to be modified by previous academic record and experience, but this does not deter most individuals from holding far too optimistic hopes for their own prospects. This optimism is understandable in view of the historical importance of education in assuring access to remunerative occupations and the fact that independence might be assumed to offer Africans new opportunities. Unfortunately enrollments at higher levels of the secondary system diminish rapidly as a result of the systematic weeding out of students, while opportunities are not expanding rapidly except in certain specific occupations, such as teaching. Under these circumstances there is always the likelihood of frustration among students. Indeed the lack of adequate opportunity in the senior cadres seems to underlie the dialogue that has continued over the last few years between the President of the Republic of the Ivory Coast and the *Union Nationale des Etudiants de la Côte d'Ivoire en France* (U.N.E.C.I.F.).[4]

Actually the generally high level of aspirations and their loose association with social or ethnic variables points again to the openness of the present status structure in the Ivory Coast. The experience of secondary education seems to exert a homogenizing influence on students that far outweighs the impact of earlier ethnic and social experience. In our initial remarks we noted that the present study could not establish the fact that schooling per se exerts a causal influence on occupational attitudes. This does not prevent us from suggesting that secondary education sets the elite apart from the mass and results in a minimal differentiation of attitudes and values.

Regardless of this putative effect of education, the fact remains that occupational aspirations are variably influenced by social and educational factors. Whereas preferences for careers in the administration or in medicine, for example, seem to be correlated with higher social background, agriculture and teaching are more frequently chosen by students from rural farming areas. By contrast, the choice of technological and scientific careers is more significantly related to academic record. In this sense the field of science and technology appears to be the one most open to talented individuals. Further, the evidence does much to dispel the myth that secondary school graduates in general are little disposed to enter careers other than those in administration. Of all male students no less than 38 per cent are interested in technical and agricultural careers.

However, a caution is necessary here. Students who choose the scientific and technical field, in particular, look toward high-level jobs. Relatively few would accept humbler types of technical work. In fact, there is a marked shift away from such careers when aspirations are contrasted with expectations. The reverse is the case with teaching; individuals who aspire to enter this occupation do not shift their pattern of preferences when asked what job they expect to enter with their present level of education. Indeed three-quarters of all students expect to enter primary school teaching or clerical work only if they are unable to continue their studies. There is, therefore, a very real

4. See Victor Dubois, *The Student-Government Conflict in the Ivory Coast* (American Universities Field Staff Reports, West Africa Series, Vol. VIII, No. 1 [1965]).

difference in the degree of commitment to various types of occupation, and it can hardly be assumed that former secondary school students will be likely to enter subordinate technical jobs in any numbers.

It could well be that this pattern reflects a fairly realistic view of opportunities. Compared with teaching and clerical work, lower level technical jobs offer fewer opportunities and also fewer advantages. This is in part reflected in the very unfortunate position of *Centres d'Apprentissage* in the present secondary school system. Few students wish to remain in them, and, as far as we can tell, the rate of unemployment is higher among their graduates than among those from other types of school. Moreover, dissatisfaction with current employment is more marked in this group. Above all, the *Centres d'Apprentissage* provide few further job opportunities for their students. Ironically the *Lycée Technique,* which enjoys relatively high prestige, does not rely upon the lower technical system for the bulk of its recruits; it prefers to enroll students from the academic schools. There can be no doubt that the *Lycée Technique* is currently successful because it does enable access to higher studies. Yet its success seems to have been achieved at the expense of the *Centres d'Apprentissage,* which now constitute a sort of backwater in the educational system. Since these schools offer hardly any opportunity for further education and provide training that is frequently ill-adapted to market needs, it is no wonder that the short technical system enjoys such low repute. One may well ask whether specific vocational education for middle-level employment would be better carried out by industrial and commercial firms themselves.[5] Clearly their own needs could provide incentives for the development of on-the-job training, and tax remissions would probably do much to stimulate adequate programs.[6]

It is instructive, however, to compare the position of the *Centres d'Apprentissage* with that of the new agricultural schools. Just over 14 per cent of all male students wish to enter agriculture in one form or another—a surprisingly high proportion. To be sure, virtually none of them want to become farmers; most aspire to jobs as agricultural

5. Some French businessmen in the Ivory Coast have expressed this view, which is also endorsed by many expatriate supervisors in Nigeria. See Alan Sokolski, *The Establishment of Manufacturing in Nigeria* (New York: Frederick Praeger, 1965), p. 75.

6. Some companies in West Africa seem to be doing a very effective job in this respect. See, particularly, Sokolski, *op. cit.,* pp. 75–76.

demonstrators and technicians. Further, only about 3 per cent expect to enter agriculture with their present level of education. The general picture seems rather similar to that in science and technology, but the attitudes of students in agricultural studies are quite distinctive. The overwhelming majority would prefer to stay in their present school, which over one-fifth of students derived from other types of institutions (mainly short cycle) would also like to enter if they had the chance. Moreover, nearly all former graduates of agricultural schools are employed in the jobs for which they have been trained. Unemployment is nonexistent among them, and levels of satisfaction are significantly higher than in most other occupations.

Although these conclusions are based on a study of a limited number of cases, it would seem that the government of the Ivory Coast has been initially successful in establishing a moderate program of agricultural education. There are, perhaps, three reasons for this: (1) Government demands for agricultural technicians and demonstrators are explicit, and clearly defined employment opportunities exist for graduates of the agricultural schools. (2) The system draws overwhelmingly from students with rural-farm backgrounds, which constitutes some guarantee of motivation. (3) A second cycle of agricultural studies has been created which makes it possible for individuals in the lower cycle to proceed further. Of course, the very newness of the system has meant that the academic schools have had to provide a proportion of recruits, but the essential fact is that agricultural instruction does not constitute a totally dead-end type of education. If present efforts to create an agricultural *Baccalaureat* are successful, it is likely that the desirability of agricultural studies will increase, as has been the case with the *Lycée Technique.*

However, one must not expect that such a development could lead to a large-scale expansion of secondary school agricultural studies, with the aim of turning out "progressive" farmers. Farming still remains one of the occupations least desired by students, and under present conditions secondary schools will probably not make any contribution in this direction. Other strategies will be necessary if the productivity of the agricultural sector is to be raised. Yet the use of extension workers and agricultural technicians, working with practicing agriculturalists, is vital to agricultural development, and it is only in the production of such personnel that the secondary schools can be expected to make a limited contribution.

Personal Preference and Development Policies

Nonetheless there are other areas where conflicts are apparent between students' aspirations and certain overall social and economic goals of government. The first of these concerns the high levels of student preference for urban employment. One well-nigh universal feature of contemporary Africa is the drift of people to the large towns and cities—most marked among those individuals with some schooling. Of course, there are good reasons for this movement: The towns are frequently the major centers of development; job opportunities there, if not commensurate with hopes, are more frequent; and, at worst, urban areas offer diversions not present in smaller rural communities.

In terms of short-run economic considerations, a good case can be made for saying that the preference for urban employment is based on sound, objective reasons and that in early stages of national growth the economic gap between urban and rural areas will necessarily become greater. Unfortunately the situation is by no means so simple. African governments cannot afford to let this gap continue to widen. In such countries as the Ivory Coast it is the cash-crop farmer who provides the wealth necessary for development schemes, and rural areas are understandably pressing for their fair share of educational, medical, and other services. Any government which fails to recognize the legitimacy of these demands runs the risk of alienating rural support. At the same time it is hard to recruit the personnel required for rural work; people are reluctant to work in these areas. Since financial incentives, such as they are, tend to increase the desirability of urban employment and since conditions in rural areas are so patently inferior, it is useless to address hortatory appeals to individuals to work in "backward" sections on the basis of "service to the community."

It is true that students expressing a desire to enter primary school teaching, some forms of medical work, and agriculture show a somewhat higher preference for work in rural areas. However, even here the figure falls far short of that required if some degree of parity is to be maintained between urban and rural services. A frequent solution to the problem is, of course, the compulsory drafting of personnel to rural districts, often immediately after they have qualified. But this is a relatively inefficient way of distributing manpower resources. It results not only in the allocation of the least experienced personnel to rural areas but in a rapid turnover, since most individuals, after their initial tour of duty, are anxious to move to more desirable areas. Because rural areas need a continuity of personnel with a lasting commitment to work there, extra incentives should be provided—for example, differential salary scales weighted in favor of rural employment and a housing policy aimed at the improvement of rural amenities. How far these and other measures would be successful is difficult to predict, but there seems to be no other way of attracting and keeping trained personnel.

A second feature in which personal aspirations are likely to clash with policy involves the high levels of commitment to government employment. This is inevitable in view of the pattern of development in the Ivory Coast. Government has always provided a substantial proportion of employment opportunities in the modern sector of the economy, while in the past it offered conditions of work usually superior to those in the private sector. But the situation is changing. Many of the larger private companies realize that their continued presence in the Ivory Coast will depend on the increased Africanization of their personnel and on better conditions of employment. At the same time official policy concerning the projected pattern of economic development has tended to be fairly pragmatic and nondoctrinaire. While exhibiting a vague commitment to planning and the enlargement of state activities, the government has not placed restrictions on foreign investment and has accepted the fact that a growing private sector is important to the economy. Thus new opportunities in the larger, foreign-controlled companies are likely to be available to individuals with secondary school training.

So far the majority of students have not been attracted by these opportunities, although from the government viewpoint it is desirable that their aspirations be more diversified; the public sector cannot constitute an unlimited source of employment for growing cohorts of secondary school graduates. Yet some interest in careers in the private sector seems to be present among a small minority, and this interest is markedly associated with social and educational background. Students who would prefer private employment are usually from superior socioeconomic backgrounds, are more likely to be in the higher cycle of secondary school study, and are more frequently planning on technical careers. From this group, which seems to be more aware of new opportunities, private business will probably draw a substantial proportion of its middle- and upper-level personnel.

However, preference for careers in the private sector is not usually associated with a desire for self-employment or for work with African business firms. Students are overwhelmingly concerned with opportunities in the larger European-controlled enterprises, and the few who would prefer to see themselves as self-employed are interested in such professions as law and medicine. There is still no evidence of any interest in the possibilities of self-owned or other African commercial enterprises, which suffer from the historical stigma of being in the hands of women or poorly educated individuals. Further, these negative attitudes toward African enterprise are reinforced by a heavy preoccupation with security, prestige, and congenial conditions of employment.

It is also striking that students attach great importance to education as a means of gaining employment and stress job proficiency as being the main determinant of success. By contrast, they feel that starting and succeeding in a self-owned business depends far more on initial wealth and family connections than it does on ability and effort. Very few students, in fact, would dream of investing resources in commercial, industrial, or agricultural enterprises. Housing (often rental housing) still remains the most desirable form of investment, followed by discharge of lineage obligations, investment in further education, and savings accounts.

One cannot suggest, therefore, that people with a secondary education are likely to make much of a contribution to the African-owned portion of the private sector. That sector will continue to be dominated by European-owned enterprises, which, to be sure, may themselves contribute substantially to Ivory Coast development. Yet one might feel happier if the African-owned enterprises would increase and generate new employment opportunities for Africans. We would hazard a guess that future development will not occur solely through the efforts of government or large-scale, foreign-controlled companies. It will depend also on the growth of a multiplicity of small-scale developments, initiated by Africans themselves, in both commerce and agriculture. This kind of thinking is often uncongenial to African governments, even if they are not hostile to the development of a private sector, because it is often easier to deal with large European-controlled concerns than it is to show an interest in small

African enterprises. The potential role of the African entrepreneur is habitually underestimated, and attitudes toward him are, to say the least, ambivalent. He tends to be the forgotten man in most development schemes, and efforts to stimulate the development of African business are often regarded as a waste of money.

Of course, there is some basis for this negative evaluation. Although in West Africa generally there is a multitude of small-scale African enterprises, their position is usually precarious. Few persist beyond the lifetime of their founder, while traditional kinship obligations tend to dissipate resources that could be ploughed back into the business. In short, new African businesses are always being created, but few of them grow.

It could be argued that one reason for this is that African business is so often controlled by illiterates or poorly educated individuals. Clearly the schools themselves cannot produce the innovators and the entrepreneurs, but perhaps if persons of this type could be trained at higher levels of formal schooling, they would be qualified to develop African business firms beyond a minimal level. Of all human resources, the innovator is the most valuable and also the most scarce. It is unfortunate that this potential resource seems so limited within the ranks of the educated themselves.

The Importance of Comparative Studies

One may well ask what relevance a specialized study of African students in one country may have for other new African states. Are we really considering a unique case here, the conclusions and findings of which have very limited applicability? We think not. We have been struck by the marked parallels between the findings of our study and those derived from an earlier, if more limited, survey in Ghana. Both show substantial similarities in student attitudes as these relate to occupational aspirations and perception of future roles. Ghanaian and Ivory Coast students are much alike in many respects. Of course, if a comparative study of political attitudes and values were undertaken, it could show marked differences between the two groups, particularly in attitudes toward the former metropole and its culture. However, differences are not apparent in economic and occupational attitudes. This is significant in that both Ghana and the Ivory Coast exhibit common economic characteristics that are far more inportant than any special differences resulting from particular patterns of colonial overrule. Both countries, in effect, share similar problems in the attempt to achieve development.

The crucial point about these two countries is that they are fairly prosperous by West African standards and their economies relatively developed. It might well be true that studies of African students in less fortunate territories, such as Mali, Senegal, or Northern Nigeria, would reveal variant configurations of student attitudes (though we suggest that the differences might be of degree rather than kind). In effect, we suggest that the axis of comparison is rather along level-of-development lines than on the basis of the particular colonial power that formerly controlled the area.

In another respect, both Ghana and the Ivory Coast are particularly important areas for study. Precisely because they are more economically and educationally developed than many African states, their present problems provide a foretaste of possible developments in other nations that have not yet been able to duplicate their achievements. Countries intending to embark on programs of educational expansion would do well to consider both the Ivory Coast and the Ghana experiences.

APPENDIX A

Interviewing Techniques and Representativeness of the Sample

STUDENTS WERE INTERVIEWED in their classrooms between March 15 and May 28, 1963, by one of the present writers. The completion of this task was made difficult by the proximity of the examination period and by the long Easter vacation. Yet it would have been difficult to begin the survey earlier, since the academic year in the Ivory Coast is rather short. European teachers tend to arrive in the country late in the fall, and the system does not function properly before the early part of November. An extension of the interviewing period would probably have disturbed the progress of students, who were already handicapped by the late commencement of the school year. Higher officials of the Ministry of Education and the principals of each school, however, greatly facilitated the task.

The final sample included 2,176 individuals, but of these, 102 cases were discarded because of incomplete questionnaires. The final 2,074 cases (1,837 boys, 237 girls) were drawn from 49 institutions. In fact, only one *Cours Normal* (Guiglo) and three *Cours Complémentaires* (Bouaflé, Dimbokro, and Bondoukou) were not surveyed, either because of lack of time or because they were too remote from the main roads and thus difficult to reach during the rainy season. However, the representativeness of the sample is high and does not vary greatly between stream and cycle (Table A1). Slight underrepresentation is observable in the case of the *Ecole Normale,* the *Cours Complémentaires,* and the *Lycée Technique.*

TABLE A1. Representativeness of the Sample *

	LYCEES AND COLLEGES		COURS NORMAUX		COURS COMPLEMENTAIRES	ECOLE NORMALE	CENTRES D'APPRENTISSAGE †		LYCEE TECHNIQUE ‡	CENTRE DE FORMATION RURALE	COLLEGE TECHNIQUE D'AGRICULTURE	TOTAL
	Public	Private	Public	Private	Public	Public	Public	Private	Public	Public	Public	
Total enrollment	1,039	237	329	53	608	82	181	8	131	30	14	2,712
Student response	838	206	253	51	391	40	168	7	81	26	13	2,074
Response percentage	80.7	86.9	76.9	96.2	64.3	48.8	92.8	87.5	61.8	86.7	92.9	76.5

* European students have been excluded from this total. There are no private agricultural institutions, nor is there a private *Ecole Normale.*
† The population of the vocational training schools has been estimated.
‡ This total includes the population of the *Ecole Normale Ménagére.*

APPENDIX B

Questionnaire Submitted to Secondary School Students
(Translated from the French)
University of Paris (I.E.D.E.S.) and the University of Chicago
Study of Postprimary Education

The Universities of Paris and Chicago are currently involved in a study of the school systems of various countries and particularly of the kind of problems you have faced since you completed primary school. We should like to know the activities in which you want to engage in the future when you have finished your present studies.

Your answers will be very useful, since they will enable the government to gain a better understanding of your problems. They will also enable your younger schoolmates to begin their studies under better conditions.

Of course, this questionnaire is not an examination. There are no right or wrong answers, and you should, therefore, be as accurate as possible in your replies. You can see that we do not ask for your name, and you can be sure that nobody outside our staff will see what you have written. . . . The answers are strictly confidential. Please answer the questions in the order in which they are given, so that you will not forget any. This will also make it easier for us to help if you need any assistance. Do not copy from your neighbor; it is your opinion that is important and not the views of others. You will see that you do not have a lot to write. Most of the time it will be enough to indicate your views by putting a small cross in a box, like this ☒, or by putting a number on a line, like this 3. If you have any difficulty, please raise your hand, and we shall come to help you. Do not hurry; you will have plenty of time, and try not to leave out any question. Above all, answer frankly and try to forget about what other people might be writing. We repeat, the questionnaire is *strictly confidential.*

1–4. Interview number _______

5–6. Name of your present school ____________________

7. Is this school ☐ public?
☐ private?

8–9. In which form are you at present? ______

10. Are you ☐ a boy?
☐ a girl?

11–12. What is your age? ______

13. Are you ☐ a boarder?
☐ a part boarder?
☐ a day scholar?

14–15. What is your tribe or people? ______

16–18. Where were you born? Please write down: The name of the place ______ The district ______ The region ______ The country ______

19–21. When you are not at school where is your principal place of residence? Please write down: The name of the village or town ______ The district ______ The region ______ The country ______

22. Does your father read *and* write French?
☐ Yes
☐ No

23. What level of education did he reach? Put a cross in the box that best describes his level of studies.
☐ Did not go to school
☐ Went to primary school but did not obtain the C.E.P.
☐ Went to primary school and obtained the C.E.P.
☐ Went to senior primary school (e.g., William Ponty or another)
☐ Went up to the *Baccalaureat* level or beyond
☐ After primary school, undertook some other kind of study. If so, what? ______

24–25. What is the present occupation of your father? Describe in as much detail as you can the type of activity in which he is currently engaged, or in which he was engaged if he is dead, retired, or presently unemployed. ______
______
______

26. Who is (or was) his employer?
☐ The administration. If so, what ministry? ______
☐ A large-scale private company. If so, which one? ______
☐ A small European firm or individual? ______
☐ Another small firm or individual ______
☐ Self-employed ______

27. Has your father more than one wife at present?
    ☐ Yes
    ☐ No
28. Does your mother read *and* write French?
    ☐ Yes
    ☐ No
29. What level of education did she reach? Put a cross in the box that best describes her level of studies.
    ☐ Did not go to school
    ☐ Went to primary school but did not obtain the C.E.P.
    ☐ Went to primary school and obtained the C.E.P.
    ☐ Went to senior primary school (e.g., William Ponty or another)
    ☐ Went up to the *Baccalaureat* level or beyond
    ☐ After primary school, undertook some other kind of study. If so, what? ____________________
30. Does your mother have an independent income of her own? Or did she, if she is now dead, retired, or unemployed?
    ☐ Yes
    ☐ No

31–32. If so, what is the origin of this income?
    ☐ She works in the fields and sells a share of the crop.
    ☐ She is an independent trader.
    ☐ She has another occupation. If so, what? ____________

33–35. Write down the name and address of the schools you have attended since gaining your C.E.P. If you have not been in any other postprimary school besides your present one, please write "None."

Name of the school *Address*

1. ____________________
2. ____________________
3. ____________________
4. ____________________

36–37. What is the *most important* thing that influenced your attendance at your present school? Put a cross in the most appropriate box.
    ☐ It is near home.
    ☐ The curriculum is not too demanding.
    ☐ Fees are low.
    ☐ This kind of school offers the best preparation for the future.

☐ Relatives of mine have already attended this school.
☐ I had no other alternatives.
☐ The quality of teaching is high so that my examination chances are good.
☐ Any other reason? If so, what? ____________________

____

____

38. Since you entered the postprimary system have you ever been obliged to repeat a class?
☐ Yes
☐ No

39. If you were able to rank all the students in your class in order of their academic ability, in which quarter of the class would you place yourself?
☐ Top quarter (the best)
☐ Second quarter
☐ Third quarter
☐ Fourth quarter

40. If you were *absolutely free* to choose your postprimary course all over again, where would you prefer to go? Give *one* choice only.
☐ *Ecole Normale*
☐ *Centre d'Apprentissage*
☐ *Lycée*
☐ *Lycée Technique*
☐ *Cours Normal*
☐ *Collège d'Agriculture*
☐ Any other? If so, what? ____________________

41. In your opinion, what is the most important thing for a student to have in order to gain the esteem of his schoolmates? Put a cross in the *one* box that best describes your view.
☐ To be a good student academically
☐ To be good at sports
☐ To be a nice fellow
☐ To have plenty of money
☐ To have a father who has a lot of status in the administration
☐ To have a father who is a traditional chief
☐ Any other thing? If so, what? ____________________

42. People want to attend school for different reasons. What, in your opinion, is the best among the following reasons for at-

tending postprimary school? Put a cross in the *one* box that best expresses your views.

☐ In order to gain the respect of others
☐ In order to enter the kind of job that most attracts you
☐ In order to enter a well-paid job
☐ In order to be able to give orders to others

43. Perhaps you feel that these reasons are not enough. Is there a reason that you think is *more* important?

☐ Yes
☐ No

If so, what is the reason? ______________________________
____
____

44. When you return home on vacation, how do the people in your community regard you? Put a cross in the *one* box that best describes their attitude.

☐ They are friendly and treat me with respect because I am a student.
☐ They respect me, but at the same time they are envious and jealous of my success.
☐ They treat me the same way as anyone else. They don't judge people on the basis of their education.

45–49. Everywhere fathers punish their children when they do something wrong. Here are five things that might make your father angry. Please rank these items in the order of their importance. In other words, put a 1 against the thing that makes your father most angry, then a 2 against the thing that comes next, and so on.

__ When you are not polite or respectful to elder kin
__ When you refuse to help him with some task when he asks you
__ When you refuse to look after your younger brothers or sisters when asked
__ When you do poorly at school
__ When you break something valuable in the house

50–54. In the same way here are five things that might make your mother angry. Please rank these items in order of their importance. In other words, put a 1 against the thing that makes her most angry, then a 2 against the thing that comes next and so on.

__ When you are not polite or respectful to elder kin
__ When you refuse to help her with some task when she asks you
__ When you refuse to look after your younger brothers or sisters when asked
__ When you do poorly at school
__ When you break something valuable in the house

55. Who in your family manifests the greatest concern over your education?
☐ Your father
☐ Your mother
☐ Somebody else. If so, who? ____________________
☐ Nobody

56. Do you wish to continue your studies after the present academic year?
☐ Yes
☐ No

57. *Realistically,* what do you think your chances are of continuing with your schooling after the present academic year?
☐ I am sure to continue.
☐ I have a good chance of continuing.
☐ I have little chance of continuing.
☐ I have no chance of continuing.

58. If, unfortunately, you think you have *little or no* chance of continuing your studies, what do you think will be the principal reason for stopping them? Put a cross in the *one* box that best describes your view.
☐ Lack of money
☐ Parental opposition
☐ Poor academic record
☐ No desire to continue
☐ Any other reason? If so, what? ____________________

59–60. If, on the other hand, you think it is likely that you will continue your studies next year what course would you like to undertake? Be *realistic* and indicate only one choice that seems feasible to you.
☐ Prepare for the technical or academic *Baccalaureat*
☐ Attend the *Ecole Normale*
☐ Prepare for the B.E.I. or B.E.C. at the *Lycée Technique*
☐ Prepare to enter the university. If so, in which branch of

studies? ______

☐ Attend another type of school. If so, which one? ______

☐ Undertake one of the special courses run by the administration or one of the larger companies. If so, which course? ______

61–62. If you could *freely* choose your future occupation what kind of job would you like to enter most of all? Try to be as accurate as possible. ______

63–64. Why would you choose this job? ______

65. When you finish your education and start working, where would you most like to live?
☐ In the capital
☐ In a large town with about 50,000 inhabitants
☐ In a smaller town with about 10,000 inhabitants
☐ In your home village
☐ In another village
☐ No preference

66. When you start working, for whom would you prefer to work?
☐ For the administration
☐ For a large private firm
☐ For a small European concern or individual
☐ For another type of small concern
☐ On your own account
☐ With somebody in your family

67–68. If you finish your studies this year, describe the kind of occupation that you will be most likely to enter *in fact*. Take into concern your own knowledge of the situation and the experience of your friends. Be as *realistic* and precise as possible! ______

69–71. Among the following occupations, choose the 3 that you would like the most. Put a 1 against the one that you would like best, a 2 against the next one, and so on.

For Boys Only	*For Girls Only*
__ Engineer	__ Primary school teacher
__ Businessman	__ Secretary
__ Lawyer	__ Businesswoman
__ Teacher in a *Lycée*	__ Teacher in a *collège*
__ Farmer	__ Social worker
__ Industrial manager	__ Midwife
__ University professor	__ Beautician
__ Medical doctor	__ Saleswoman in a fashion house

72. In your opinion, what is the best way of getting ahead in an occupation? Check the *one* box that best describes your view.
   - ☐ To be intelligent
   - ☐ To be efficient at your job
   - ☐ To work hard
   - ☐ To gain seniority on the job
   - ☐ To know how to get on with people
   - ☐ To have kin in the right places
   - ☐ To have a good academic record
   - ☐ To be older than other employees
73. What is your religion?
   - ☐ Harriste
   - ☐ Moslem
   - ☐ Catholic
   - ☐ Protestant
   - ☐ Traditional
   - ☐ Other
   - ☐ No religion
74. If you wanted to start a business on your own, what do you think would be the most important thing to have? Check the *one* box that best describes your view.
   - ☐ To have a good deal of money
   - ☐ To work hard
   - ☐ To have relatives already in the business
   - ☐ To be intelligent
   - ☐ To come from an area where people have a tradition of commercial know-how
   - ☐ To have a good education

75–76. If you were suddenly to be left a million francs that you were free to do with as you liked, how would you use it?

____

____

____

1–4. Interview number.

5–9. Here are a number of pairs of opinions concerning jobs. In each pair, choose the statement which suits you best and check it. Do not forget any pair, and make sure that you have checked only *one* statement in each pair.

I
- ☐ A steady and secure job but which does not carry much prestige

  or
- ☐ A job that carries a lot of prestige but which is not very secure

II
- ☐ A job which is well paid but which is unpleasant

  or
- ☐ A job which is pleasant but poorly paid

III
- ☐ A job which is pleasant but offers little chance of promotion

  or
- ☐ A job with good opportunities for promotion but which is not pleasant

IV
- ☐ A job which is well paid but does not carry much prestige

  or
- ☐ A job which is not well paid but which carries a good deal of prestige

V
- ☐ A job which is unpleasant but steady and secure

  or
- ☐ A job which is pleasant but not steady and secure

10–34. Here is a list of jobs which people do in your country. Read this list carefully and indicate the amount of prestige that you feel each job carries. As you see, we have put five columns against each occupation so that you can indicate whether it carries very high prestige, high prestige, average prestige, low prestige, or very low prestige. Check the column of your choice.

Occupation	Very High Prestige	High Prestige	Average Prestige	Low Prestige	Very Low Prestige
10. Clergyman					
11. Lawyer					
12. Policeman					
13. Primary school teacher					
14. Salesman					
15. Carpenter					
16. Government clerk					
17. Traditional Chief					
18. Farmer					
19. Electrician					
20. Street cleaner					
21. Radio announcer					
22. Automobile mechanic					
23. University lecturer					
24. Soldier					
25. Peddler					
26. *Lycée* professor					
27. Engineer					
28. Agricultural laborer					
29. Nurse					
30. *Collège* professor					
31. Minstrel					
32. Proprietor of a road transport firm					
33. Medical doctor					
34. Bank clerk					

35–59. Here are the same jobs again. Now we should like you to indicate how well paid you think they are. There are five columns: very high income, high income, average income, low income, very low income. Check the column of your choice.

Occupation	Very High Income	High Income	Average Income	Low Income	Very Low Income
35. Clergyman					
36. Lawyer					
37. Policeman					
38. Primary school teacher					
39. Salesman					
40. Carpenter					
41. Government clerk					
42. Traditional Chief					
43. Farmer					
44. Electrician					
45. Street cleaner					
46. Radio announcer					
47. Automobile mechanic					
48. University lecturer					
49. Soldier					
50. Peddler					
51. *Lycée* professor					
52. Engineer					
53. Agricultural laborer					
54. Nurse					
55. *Collège* professor					
56. Minstrel					
57. Proprietor of a road transport firm					
58. Medical doctor					
59. Bank clerk					

60–64. Here again are five new pairs of opinions concerning jobs. In each pair choose the statement which suits you best and check it. Do not forget any pair and make sure that you have checked only one statement in each pair.

VI
- ☐ A job which is well paid but offers little chance of promotion

  or
- ☐ A job which is poorly paid but which offers good chances of promotion

VII
- ☐ A steady and secure job but which is poorly paid

  or
- ☐ A job which is well paid but is not steady or secure

VIII
- ☐ A job which carries a lot of prestige but offers little chance of promotion

  or
- ☐ A job which carries little prestige but offers good chances of promotion

IX
- ☐ A steady and secure job but which offers little chance of promotion

  or
- ☐ A job which offers good chances of promotion but which is not steady or secure

X
- ☐ A job which is unpleasant but carries a lot of prestige

  or
- ☐ A job which is pleasant but which carries little prestige

APPENDIX C

Gamma Coefficients of Correlation between Occupational Aspirations and Socio-economic Background

OCCUPATIONAL CHOICE	SIZE OF PLACE OF RESIDENCE	AREA OF RESIDENCE	LEVEL OF PATERNAL EDUCATION	PATERNAL OCCUPATION	LEVEL OF ACCULTURA-TION
Teaching	−.358	+.066	−.222	−.305	−.501
Scientific and technological	−.121	−.089	−.036	+.076	+.462
Medicine and nursing	+.278	−.108	+.238	+.234	−.028
Agriculture	−.228	−.203	−.309	−.298	−.645
Administration	+.173	+.077	+.224	+.228	+.465
Military and police	−.112	−.140	−.297	−.219	−.159

APPENDIX D

Gamma Coefficients of Correlation between Occupational Aspirations and Academic Achievement

OCCUPATIONAL CHOICE	PRESENT CYCLE OF STUDY	SELF-ASSESSMENT OF PRESENT ACADEMIC STATUS	SELF-ESTIMATE OF CHANCES OF CONTINUING EDUCATION
Teaching	−.253	−.123	−.205
Scientific and technological	+.075	+.207	+.144
Medicine and nursing	+.061	−.037	+.050
Agriculture	−.071	+.032	−.004
Administration	+.207	+.054	+.142
Military and police	−.149	−.195	−.274

APPENDIX E

Questionnaire Sent to Former Secondary School Students
(Translated from the French)
University of Chicago (Comparative Education Center)
and the University of Paris (I.E.D.E.S.)

Dear Sir or Madam:

The universities of Paris and Chicago are currently engaged in a study of the degree to which postprimary schooling meets the needs and aspirations of youth. For this reason we should like to find out the kind of occupations now entered by former students of various kinds of postprimary school. We should also like to discover whether former students are satisfied with the kind of jobs they have been able to find since completing secondary school. The Ministry of Education was kind enough to provide us with your name and address, and this is why we have been able to write to you.

As you will understand, the value of the information that we collect depends greatly upon the frankness of your reply. Enclosed with this questionnaire is a stamped and addressed envelope which you can use to return it to us. The questionnaire is strictly *anonymous,* and we shall not quote from any specific person in our report. What is of interest to us is the opinion of the majority.

In returning the questionnaire you will help us to suggest some ways in which the present curricula of the schools might be improved.

You do not need to write a great deal. Most of the time we suggest several answers to the questions that we ask you. Among these answers, we want you to choose that which corresponds *best* to your own situation or your own opinion. Please check the one box of your choice like this ☒.

1–4. Interview number ______

5–7. What is your present address? Indicate the name of the village or of the town ______ District ______ Region ______ Country ______

8. Is this place the same as your place of birth?
☐ Yes
☐ No

9–10. How old are you? Try to be as precise as possible ________

11. Are you
    - ☐ Male
    - ☐ Female

12–13. What is your tribe or people? (I.e., please indicate whether you are Agni, Bété or Senoufo, etc.) ____________

14–15. What is your father's occupation? Please try to be as accurate as possible. (If he is dead, retired, or presently unemployed, describe his former occupation.) ____________

____

____

16. Occupation. (Put a cross in the box which best describes your current situation.)
    - ☐ You have finished your schooling and are currently unemployed.
    - ☐ You have finished your schooling and are currently employed.
    - ☐ You are still attending school.

The present questionnaire is divided into two parts, Part A and Part B. Part A is to be filled in only by those who have already completed their schooling. Part B is to be filled in only by those who are still attending school.

PART A

17. After you left ______ * in ______ * were you able to continue further with your schooling?
    - ☐ No
    - ☐ Yes

18–19. If you were able to continue, please indicate below the school or schools that you attended and the course you took. If you did not continue, please write "No other courses."

Course	Dates		Name and Address of the School
	From	To	
1.			
2.			
3.			

* In the mailed-out questionnaire these sections were completed by the investigators on the basis of existing school records.

20–21. What certificates or diplomas have you obtained *since* completing your primary schooling? If you have not obtained any, please write "None." ______________________

22. How many jobs have you held since you left school for good? Indicate the number only. Do not give details.
Number ______

23–24. What is your present occupation? Please give as many details as possible. (If you are currently unemployed, please write "Unemployed.") ______________________

25. Who is your current employer?
☐ You are unemployed.
☐ The administration. If so, which ministry? ____________
☐ A large private firm. If so, which one? ____________
☐ A small European concern or individual.
☐ Another type of small firm or individual employer.
☐ A relative of yours.
☐ You are self-employed.

26. How much money do you earn a month? (If you are currently unemployed, write "Unemployed.") ______________

27. What is your present status under the collective bargaining classification?

Unemployed	Unknown	1	2	3	4	5	6	7	8
☐	☐	☐	☐	☐	☐	☐	☐	☐	☐

28. Since you left school, have you, on the whole, been satisfied or dissatisfied with the various jobs that you have held?
☐ I have never been employed.
☐ On the whole, I have been satisfied.
☐ On the whole, I have been dissatisfied.

29–30. If you are currently employed, what do you feel are the main advantages and shortcomings of your present occupation? Check the *one* box corresponding to what you feel is its main advantage and its main shortcoming. If you are currently unemployed, do not answer this question.

Main Advantage
☐ It is well-paid.
☐ It is easy to perform.
☐ There are good opportunities for promotion.
☐ It carries a good deal of prestige.

Main Shortcoming
☐ It is difficult to perform.
☐ I don't get along with my fellow workers.
☐ It is an unsteady and insecure occupation.
☐ There are few opportuni-

☐ It is near my home.
☐ It is a steady and secure occupation.
☐ I get along with the employer.
☐ Another advantage? If so, what? ________________
____

ties for promotion.
☐ I don't get along with my employer.
☐ The pay is poor.
☐ It is far from my home.
☐ Another shortcoming? If so, what? ________________
____

31. In your opinion, what does it take to get ahead in the job in which you are currently engaged? (Check the *one* box against the thing you feel is most important.)
☐ To be intelligent
☐ To be efficient at the job
☐ To work hard
☐ To know how to get along with people
☐ To acquire seniority in the firm
☐ To have the "right contacts," who can give you a push at the right time
☐ To be older than the other workers
☐ To have a good education
☐ Any other thing? If so, what? ________________

32–34. If you are currently employed, do you intend to
☐ Remain in the same job with the same employer?
☐ Remain in the same kind of job but with a different firm?
☐ Change your kind of job altogether? If so, indicate the type of occupation that you are looking for. ________________
____
____
____

35–37. Are you currently unemployed? Describe in as much detail as possible the kind of job you are trying to find. (If you are currently employed, do not answer this question.) ________________
____
____
____

38. If you are currently unemployed, how do you get by? (Check the *one* box which best corresponds to your situation.)
☐ I help relatives or friends on their farms.
☐ I help relatives or friends with their business (taxis, trading, etc.).

☐ I help relatives or friends in their households.
☐ I have other ways to manage. If so, what? ____________

____

39. Since you left school, would you say that it has been difficult to enter the type of job which you feel suits you best? (Check only one box.)
☐ Very difficult
☐ Difficult
☐ Easy
☐ Very easy

40. Are you currently taking part-time courses under your employer's auspices?
☐ No
☐ Yes. If so, what kind of course? ____________

41. Have you registered *on your own initiative* for part-time courses, or specialized training (e.g., night courses, correspondence courses, etc.)?
☐ No
☐ Yes. If yes, what type of course? ____________

42. Looking back, do you think that the school you attended could have provided you with a more adequate preparation for the kind of life that you currently lead?
☐ No
☐ Yes

43–75. If you think that this school could have done a better job, could you explain why in as much detail as you can? This will be of great assistance to us.

PART B

17–18. What school are you currently attending? ____________

19. For which examination are you preparing? ____________

20–21. What diplomas or certificates have you obtained since you entered postprimary education? ____________

22. After you have sat for the examination for which you are currently preparing, do you intend to continue your education?
☐ No
☐ Yes

23. If you intend to continue, what type of studies do you hope to undertake? ____________

24. Where? ____________

25. Since you left ________________ * class in ________________ * school, have you ever been obliged to interrupt your education and take a job?
   - ☐ No
   - ☐ Yes

26–27. If you have been obliged to work, please describe in as much detail as possible the type of jobs that you have held. (If you have never been employed, please write "Never employed.")

____

____

28–29. When you leave school for good, what is the type of occupation that you would most like to enter? Be as accurate as possible.

____

____

____

30. Where would you like to work? (Check only *one* box.)
   - ☐ In the capital city
   - ☐ In a large town with a population of around 50,000 inhabitants
   - ☐ In a smaller town with a population of around 10,000 inhabitants
   - ☐ In your home village
   - ☐ In another village

31. For whom would you like to work most? (Check only *one* box.)
   - ☐ The administration
   - ☐ A large company
   - ☐ A small European enterprise or individual employer
   - ☐ Another type of small concern or individual
   - ☐ Relatives
   - ☐ On your own account

32–33. If you are *unable* to continue your studies, what kind of occupation are you most likely to enter, from what you know and from the experiences of your friends? Be realistic and accurate.

* In the mailed-out questionnaire these sections were completed by the investigators on the basis of existing school records.

INDEX